The media's
Here's a sar

"Lawyers looking for the scoop on the nation's biggest law firms now have a place to go."
– *The Wall Street Journal*

"With reviews and profiles of firms that one associate calls 'spot on', [Vault's] guide has become a key reference for those who want to know what it takes to get hired by a law firm and what to expect once they get there."
– *New York Law Journal*

"The best place on the web to prepare for a job search."
– *Fortune*

"Vault is indispensable for locating insider information."
– *Metropolitan Corporate Counsel*

"[Vault's guide] is an INVALUABLE Cliff's Notes to prepare for interviews."
– *Women's Lawyer's Journal*

"For those hoping to climb the ladder of success, [Vault's] insights are priceless."
– *Money Magazine*

"[Vault guides] make for excellent starting points for job hunters and should be purchased by academic libraries for their career sections [and] university career centers."
– *Library Journal*

VAULT
> the most trusted name in career information™

TOP CHICAGO LAW FIRMS, ASSOCIATES, AND PARTNERS KNOW WHERE TO FIND THE LARGEST NUMBER OF PARTNER AND ASSOCIATE JOBS.

LAWCROSSING is America's largest legal job board. In one place you will find virtually every attorney job advertised by a law firm, corporation, or government agency. LawCrossing contacts more than 500,000 legal employers monthly to bring you practically every legal position as soon as it becomes available. As a result, you benefit from real-time, up-to-the-hour information that gives you jobs, jobs, and more jobs.

Visit LawCrossing today! Your next job and a better future could be waiting.
www.lawcrossing.com

VAULT GUIDE TO THE TOP
CHICAGO & MIDWEST LAW FIRMS

© 2005 Vault Inc.

BAKER & McKEN

Be world class!

38 nations

60 languages

3,100 lawyers

Many cultures. One team.

Are you fascinated by diverse cultures? Are you determined to practice law with an international flavor? Do you meet the high standards a worldwide practice demands?

If you do, talk to us and see the difference.

www.bakernet.com

VAULT GUIDE TO THE TOP
CHICAGO & MIDWEST LAW FIRMS

VERA DJORDJEVICH
AND THE STAFF AT VAULT

© 2005 Vault Inc.

Copyright © 2005 by Vault Inc. All rights reserved.

All information in this book is subject to change without notice. Vault makes no claims as to the accuracy and reliability of the information contained within and disclaims all warranties. No part of this book may be reproduced or transmitted in any form or by any means, electronic or mechanical, for any purpose, without the express written permission of Vault Inc.

Vault, the Vault logo, and "the most trusted name in career information™" are trademarks of Vault Inc.

For information about permission to reproduce selections from this book, contact Vault Inc., 150 W. 22nd St., 5th Floor, New York, NY 10011, (212) 366-4212.

Library of Congress CIP Data is available.

ISBN 1-58131-312-8

Printed in the United States of America

ACKNOWLEDGEMENTS

Thank you to writers Mark Fass, Meredith Strauss, Neeraja Viswanathan and Amy Watkins. Thanks also to the Vault sales, graphics, editorial and IT staff for their tireless work.

A special thank you to the hundreds of law firm recruiting professionals and hiring partners who put up with our tight deadlines, frantic phone calls and repeated requests for information.

And a sympathetic and heartfelt thanks to all the vast number and array of law firm associates who take the time in between their document reviews, closing checklists, deposition transcripts, term sheets, recruiting efforts, diversity initiatives, pro bono contributions, etc. to complete our surveys. We've been there too.

Upon hearing Mayer, Brown, Rowe & Maw
had been named Chambers 2004 UK Law Firm of the Year,
we reacted with typical British reserve.

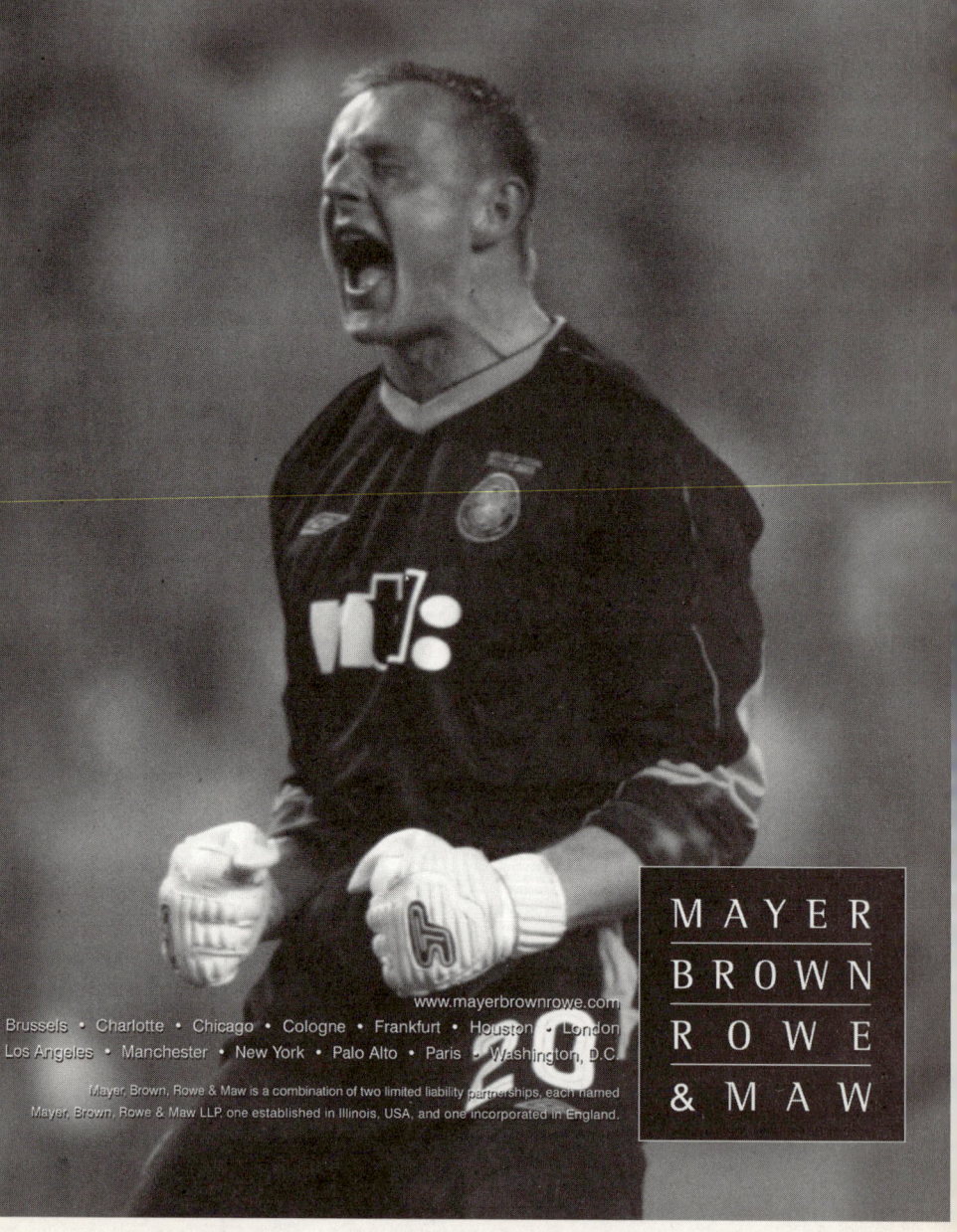

www.mayerbrownrowe.com

Brussels • Charlotte • Chicago • Cologne • Frankfurt • Houston • London
Los Angeles • Manchester • New York • Palo Alto • Paris • Washington, D.C.

Mayer, Brown, Rowe & Maw is a combination of two limited liability partnerships, each named
Mayer, Brown, Rowe & Maw LLP, one established in Illinois, USA, and one incorporated in England.

MAYER
BROWN
ROWE
& MAW

Table of Contents

INTRODUCTION 1

A Guide to this Guide 3
The Year in Law 5

LAW FIRM PROFILES 9

Arnstein & Lehr LLP 10
Baker & Daniels 14
Baker & Hostetler LLP 20
Baker & McKenzie LLP 25
Banner & Witcoff, Ltd. 29
Barack Ferrazzano Kirschbaum Perlman & Nagelberg LLP 32
Barnes & Thornburg LLP 36
Bell, Boyd & Lloyd LLC 42
Bollinger, Ruberry & Garvey 47
Brinks Hofer Gilson & Lione 50
Bryan Cave LLP 54
Butzel Long 59
Calfee, Halter & Griswold LLP 62
Chapman and Cutler LLP 66
Clark Hill PLC 71
Clausen Miller, P.C. 74
Dickinson Wright PLLC 78
DLA Piper Rudnick Gray Cary US LLP 82
Dykema Gossett PLLC 88
Foley & Lardner LLP 92
Freeborn & Peters LLP 97
Frost Brown Todd LLC 102
Gardner Carton & Douglas LLP 107
Godfrey & Kahn, S.C. 111
Goldberg Kohn Bell Black Rosenbloom & Moritz, Ltd. 114
Greenberg Traurig, LLP 118
Hinshaw & Culbertson LLP 123
Holland & Knight LLP 126

"A HAPPY BUNCH, THOSE WINSTON ASSOCIATES ARE."
—Vault Guide to the Top 100 Law Firms, 6th Ed.

HAPPY THEN, HAPPY NOW

Ranked in the Top 3 in

"Best Firms to Work For"

for five consecutive years.

THIS YEAR, ALSO RANKED TOP 5 IN...
Satisfaction, Offices, Compensation, Mentoring, Diversity for Minorities, Associate/Partner Relations, Pro Bono, and Overall Diversity.

Vault Guide to the Top 100 Law Firms, 7th Ed.

WINSTON & STRAWN LLP

CHICAGO   GENEVA   LONDON   LOS ANGELES   NEW YORK   PARIS   SAN FRANCISCO   WASHINGTON, D.C.

Honigman Miller Schwartz and Cohn LLP 131
Husch & Eppenberger, LLC 134
Ice Miller® 138
Jenkens & Gilchrist, a Professional Corporation 142
Jenner & Block LLP 148
Jones Day 154
Katten Muchin Zavis Rosenman 158
Kirkland & Ellis LLP 164
Latham & Watkins Illinois LLP 170
Leydig, Voit & Mayer, Ltd. 175
Lord, Bissell & Brook LLP 178
Marshall, Gerstein & Borun LLP 182
Mayer, Brown, Rowe & Maw LLP 185
McDermott Will & Emery 188
McGuireWoods LLP 193
Michael Best & Friedrich LLP 198
Miller, Canfield, Paddock and Stone, P.L.C. 203
Miller, Johnson, Snell & Cummiskey, P.L.C. 207
Much Shelist Freed Denenberg Ament & Rubenstein, P.C. 210
Neal, Gerber & Eisenberg LLP 213
Pattishall, McAuliffe, Newbury, Hilliard & Geraldson LLP 217
Pedersen & Houpt 220
Porter Wright Morris & Arthur LLP 224
Quarles & Brady LLP 228
Reinhart Boerner Van Deuren S.C. 231
Sachnoff & Weaver, Ltd. 234
Schiff Hardin LLP 239
Schwartz, Cooper, Greenberger & Krauss 243
Seyfarth Shaw LLP 246
Shefsky & Froelich Ltd. 249
Sidley Austin Brown & Wood LLP 252
Skadden, Arps, Slate, Meagher & Flom LLP and Affiliates 258
Sonnenschein Nath & Rosenthal LLP 264
Squire, Sanders & Dempsey L.L.P. 270
Taft, Stettinius & Hollister LLP 275
Thompson Coburn LLP 278
Thompson Hine LLP 282

VAULT
THE MOST TRUSTED NAME IN CAREER INFORMATION

"With reviews and profiles of firms that one associate calls 'spot on,' [Vault's] guide has become a key reference for those who want to know what it takes to get hired by a law firm and what to expect once they get there."

– New York Law Journal

"To get the unvarnished scoop, check out Vault."

– SmartMoney magazine

VAULT

"Vault is indispensable for locating insider information."
- Metropolitan Corporate Counsel

Ungaretti & Harris LLP 287
Vedder, Price, Kaufman & Kammholz, P.C. 292
Vorys, Sater, Seymour and Pease LLP 296
Warner Norcross & Judd LLP 299
Welsh & Katz, Ltd. 303
Whyte Hirschboeck Dudek S.C. 306
Wildman Harrold 309
Winston & Strawn LLP 314

What Latham & Watkins can do for your career.

From the global capabilities of our 22 offices worldwide to the abundant and challenging opportunities that even our newest associates enjoy, Latham & Watkins is the perfect place for you to soar. True, our hiring standards are rigorous, but imagine working among some of today's best legal minds.

As a Latham associate you'll thrive in a collegial atmosphere and benefit from our stellar training and award-winning pro bono programs.

Together with our dedication to diversity and equal opportunity, you'll find that at Latham & Watkins, the sky really is the limit for your career. Find out more on campus or visit us online at www.lw.com.

LATHAM & WATKINS LLP

Boston	New York
Brussels	Northern Virginia
Chicago	Orange County
Frankfurt	Paris
Hamburg	San Diego
Hong Kong	San Francisco
London	Shanghai
Los Angeles	Silicon Valley
Milan	Singapore
Moscow	Tokyo
New Jersey	Washington, D.C.

Latham & Watkins operates as a limited liability partnership worldwide with an affiliate in the United Kingdom and Italy, where the practice is conducted through an affiliated multinational partnership.

Introduction

Welcome to the new, expanded edition of the *Vault Guide to the Top Chicago & Midwest Law Firms*. For the last several years, we have published comprehensive guides to the most prestigious law firms throughout the United States. We realized, however, that those national guides only scratched the surface of the vibrant law community in the Midwest, and in 2003 we released our first *Vault Guide to the Top Chicago Law Firms*. This year, we have expanded the guide to include top firms throughout the Midwest. We invited associates at the region's top law firms to tell us about their jobs, offer suggestions to prospective associates and rate their employers on subjects such as hours, compensation, treatment by partners, training and office space. The candid assessments of these associates regarding life at their firms are included in our profiles, which also contain information on major practice areas, recruiting contacts and the most notable perks each firm offers its attorneys.

When we asked associates to tell us why they chose to practice in the Midwest, we drew a range of responses – from eager, urban sophisticates ("I love Chicago!") to laid-back lawyers in Milwaukee looking "to get away from the big-city life." Chicagoland associates proudly tout their city's legal market, citing its "strong, sophisticated client base," as well as its "urban amenities," including "beautiful architecture, museums, theatre and music." Eschewing the charms of California and New York, many "prefer the Midwest over either coast" and claim that "Chicago has all the advantages of New York City without the stress." "Chicago is the perfect city," declares one insider: "huge, but livable."

In fact, "livability" seems to be one of the region's biggest attractions, whether associates work in Chicago, Cleveland or Grand Rapids, Mich. Our contacts enjoy the "pace of the Midwestern lifestyle" and share a sense that the middle of the country is "more family-friendly" than either coast. Chicago may be "one of the best markets for practicing law," according to Windy City associates, but Ohio also offers "challenging and sophisticated work" in a "family-oriented" environment. "West Michigan is a great area to raise a family," says one lawyer, and so, according to others, is Indianapolis. The region's frequently cited "low cost of living" is undoubtedly one of its attractions.

Many associates are native Midwesterners who have lived elsewhere but returned to be near friends and relatives or to raise their own families. Some simply never left. Says one Ohio lawyer, "I have always lived in this geographic area and have never had any desire to leave." Other associates are escapees from the Big Apple who longed for a more "balanced" life. One attorney who stayed in Ohio after attending law school there explains, "I thought there was an opportunity to make a difference in this town."

Whether you already call the Midwest home or hope to relocate there, we're confident that with the *Vault Guide to the Top Chicago & Midwest Law Firms* you'll have access to the best information to prepare yourself for interviews at the region's top firms.

A GUIDE TO THIS GUIDE

If you're wondering how our entries are organized, read on. Here's a handy guide to the information you'll find packed into each entry of this book.

The Profiles

Our profiles are divided into three sections: The Scoop, Getting Hired and Our Survey Says. Only profiles of firms for which we have associate survey data contain an Our Survey Says section. We received survey data either when a law firm chose to participate in our 2004 national or regional associate survey or when Vault contacted firm associates independently, without the participation of the firm.

The Scoop: The firm's history, major clients, recent deals, major firm developments and other points of interest.

Getting Hired: Qualifications the firm looks for in new associates, tips on getting hired, information about the firm's summer associate program and other notable aspects of the hiring process.

Our Survey Says: Actual quotes from surveys and interviews with current associates in the firm's Midwestern office(s) on topics such as the firm's assignment system, work feedback, partnership prospects, levels of responsibility, summer associate program, culture, hours, compensation, training and much more.

Firm Facts

Locations: A listing of the firm's offices, with the headquarter office bolded. You may see firms with no bolded location. This means that these are self-proclaimed decentralized firms without official headquarters.

Major Departments & Practices: Practice areas that employ a significant portion of the firm's attorneys as reported by the firms.

Base Salary: The firm's base salary in the Midwestern office(s). Pay is for 2005 except where noted. Some firms have chosen not to list any salary information at all.

Notable Perks: A listing of impressive, interesting or unusual perks and benefits outside the norm. (For example, we do not list health care, as every firm we surveyed offers a health care plan.)

Uppers and Downers: Good points and bad points about working at the firm, as gleaned from associate surveys. Uppers and downers are the impressionistic perceptions of insiders and are not based on statistics. (Note that only profiles of firms for which we have associate survey data contain Uppers and Downers.)

Employment Contact: The person the firm identifies as the primary contact to receive resumes or to answer questions about the recruitment process.

The Stats

No. of attorneys firm-wide: The total number of attorneys in all offices as of December 2004.

No. of attorneys in the firm's largest Midwestern office(s): The total number of attorneys at the firm's largest Midwestern regional office(s) as of December 2004.

No. of offices: The firm's total number of offices worldwide.

Summer associate offers firm-wide: The firm-wide number of second-year law students offered full-time associate positions by the firm in 2004, as well as the number of second-year law students who participated in the firm's summer program that year.

Summer associate offers in the firm's largest Midwestern office(s): The number of second-year law students offered full-time associate positions in the firm's largest Midwestern office(s) in 2004, as well as the number of second-year law students who participated in the firm's summer program in those offices that year.

Chairman, Managing Partner, etc.: The name and title of the leader of the firm. Sometimes more than one name is provided.

Hiring Partner, Hiring Attorney, etc.: The name and title of the attorney in charge of the firm's hiring efforts. Sometimes the Midwestern regional hiring partner's name is given.

THE YEAR IN LAW

Getting better all the time

Things are looking up for law firms all over the country, and the economic recovery in the Midwest is part of the reason. Not only were 15 percent of *The American Lawyer's* 200 top-grossing firms from the Midwest, but one (Jenner & Block) even made the national publication's elite "A-List." Jenner's successful practice and pro bono performance, combined with its diversity and decent treatment of associates, put it at No. 19 among the top 20 firms in the country. Baker & McKenzie remained at No. 6 on *Corporate Board Member's* list of the top 20 law firms in the nation, with Chicago rivals Jones Day, Kirkland & Ellis and Sidley Austin Brown & Wood not far behind (Kirkland & Ellis was actually named the leader in the Chicago market).

It's (almost) all good

The past year has been a lively one for most law firms, with the Midwest receiving its share of the country's big-ticket litigation. Sonnenschein Nath & Rosenthal received considerable attention last spring when it persuaded a jury to return a complete defense verdict in a 30-state, class-action lawsuit against Allstate Insurance Company. At the same time, Sonnenschein's Chicago lawyers helped ink out a $2 billion settlement for a client in an antitrust lawsuit. Vorys, Sater, Seymour and Pease found itself touted in the papers for defending (and ultimately helping to settle) three employment discrimination lawsuits that sought up to $50 million in damages against Abercrombie & Fitch. Meanwhile, Sidley Austin Brown & Wood successfully represented Tyson Foods against a claim that the company had been smuggling illegal aliens into the country to work at its poultry processing plants. (But not everything has been good for Sidley: both Sidley and Jenkens & Gilchrist experienced their own legal troubles in 2004 when they were sued by former clients over tax-shelter advice provided several years ago.)

Merger and acquisitions work also brought in a lot of money for Midwest law firms, especially in the first part of 2004. Katten Muchin Zavis Rosenman made it to *Corporate Board Member's* ranking of the top five corporate law firms in Chicago, in no small part because of a $76 million deal it completed in the summer on behalf of client InstallShield Software Corporation. Jones Day once again topped the lists compiled by Thomson Financial and Bloomberg for the most deals completed worldwide. Among some of the biggest deals in which Jones Day's Midwestern offices had a hand in 2004 were the $46.5 billion merger between Jones Day client Nextel Communications and Sprint and the acquisition by Albertson's of Shaw's Supermarkets for $2.5 billion.

Meanwhile, many firms continued to grow their intellectual property practices with much success. Foley & Lardner, for example, now represents four of the 10 hottest nanotechnology university labs, including Northwestern. The only lag overall was in bankruptcy, thanks to rebounds in the economy. But even there, some Midwest firms prospered. United Air Lines, which has been in Chapter 11 since December 2002, had racked up $235 million in professional fees by the end of June, no small amount of which went to lead bankruptcy counsel Kirkland & Ellis. The Chicago office of Latham & Watkins had 24 active insolvency cases in the first half of 2004, earning it the No.-1 ranking among the "Top 10 Bankruptcy Lender Law Firms," a list compiled by *The Deal: Bankruptcy Insider*. Another firm to get in on the action: Skadden, Arps, Slate, Meagher & Flom, which filed a notable bankruptcy action on behalf of Interstate Bakeries, the Missouri-based company responsible for Twinkies, Ho-Hos and Ding Dongs. To the relief of many grateful sweet-tooths, the company is still in operation.

More money, more mergers

Building on the economic recovery they experienced last year, most Midwestern law firms reported stronger revenues in 2004 and increased their expenses by close to 10 percent. The surge in litigation, especially securities class actions, boosted revenues by 16.5 percent at Chicago firms. To keep up with the work, Midwestern firms brought on more and more lawyers, and they haven't let go yet. In fact, news reports say that many have raised their billable rates, and the clients keep on coming.

Some firms, such as Piper Rudnick, have grown so much they've become unrecognizable. Now DLA Piper Rudnick Gray Cary, LLP, the firm negotiated two mammoth mergers last year, both of which became effective on New Year's Day, 2005. After announcing a cross-country union with Silicon Valley's Gray Cary Ware & Freidenrich LLP, Piper Rudnick reached across the Atlantic to merge with the U.K.-based DLA. While the former Piper Rudnick was comparatively large with close to 1,000 attorneys last year, DLA Piper is now the third-largest firm in the world, with over 2,800 attorneys in 18 countries and revenues of more than $1 billion.

Other Midwestern law firms which experienced significant growth in 2004 include Dykema Gossett, which scooped up 78 attorneys when it merged with Rooks Pitts (it also added four lawyers from the Washington, D.C., securities and corporate boutique, Jones & Blouch, and three real estate attorneys from Michigan's Howard & Howard). Honigman Miller Schwartz and Cohn also underwent a few changes in 2004, first adding nine IP attorneys to its ranks and then gobbling up several partners from now-dissolved Miro, Weiner, & Kramer.

But not everyone likes change, even if it comes with more resources and bigger name recognition. Holland & Knight suffered a blow after acquiring Chicago-based McBride Baker & Coles in 2002 and taking on five real estate attorneys from Piper Rudnick. Three partners and several other associates from the firm's real estate practice left for smaller pastures. DLA Piper's last round of mergers has the potential for so many conflicts that some attorneys worried they will be forced to move to keep their business.

Bonus blues

Despite the continued upturn and the increase in bonuses at many East Coast firms at the end of the year, many Midwest firms kept their year-end perks relatively stagnant. At the Missouri offices of Bryan Cave, for example, associates were only entitled to the same bonus amounts they received for 2003, assuming they met billable hours and otherwise qualified for a bonus. (If they did qualify, however, those bonuses were by no means paltry: a member of the 2003 class was eligible for a bonus of up to $20,000, and some senior associates received double that amount.) Chicago's Mayer, Brown, Rowe & Maw also stuck with last year's bonus plan, at least for associates who weren't working in New York.

New digs

For some firms, any extra money they received may have been spent on new or renovated offices. Mayer Brown will soon become the anchor tenant in the new 47-story Hyatt Center just north of the Sears Tower, while Bollinger, Ruberry & Garvey increased its office space in Chicago's all-glass Citicorp building and then renovated it. On the horizon: Lord Bissell & Brook is expected to move to The John Buck Co.'s $300 million, 51-story building, which is opening this summer.

To get the best law jobs, you need the best legal career advice.

That's where Vault's expertise in the legal field can help you. We wrote the book on top law firms. Now we can help you reach the next stage in your legal career.

Law Resume Writing and Resume Reviews

- Have your resume reviewed by a legal resume expert.
- For resume writing, start with an e-mailed history and 1- to 2-hour phone discussion. Our experts will write a first draft, and deliver a final draft after feedback and discussion.
- For resume reviews, get an in-depth, detailed critique and rewrite within TWO BUSINESS DAYS.

Law Career Coaching

Need Vault's help in solving a pressing legal career question? We've got experts ready to assist you.

- Looking to leave Big Law?
- Ready to move to another law firm?
- Considering a switch from private practice to government work?
- Just graduating from law school and unsure where to begin?

"It was well worth the price! I have been struggling with this for weeks and in 48 hours you had given me the answers! I now know what I need to change."

-- T.H., Attorney, Pasadena, CA

"Law school taught me to be precise, your comments helped me to see the bigger picture and make the resume more accessible to a hiring manager."

-- A.J., Recent Law School Graduate, Chicago, IL

"Thank you for your time and patience, I really felt like you heard what I had to say and made great suggestions!"

-- R.F., Attorney, Chicago, IL

For more information go to www.vault.com/law

VAULT
> the most trusted name in career information™

LAW FIRM PROFILES

Arnstein & Lehr LLP

120 South Riverside Plaza
Suite 1200
Chicago, IL 60606-3910
Phone: (312) 876-7100
www.arnstein.com

LOCATIONS

Chicago, IL (HQ)
Boca Raton, FL
Hoffman Estates, IL
Miami, FL
Milwaukee, WI
Tampa, FL
West Palm Beach, FL

MAJOR DEPARTMENTS & PRACTICES

Antitrust & Trade Regulation
Bankruptcy
Banks & Financial Institutions
Business/Corporate
Employment & Employee Benefits
Environmental
Estate Planning/Probate
Health Care
Insurance
International
Litigation
Real Estate
Taxation
Trademark
White-Collar Criminal Defense

THE STATS

No. of attorneys:
   firm-wide: 131
   Chicago: 95
No. of offices: 7
Summer associate offers:
   Chicago: 3 out of 4 (2004)
Executive Committee Chair: Raymond J. Werner
Hiring Partner: Robert D. Butters

NOTABLE PERKS

- Bar review expenses
- Bonus upon completion of 2,000+ billable-hours
- ARDC registration fees

BASE SALARY

Chicago, IL (2005)
1st year: $110,000
Summer associate: $2,115/week

EMPLOYMENT CONTACT

Ms. Kathleen A. Hanus
Hiring Coordinator
Phone: (312) 876-7100
Fax: (312) 876-0288
E-mail: kahanus@arnstein.com

THE SCOOP

Since its inception in 1893, Arnstein & Lehr has represented landmark Chicago clients. In the early days of the firm, Arnstein & Lehr serendipitously landed Sears, Roebuck and Company as a client. Just two years after the firm's formation, Richard Sears, Aaron Nussbaum and Julius Rosenwald sought to reorganize their company with equal ownership among the three partners. According to firm lore, the men could not reach their usual counsel one night, when they saw the lights on at Loeb & Adler, Arnstein's ancestral firm. The company retained the young firm and has been a client ever since. In the 1970s, Arnstein represented Sears in a dispute that arose during the construction of the Sears Tower. When the famed skyscraper was half-built, the state of Illinois commenced a lawsuit against the builders, complaining that the finished structure would interfere with television reception in the surrounding neighborhood. Arnstein & Lehr successfully defended the suit, and the tower was finished as planned in 1973.

In another key victory for the firm, Arnstein represented the Drake Hotel in litigation that could have cost the hotel $100 million. The dispute surrounded a building appraisal that would have raised the hotel's ground rent payments exponentially; but the Arnstein lawyers argued that a clause in the lease limited the potential uses for the structure and thus the value of the land. Accordingly, the court reduced the appraisal and the computation of the rent payments.

Although Arnstein & Lehr has five main practice areas (business transactions, litigation, real estate, tax and estate planning, and local government), the firm is especially known for its strong litigation practice. Litigators handle all kinds of commercial litigation as well as malpractice and product liability defense, creditors' rights issues and criminal defense. In addition, a growing number of the firm's 120 lawyers are dedicated to transactional and real estate matters. Clients range from individuals to small and growing businesses to large, multinational corporations. In many cases, as with Sears, the attorney-client relationship has spanned several decades.

In recent years, the firm has branched out from its Windy City headquarters, establishing offices in warmer outposts in West Palm Beach, Boca Raton, Miami and Tampa, Fla. Arnstein & Lehr also has offices in Milwaukee, Wis., and Hoffman Estates, Ill. In August 2004, the Chicago office welcomed three new attorneys, partner Michael J. Zdeb and associates A. Thomas Skallas and Joy E. Mason, who bring to the firm broad experience in corporate law, trusts and tax planning, and bankruptcy litigation.

GETTING HIRED

Although the firm does hire laterally, it takes pride in developing young lawyers, and the summer program for second-year law students is at the heart of the firm's hiring practice. In evaluating candidates, Arnstein & Lehr balances class rank against law school prestige. It expects students from "first-tier" schools to be in the top half of their class, while applicants from lower-tier schools should be within the top 25 percent. The selection process is not all about academics, however; the firm also gives weight to extracurricular activities like moot court and journal experience.

Arnstein & Lehr interviews at law school campuses throughout the Midwest, including Chicago-Kent, DePaul, University of Illinois, Indiana University at Bloomington, University of Iowa, John Marshall Law School, Loyola University, University of Michigan, Northwestern University, Washington University in St. Louis and the University of Wisconsin. In addition, as part of its effort to increase the diversity of its attorneys, Arnstein & Lehr conducts on-campus interviews at Howard University in Washington, D.C., and participates in the Cook County Bar Association Minority Job Fair.

Those who succeed in landing a job at Arnstein & Lehr should expect to work hard; the minimum annual billable requirement is 2,000 hours. But there are rewards in store for those who meet or exceed the billable-hours target. At 2,000 hours, associates receive a guaranteed $10,000 bonus, and additional bonuses are available for every additional hour billed over and above the target.

Use the Internet's
MOST TARGETED
job search tools.

Vault Job Board

Target your search by industry, function, and experience level, and find the job openings that you want.

VaultMatch Resume Database

Vault takes match-making to the next level: post your resume and customize your search by industry, function, experience and more. We'll match job listings with your interests and criteria and e-mail them directly to your inbox.

VAULT
> the most trusted name in career information™

Baker & Daniels

300 North Meridian Street
Suite 2700
Indianapolis, IN 46204
Phone: (317) 237-0300
www.bakerdaniels.com

LOCATIONS
Elkhart, IN
Fort Wayne, IN
Indianapolis, IN (two offices)
South Bend, IN
Washington, DC
Beijing
Qingdao

MAJOR DEPARTMENTS & PRACTICES
Business Litigation
Commercial & Bankruptcy
Construction & Real Property Litigation
Corporate Finance
Employee Benefits
Government Services
Health Care
Insurance & Financial Services
Intellectual Property
International
Labor & Employment
Not-for-Profit
Public Finance
Real Estate
State & Local Taxation
Strategic Business Services
Trusts & Estates

THE STATS
No. of attorneys:
  firm-wide: 299
  Indianapolis: 202
  Fort Wayne: 49
  South Bend: 26
No. of offices: 8
Summer associate offers:
  firm-wide: 10 out of 11 (2004)
  Indianapolis: 8 out of 9 (2004)
  Fort Wayne: 1 out of 1 (2004)
  South Bend: 1 out of 1 (2004)
Chair and CEO: Brian K. Burke
Managing Partner, Professional Personnel: Francina A. Dlouhy

UPPERS
- National and global focus with a regional "feel"
- Family-friendly attitude and associate camaraderie

DOWNERS
- No billable credit for pro bono work
- Lack of communication about partnership

NOTABLE PERKS
- Subsidized health club membership
- Firm-covered BlackBerry services
- Annual firm formal
- "Wonderful" administrative and IT support

BASE SALARY
Indiana offices (2005)
1st year: $85,000
Summer associate: $1,550/week

EMPLOYMENT CONTACTS
Indianapolis
Ms. Kristin Givens
Legal Recruiting Administrator
Phone: (317) 237-1299
Fax: (317) 237-1000
E-mail: kristin.givens@bakerd.com

Fort Wayne
Dave Kuker, Esq.
Hiring Attorney
Phone: (260) 460-1694
Fax: (260) 460-1700
E-mail: dave.kuker@bakerd.com

South Bend
Ms. Beckie Mills
Recruiting Coordinator
Phone: (574) 239-1974
Fax: (574) 472-4584
E-mail: beckie.mills@bakerd.com

THE SCOOP

For three years running, Baker & Daniels has been deemed the best law firm in Indianapolis by the country's corporate directors and the editors of *Corporate Board Member* magazine. The firm also topped *Chambers USA*'s 2004 rankings of the best Indiana firms in the areas of litigation, corporate mergers and acquisitions, and employment. In another home-state honor, Baker & Daniels had 45 lawyers selected for the 2005–2006 edition of *The Best Lawyers in America*, the most attorneys of any Indiana law firm.

Baker & Daniels started out in 1863 as Hendricks & Hord, a two-man Indianapolis law office launched by Thomas A. Hendricks, who later served as vice president to Grover Cleveland, and Oscar B. Hord, who had been attorney general of Indiana. The masthead partners, Conrad Baker and Edward Daniels, joined the practice in 1873 and 1879, respectively. Today, the firm's nearly 300 attorneys work in five Indiana offices, a branch in the nation's capital and two law offices in China.

The practice at Baker & Daniels offers many of the traditional law firm areas of expertise, such as litigation, labor and tax; but the firm has branched out into more specialized practices, including sports and entertainment, life sciences, immigration and construction. Most notably, Baker & Daniels has established a thriving practice centered on China: the firm frequently counsels clients on the legal and strategic ramifications of developing business in China. Baker & Daniels has also posted attorneys in three Chinese cities to act as liaisons between American clients and the Chinese government.

GETTING HIRED

The "utmost integrity" and a high degree of intelligence are "the bare minimum to get in the door for an interview," says one Baker & Daniels source. "To get hired, we're looking for a lot more than just those two qualities." Another associate agrees: "It is a very competitive process. We are seeking applicants who are seeking to perform challenging work for an Indiana-based law firm with a national perspective, but hope to retain a high quality of life that is not prevalent in many other cities." A veteran of the firm adds, "The firm spends a lot of time finding the right people and takes the interview/recruiting process very seriously. Besides being smart and willing to work hard, I believe the firm is looking to hire those who have an ownership mentality from the start and who can be good team players."

OUR SURVEY SAYS

For the most part, associates at Baker & Daniels display almost unbridled enthusiasm for their firm. "According to all of my friends from law school, I am one of the only ones that truly loves my job after two full years out in the field. I attribute that to Baker & Daniels being such a wonderful place to work," declares one happy camper. Says another, "I work with a fantastic group of smart, caring people, and I have been put in a position as a young associate to help craft creative ways to assist our clients in accomplishing their objectives." A litigator observes that the firm culture "reflects Midwestern values – a spirit of cooperation and collegiality combined with an ethic of hard work, professionalism and dedication to client service."

Thanks to the firm's carefully balanced ratio, associates get a lot of quality time with partners. "Our one-partner, one-associate rule makes this a fantastic place to practice," comments a junior attorney. Partners seem to welcome the opportunity to mentor newer members of the profession. "The firm's culture is one of respect and openness," says an associate, "where doors remain open and associates are welcome to drop into partners' offices to ask questions or just chat." On a more structured basis, Baker & Daniels provides some training, but many find that the off-the-cuff mentoring is more effective. "The firm has some formal training on topics of general interest. They are of limited use, however," remarks an insider. According to another, "Practical team training sessions are essentially non-existent. However, the firm as a whole does a wonderful job at providing rainmaking/business development training."

Associates take the hours required of them in stride. "I am very satisfied in that the firm does not place any pressure on me to bill hours in excess of 1,850. However, I end up working more hours every year because we get interesting cases on which I want to work and I volunteer for those assignments," reports a midlevel attorney. A young corporate associate says, "I have had a few long days, but I don't feel pressure to bill as of yet. Additionally, it is acceptable to bill hours from home if need be, so I don't feel the need to be physically present in the office." The firm places emphasis on family time, which insiders appreciate. "I still have plenty of time to have a full life outside of work," says a midlevel associate. "Baker & Daniels definitely encourages its lawyers (including associates on every level) to prioritize family and get involved in activities that we each enjoy out of the office."

Considering the low cost of living in the region, Indiana associates find their salaries satisfactory. A transactional attorney observes, "The firm has taken steps to reduce salary compression that prevails in Indianapolis and other medium-sized cities. Essentially being paid overtime in the form of a bonus for billable-hours is also rewarding. In comparison to large firms in Chicago, there is no comparison in terms of associate compensation. In my experience though, the lower cost of living and reduced billable-hour expectations in Indianapolis result in more satisfied associates." One pleased midlevel notes that "Baker & Daniels has chosen to provide associates with salaries and production bonuses above the competition, while at the same time not increasing billable goals or hindering associate quality-of-life matters."

"Baker & Daniels has chosen to provide associates with salaries and production bonuses above the competition, while at the same time not increasing billable goals or hindering associate quality-of-life matters."

— *Baker & Daniels associate*

Baker & Hostetler LLP

3200 National City Center
1900 East 9th Street
Cleveland, OH 44114-3485
Phone: (216) 621-0200
www.bakerlaw.com

LOCATIONS
Cleveland, OH (HQ)
Cincinnati, OH
Columbus, OH
Costa Mesa, CA
Denver, CO
Houston, TX
Los Angeles, CA
New York, NY
Orlando, FL
Washington, DC

MAJOR DEPARTMENTS & PRACTICES
Business
Employment & Labor
Health Care
Hospitality
Intellectual Property
International
Litigation
Media Law
Tax, Personal Planning & Employee Benefits
Transportation

THE STATS
No. of attorneys:
   firm-wide: 599
   Cleveland: 195
   Cincinnati: 15
   Columbus: 71
No. of offices: 10
Summer associate offers:
   firm-wide: 52 out of 58 (2004)
   Cleveland: 16 out of 16 (2004)
   Cincinnati: 2 out of 2 (2004)
   Columbus: 9 out of 10 (2004)
Executive Partners: R. Steven Kestner and Alec Wightman
Hiring Partners:
   Cleveland: Ronald A. Stepanovic
   Cincinnati: David Holcombe
   Columbus: Mark D. Senff

UPPERS
- Diversity and quality of work
- Collegial, friendly atmosphere

DOWNERS
- Limited formal training
- Low salary increases for first few years

NOTABLE PERKS
- Tickets to sporting events
- Monthly wine and cheese parties
- Six months maternity leave (including 12 weeks paid)
- Bar exam stipend, payment of bar and moving expenses

BASE SALARY

Cleveland, OH (2005)
1st year: $105,000
Summer associate: $7,500/month

Cincinnati, OH (2005)
1st year: $90,000
Summer associate: $1,635/week

Columbus, OH (2005)
1st year: $100,000
Summer associate: $1,744/week

EMPLOYMENT CONTACTS

Cleveland
Ms. Jennifer Pethel
Recruiting Coordinator
Phone: (216) 861-7113
Fax: (216) 696-0740
E-mail: jpethel@bakerlaw.com

Cincinnati
Ms. Kimberlee Nickolas
Recruiting Coordinator
Phone: (513) 929-3480
Fax: (513) 929-0303
E-mail: knickolas@bakerlaw.com

Columbus
Ms. Jeanie Fulton
Recruiting Coordinator
Phone: (614) 462-4703
Fax: (614) 462-2616
E-mail: jfulton@bakerlaw.com

THE SCOOP

Over the course of its 88-year history, Baker & Hostetler has attracted an enviable list of clients, such as General Electric and Major League Baseball. With several former journalists on staff, including attorneys who have written for *The Wall Street Journal* and *The Washington Post*, the firm has a particularly impressive media practice. One of Baker & Hostetler's most celebrated achievements in this area was the international licensing of the PEANUTS® gang for client United Features Syndicate. Other clients of the firm's media group are FOX Television, Random House and the Hearst Corporation.

Baker & Hostetler's nearly 600 lawyers frequently work on cases and transactions that cross the boundaries of practice areas and office locations. In one recent case, attorneys from the firm's litigation and tax departments teamed up on a tax controversy, successfully representing a financial services institution in the recovery of an $80 million refund. Meanwhile, the firm's transactional lawyers counseled client Interval International, a timeshare-swapping network with over 1,900 resorts and 1.5 million family members worldwide, in its all-cash $578 million sale to USA Interactive, an electronic travel services conglomerate. In another landmark media deal, Baker & Hostetler advised longtime client The E.W. Scripps Company, which owns Home & Garden Television, in a transaction that resulted in the $775 million purchase of several print and broadcast concerns, including the Food Network.

GETTING HIRED

According to one insider at Baker & Hostetler, "it is much more difficult to get an interview than it is to get hired after you are invited to interview." Pedigree counts, as a threshold matter: "The firm's recruiting appears to be focused on second- and third-tier students at Ivy League or 'Ivy League equivalent' schools." But that's not all; Baker is also "very focused on personality – they want lawyers who will work hard and play hard." A midlevel observes that "the firm seeks to hire individuals who are bright and motivated, who fit into the congenial atmosphere and who would be committed to the practice of law." The source adds that long-term potential is a factor: "Associate retention at the firm is important – the firm looks to hire those individuals who would want to help the firm grow and expand. In other words, I believe that the firm looks to hire associates who could be a partner someday."

OUR SURVEY SAYS

Baker & Hostetler maintains a formal dress code in a business casual world, but the firm's personality is much more Banana Republic than Savile Row. As one source puts it, the firm is "very laid-back, respectful and kind. Partners socialize with associates and associates socialize regularly." Another insider characterizes the firm culture as "very friendly," adding that attorneys are "formal when they need to be, laid-back when they can be." To some degree, the culture varies by department; in certain groups, says an associate, "there is a pretty wide divide between us and the partners."

In many practice groups, however, partners demonstrate an admirable commitment to associate development. "I cannot overemphasize the value of the informal training I have received from the three or four partners that I do most, if not all, of my work for," raves a third-year. "They have gone out of their way to mentor me on things other than substantive work. They have taken an interest in my quality of life and seem genuinely interested in grooming me for partnership down the road." A more senior associate is slightly less enthusiastic: "Partners do sometimes go out of their way to provide tips and insights and to advise you on how to better handle different situations. But most learning is just by trial and error, and while there does not seem to be much penalty for being on the 'error' side, it is not a very efficient system for learning." On a more structured level, the firm provides training programs for junior attorneys, including the four-day Associate Academy, and midlevel training through practice group retreats. Some departments also hold monthly training meetings and participate in bar association programs.

Some insiders at Baker & Hostetler report that the firm's expectations for billable-hours are "altogether reasonable." One associate states, "You see few people after 7:00 or so, and those that are here are here because they need to be." Others laud the lack of face time: "I do a lot of work at home," says a midlevel lawyer. "The firm is very flexible in that regard and does not have a problem with me spending less time at the office." One junior associate cautions that Baker is leaning toward a greater emphasis on billable-hours: "The firm is attempting to increase associate hours as a way to be viewed by clients as a 'go-to, top' firm. This push to increase hours changes the work/life balance that Baker has had a reputation for keeping positive." The firm has a part-time program and those who take advantage of it find that the firm is supportive. Pro bono hours do not count toward billable totals, "unless the project is something substantial enough, and the associate goes through a process to get approved."

"At the first-year level," according to several Baker & Hostetler insiders, "compensation is competitive, but after that the firm is very stingy with increases." One Cleveland lawyer complains that "raises are below inflation." On the other hand, another Ohioan believes that "compensation is more than fair for the billable-hours requirement." Bonuses are tied directly to billable-hours. Associates receive a 5 percent bonus for hitting 1,950 hours and a 7.5 percent bonus for billing 2,100 hours. Beyond the first year or two, associates may be eligible for additional, discretionary bonuses if they hit the 1,950-hour threshold.

Baker & McKenzie LLP

One Prudential Plaza
Chicago, IL 60601
Phone: (312) 861-8000
www.bakernet.com

LOCATIONS

Chicago, IL (HQ)
Dallas, TX
Houston, TX
Miami, FL
New York, NY
Palo Alto, CA
San Diego, CA
San Francisco, CA
Washington, DC
+ 60 other offices worldwide

MAJOR DEPARTMENTS & PRACTICES

Antitrust & Trade
Banking & Finance
Corporate
Employment
Information Technology & Communications
Insurance
Intellectual Property
International & Commercial Litigation
Major Projects & Project Finance
Real Estate, Construction, Environment & Tourism
Tax

THE STATS

No. of attorneys:
firm-wide: 3,225
Chicago: 177
No. of offices: 69
Summer associate offers:
Chicago: 8 out of 9 (2004)
Chairman of Executive Committee: John Conroy
Hiring Partner: Nam H. Paik (Chicago)

UPPERS

- International practice with sophisticated work
- Diverse, smart associates

DOWNERS

- Excessive bureaucracy
- Uneven workload

NOTABLE PERKS

- Free weekend parking
- Discount movie tickets
- Daily soup lunch
- In-house training at resort locations

BASE SALARY

Chicago, IL (2005)
1st year: $125,000
Summer associate: $2,400/week

EMPLOYMENT CONTACT

Ms. Eleonora Nikol
Recruitment Coordinator
Phone: (312) 861-2924
Fax: (312) 861-2898
E-mail: eleonora.nikol@bakernet.com

THE SCOOP

Few law firms have reached "behemoth" status, but Baker & McKenzie is surely among the handful that have. What started out as a small practice, founded by a young Texan who had paid his way through the University of Chicago Law School by working as a professional prizefighter, has mushroomed over the last 80 years into the 3,200-attorney, 69-office worldwide sprawl that is Baker & McKenzie today.

Even the domestic offices of Baker & McKenzie handle matters on an international scale. In July 2004, a team of lawyers in Chicago worked with Baker attorneys in the New York and Buenos Aires offices to advise an Argentinean water concession company, Aguas Argentinas S.A., and its principle shareholders on a debt repurchase agreement with the company's creditors. The $145 million refinancing will help to resolve a dispute between the firm's client and the government of Argentina that has been ongoing since 2002, and many hope that the deal will help stabilize conditions in the concession industry. In another recent interoffice, interdisciplinary matter, Baker-Chicago attorneys teamed with partners and associates from no less than eight other offices on client Clariant International AG's sale of its AZ Electronic Materials business to The Carlyle Group. The Carlyle Group manages $18.3 billion in private equity, while AZ Electronic provides supplies to semiconductor and flat panel display manufacturers around the world and operates in several countries in Asia, Europe and North America.

GETTING HIRED

Associates disagree on how difficult it is to get hired at Baker & McKenzie. According to one source, "It's getting harder and harder these days. Great academic credentials are a prerequisite. [A] well-rounded personality and extracurricular qualifications (languages, having lived abroad) make the difference." Another associate notes that, given its longstanding reputation and its global reach, "the firm is still able to attract students from the best law schools." However, a senior associate opines, "I think we should be more selective. We do not have enough hiring personnel facilitating the process and this leads to disorganization and poor hires in many circumstances." However high the bar for getting that foot in the door, the firm is basically looking for "a candidate with both a solid academic record and strong interpersonal skills."

OUR SURVEY SAYS

As one of the world's largest law firms, Baker & McKenzie "is very diverse and each group has its own microcosm. There is no way to describe the firm as a whole." A young associate in the Chicago office enthuses, "Words don't really do the firm justice. I'm sure a lot of people have good things to say about their firms, but Baker really is special. It truly is international. We have people from Mexico, Australia, England, Japan, Germany and the United States on my floor alone. It's very friendly here," the associate continues, "we hang out together. Some of my best friends work here. Sorry to sound corny, but every morning I go to work with a smile on my face." Another insider comments that most of the practice groups "are laid-back and friendly, and there is significant socializing."

Associates at Baker & McKenzie put in plenty of hours, but some are relieved to report that, "if something needs to be done, you just get it done, irrespective of how long it ends up taking. But if you have a slow day, no one gives you a hard time if you leave early." Not everyone agrees with this assessment, however. Says one litigator, "Associates are expected to be in the office 9-to-5, no matter what, plus evenings and weekends when needed, plus when the partners are in the office, plus when the partners are out of the office. The attitude is that there should be 2,500 hours per year, 2,100 of which should be billable and the rest which should be a 'contribution' to the firm in other ways."

While insiders note that associates learn through "very little formal training, more in the line of fire" at Baker, they also feel that they "can ask anybody any question any time." Nevertheless, one source gripes, "There is extensive formal training, but little of it is valuable. Those in charge of much of the training don't prepare well and end up foregoing complete and accessible presentations for high-level and scattered discussions that are a waste of everyone's time." However, help is on the way: "A person has just been hired who is responsible solely for the professional and educational development of associates."

Compensation merits a mixed bag of opinions. One associate remarks, "I have a great life here. Compensation is more than enough." Another

Chicagoan notes, "I am told we are below other comparable firms in the city, but I have always felt we make a lot of money for what we do, particularly when fewer than 50 percent of associates make 2,000 billable-hours. Every year associates seem angry about bonuses, but I'm happy to work the hours I do (less than 2,000) and not get a bonus. I do, however, suspect our bonuses are lower than other firms in the city." A more disgruntled insider complains, "Baker & McKenzie steals from its associates by delaying their raises for class ascension and delaying performance-based bonuses for eight months from the end of the billable year."

When it comes to pro bono, most Midwesterners agree that the firm is committed, but according to some, Baker "could do more to incorporate pro bono work into [the] billable-hour requirement," since, as one midlevel observes, "We are to bill 60 pro bono hours on top of 2,100 billable-hours." On the other hand, "The firm's pro bono practice is perhaps one of the best in the region."

Banner & Witcoff, Ltd.

Ten South Wacker Drive
Suite 3000
Chicago, IL 60606-7407
Phone: (312) 463-5000
www.bannerwitcoff.com

LOCATIONS

Chicago, IL (HQ)
Boston, MA
Portland, OR
Washington, DC

MAJOR DEPARTMENTS & PRACTICES

Intellectual Property

THE STATS

No. of attorneys:
    firm-wide: 82
    Chicago: 34
No. of offices: 4
President: J. Pieter van Es

NOTABLE PERKS

- Year-round business casual dress
- Flexible work schedules
- Reimbursement of CLE and local bar dues
- Profit-sharing 401(k) plan

BASE SALARY

Chicago, IL (2005)
1st year: $120,000/$135,000*
Summer associate: $2,300/week

*1,850/2,000 billable hours

EMPLOYMENT CONTACT

Recruiting Coordinator
Phone: (312) 463-5000
Fax: (312) 463-5001
E-mail: chicagojobs@bannerwitcoff.com

THE SCOOP

In April 2004, a team of lawyers from Banner & Witcoff won summary judgment on behalf of client Nike, Inc., in a case brought by an individual plaintiff who claimed that Nike had incorporated his trade secret-protected cushioning technology in the popular Nike Shox footwear line. The firm prevailed on a threshold issue, convincing the federal court that the plaintiff, Roy Dixon Jr., had failed to demonstrate that he had taken reasonable steps to protect the alleged secrecy of his "Shockee 2000" shoe design. Accordingly, the court did not reach Nike's substantive defenses, such as whether or not the titan athletic wear company had actually used the disputed technology.

This kind of cutting-edge, high-profile case is typical for Banner & Witcoff, which has been one of the country's leading intellectual property practices since its creation in 1920. The firm that was once paid by its clients in crops and produce now caters to blue-chip clients including Microsoft, General Electric and General Motors. Banner & Witcoff's history reflects the growth of technology and intellectual property law over the last 80 years; the firm has represented high-tech pioneers, such as the inventor of the first electronic computer, and has litigated ground-breaking IP cases like *Mazer v. Stein*, in which the United States Supreme Court held that inventions can be protected by both patents and copyrights. In recent years, the firm's 82 attorneys have garnered a design patent for Nike's Michael Jordan athletic shoe and used the Digital Millennium Copyright Act to shut down offensive web sites.

With offices in Chicago, Boston, Portland, Ore., and Washington D.C., the firm has earned industry praise as a leader in intellectual property law. Banner & Witcoff is particularly known for its work preparing, defending and prosecuting patents. In March 2004, *Intellectual Property Today* named Banner & Witcoff a "Top Patent Firm." The firm ranked No. 28 on a list of 373 firms. Two months later, *IP Today* lauded Banner & Witcoff for its success as a "Top Trademark Firm." And in the 2003 edition of "Who Protects IP America," *IP Law & Business*'s annual survey of Fortune 250 companies, Banner & Witcoff was cited by corporate counsel as one of the 10 firms in the United States most frequently called on for patent prosecution and litigation.

Among other recent litigation, in 2004 the firm recorded victories relating to radar guns, railroad cars and educational toys. In the spring, Banner & Witcoff persuaded a federal appeals court in Chicago to rule in favor of Peaceable Planet, a small toy company based in Georgia, and against industry giant Ty Inc., maker of Beanie Babies, in a trademark appeal. In reversing the lower court decision, the 7th U.S. Circuit Court of Appeals held that the name "Niles" for a plush toy camel produced by Peaceable Planet is a protectable trademark. A couple of months earlier, Banner & Witcoff had won summary judgment in a Pennsylvania federal court for Toshiba International Corp. Halmar Robicon Group, Inc., a Pittsburgh company that makes medium-voltage power drives, accused Toshiba International (a Houston, Texas-based subsidiary of Toshiba Corporation) of willfully infringing one of Robicon's patents for its own medium-voltage power drives. In February 2004, the U.S. District Court for the Western District of Pennsylvania found no infringement.

This success followed on the heels of a landmark decision in which the U.S. Court of Appeals for the Federal Circuit accepted a first-of-its-kind patent infringement defense argued by Banner & Witcoff on behalf of Canadian Pacific Ry, Ltd. The court held that railcars that travel through the United States to load and unload cargo and then return to Canada are only "temporarily" in the country and therefore not subject to charges of patent infringement. More recently, Banner & Witcoff obtained another Federal Circuit win when the appeals court affirmed a ruling in October 2004 that client Applied Concepts, Inc. did not infringe Kustom Signals, Inc.'s patent covering a police radar gun.

GETTING HIRED

As an intellectual property boutique, Banner & Witcoff is looking for candidates with strong academic qualifications and, preferably, an undergraduate degree in engineering or one of the sciences. A technical background is essential for patent attorneys, as is eligibility to take the patent bar exam. Other applicants without science or engineering degrees might get away with stellar law school credentials and "a demonstrated interest in trademark matters."

Barack Ferrazzano Kirschbaum Perlman & Nagelberg LLP

333 West Wacker Drive
Suite 2700
Chicago, IL 60606
Phone: (312) 984-3100
www.bfkpn.com

LOCATION

Chicago, IL

MAJOR DEPARTMENTS & PRACTICES

Bankruptcy & Creditor Rights
Corporate Finance
Corporate & Securities
Employee Benefits, Executive Compensation & Human Resource Practice
Financial Services
Franchise & Product Distribution
Intellectual Property
Litigation
Real Estate
Tax & Business Planning

THE STATS

No. of attorneys: 75
No. of offices: 1
Summer associate offers firm-wide: 2 out of 2 (2004)
Co-Managing Partners: Howard J. Kirschbaum and Charles H. Perlman
Hiring Partner: Sarah M. Bernstein

UPPERS

- Plenty of responsibility early on
- Informal atmosphere and reasonable hours

DOWNERS

- Lack of structure may not be for everyone
- Occasionally long hours

NOTABLE PERKS

- In-house ice cream parlor
- Frequent firm parties
- Free yoga classes
- No dress code

BASE SALARY

Chicago, IL (2005)
1st year: $125,000
Summer associate: $2,400/week

EMPLOYMENT CONTACT

Sarah M. Bernstein, Esq.
Phone: (312) 984-3100
Fax: (312) 984-3150
E-mail: sarah.bernstein@bfkpn.com

THE SCOOP

1984: "Owner of a Lonely Heart" topped the charts. *Dynasty* and *Dallas* duked it out for the top television drama. And four Chi-town lawyers, including two professors at Northwestern Law School, joined forces to form a boutique practice that now bears the tongue-twisting name of Barack Ferrazzano Kirschbaum Perlman & Nagelberg LLP. Still just a single office in the Windy City, Barack Ferrazzano has developed into a 75-lawyer shop with sophisticated practices in bankruptcy, corporate, securities, financial services, litigation and real estate.

Recently, Barack Ferrazzano's bankruptcy lawyers have handled notable cases on behalf of debtors, creditors' committees and third-party transferees. For example, in the 2003 case *In re Computer Engineering Associates*, the firm represented Advanced Testing Technologies, Inc., a subcontractor of the debtor in a Chapter 7 bankruptcy proceeding. The firm's client had received payments from Computer Engineering which the Chapter 7 trustee claimed were invalid transfers made within the 90-day "preference period" before the debtor filed for bankruptcy. The 1st U.S. Circuit Court of Appeals, however, ruled that the $1.2 million payments to Advance Testing were properly made because the debtor had assigned its rights to the contract with Advance Testing to a third party prior to the pre-insolvency preference period.

Barack Ferrazzano also houses a strong transactional practice. In the past few years, the firm has handled high-value deals such as the $3.2 billion acquisition by a publicly held French company of a majority interest in a global retail interest, the merger of another French corporation with an American company to form an $8 billion-a-year business travel service provider, and the merger and NASDAQ listing of two large sporting goods concerns.

GETTING HIRED

Barack Ferrazzano's low attrition rate means that getting a job here isn't easy. "We recruit only from top law schools and only the top candidates from those schools," advises a midlevel associate. "Because lawyers tend to practice here a while, we are very selective in whom we hire." A junior associate notes that the firm only takes from two to four summer associates each year, adding, "I participated in recruiting this year and watched them turn away law review editors with very high grades. Personality counts for a lot during the recruiting process here." A corporate insider agrees, observing that Barack Ferrazzano looks for "brains and a personality that will add to the mix."

OUR SURVEY SAYS

As for that "mix," Barack Ferrazzano seems to have found the ideal blend of high-quality work and down-to-earth people. One associate marvels, "This place is unlike any other working environment I've been in. [The] atmosphere is completely casual and the work is completely professional." According to a midlevel, "The culture of the firm is very collegial. The firm respects the family life of all of its employees (including associates)."

The absence of a dress code (not to mention the in-house ice cream parlor) contributes to the firm's low-key atmosphere. "I wear jeans and tennis shoes to the office almost every day," says one insider. "There is a juke box in the main lunch room and an ice cream sundae bar available year-round for snacking." In addition to free beverages of all kinds regularly on hand, "Several times a month there is a firm-catered party to celebrate someone's birthday, baby or wedding."

Between all of these celebrations, the actual work is substantive and fulfilling. "I was taken to court my first week and have never looked back," declares a junior associate. "As a litigator, I wanted to get courtroom experience and I couldn't be happier. The litigation department has great clients that provide me with the same sophisticated litigation that I would have at any bigger shop."

Substantive work can mean intense hours, but Barack associates don't seem to mind. "The hours here are wonderful!" gushes an insider. "Occasionally I have to work a week or two of long nights, but I can often leave shortly after 5 p.m. or 6 p.m." Another lawyer reports, "There is not insane pressure to bill tons of hours. The expected target is 2,000 [hours]/year. If we have a lot of work to do, we are expected to work hard getting it done. If we have a slow period, we are encouraged to enjoy it and take time for ourselves." Billing for the sake of billing is discouraged. "I have never felt pressure to increase my output. If something needs to get done, it gets done in the amount of time it requires. No more, no less," declares a second-year.

Barack Ferrazzano lawyers don't see lectures and seminars as an effective way to learn their trade. A corporate associate remarks, "What formal training? I like how they do it – it is a learn-on-the-job approach." Those who prefer a little more structure, however, do have options. According to one litigator, "If we need training on something, we are free to set it up and the firm will cover it." More meaningful than formal classes is the direct training offered by experienced attorneys. "Partner feedback is fast, constructive and helpful," comments a midlevel. "Partners are very generous in sharing the better parts of responsibility on cases." A recent hire exclaims, "The small-firm culture means that, even as a first-year, I'm getting trained directly by partners with 20 to 30 years of experience!"

"Although not discouraged," says one seasoned attorney, "pro bono work is not a focus of the firm." However, according to another, "The firm is making a strong effort to get involved in more pro bono activities." Associates at this firm have no axe to grind when it comes to their paychecks. "Who can complain [about] getting paid $125,000 for being a lawyer that is essentially a student lawyer in training?" asks a junior associate. Another satisfied insider reports that Barack Ferrazzano's salaries are "as good as it gets in the Chicago market."

Barnes & Thornburg LLP

11 South Meridian Street
Indianapolis, IN 46204-3556
Phone: (317) 236-1313
www.btlaw.com

LOCATIONS
Chicago, IL
Elkhart, IN
Fort Wayne, IN
Grand Rapids, MI
Indianapolis, IN
South Bend, IN
Washington, DC

MAJOR DEPARTMENTS & PRACTICES
Business, Tax & Real Estate
Creditors' Rights
Environmental Law
Health Care
Intellectual Property
Labor & Employment
Litigation

THE STATS

No. of attorneys:
 firm-wide: 389
 Indianapolis: 213
 Chicago: 58
 Elkhart: 15
 Fort Wayne: 24
 South Bend: 56
No. of offices: 7
Summer associate offers:
 firm-wide: 14 out of 16 (2004)
 Indianapolis: 9 out of 9 (2004)
 Chicago: 2 out of 2 (2004)
 Elkhart: 1 out of 1 (2004)
 Fort Wayne: 1 out of 2 (2004)
 South Bend: 1 out of 2 (2004)
Managing Partner: Alan A. Levin
Hiring Partners:
 Indianapolis: Joseph G. Eaton
 Chicago: Melissa A. Vallone
 Elkhart: Brian J. Clark
 Fort Wayne: Dawn R. Rosemond
 South Bend: James M. Lewis

UPPERS
- Big-firm resources with a small-firm feel
- Complex work and quality clients

DOWNERS
- Difficult to get to know everyone
- Although relatively reasonable, hours can still be long

NOTABLE PERKS
- CLE budget for travel to seminars
- On-site fitness facility
- Free soda
- Frequent tickets to fundraisers and charity events

BASE SALARY

Indiana offices (2005)
1st year: $85,000
Summer associate: $1,500/week

Chicago, IL (2005)
1st year: $95,000
Summer associate: $1,800/week

EMPLOYMENT CONTACT

All offices except South Bend
Ms. Deborah A. Snyder
Director of Recruiting
Phone: (317) 231-7289
Fax: (317) 231-7433
E-mail: dsnyder@btlaw.com

South Bend
Ms. Susan C. Haag
Recruiting Administrator
Phone: (574) 237-1268
Fax: (574) 237-1125
E-mail: shaag@btlaw.com

THE SCOOP

Despite its Midwestern location, Barnes & Thornburg has a wide-reaching practice that serves more than 12,000 clients in the United States and abroad. In 2004, for example, the firm garnered attention in the national media for its representation of the Connecticut-based General Electric Capital Corporation in the Chapter 11 proceedings of discount carrier ATA Airlines, the 10th-largest airline in the United States and one of several carriers to file for bankruptcy this year. On a global scale, Barnes & Thornburg has built a thriving international practice over the last two decades. In the late 1980s, the firm landed its first Japanese client, Kobelco Metal Powder, and just a few years later, used its growing Asia practice to attract the brass ring of international clients: Toyota. Lawyers at Barnes & Thornburg counseled the auto giant on establishing the company's first plant in Indiana. Today, the firm also advises domestic companies on exporting business and goods to countries such as India and China.

Barnes & Thornburg has the largest number of lawyers practicing in Indiana, with over 300 attorneys. The firm also has a sizeable office in Chicago, an office in the nation's capital and a growing office in Grand Rapids, Mich. Barnes & Thornburg offers a prominent intellectual property practice, which ranked at No. 2 in the United States for the number of plaintiff-side patent cases filed in 2002, and at No. 9 for the number of suits it handled for plaintiffs and defendants, combined. The firm's IP clients include pharmaceutical giants such as Eli Lilly and Roche Diagnostics, while Barnes & Thornburg's overall client roster includes household names like Johnson & Johnson, Mercedes-Benz U.S.A., Whirlpool and PepsiCo.

GETTING HIRED

Every year, Barnes & Thornburg attracts a large number of highly qualified candidates for each of its available positions. Who makes the cut? According to a seasoned associate, "The firm is looking for (1) hard workers, (2) bright people, (3) preferably with some semi-permanent connection to the Midwest or Indiana. The stated intent is to only hire people with the potential to make partner, but it seems more and more that partners are laterals or at least have some credit (JAG, clerkships and so on) when they walk in the door." A more recent hire describes the ideal applicants as "intelligent, outgoing and thoughtful people that can one day potentially be partners." Procedurally, a litigator notes, "The interview process is typical of most big firms. The callback process is prompt, a factor which I really appreciated in making my decision to come to work here."

OUR SURVEY SAYS

The primary emphasis at Barnes & Thornburg is on professionalism and client service, but not to the exclusion of social interaction. As a midlevel associate puts it, the firm's "attorneys are focused on providing clients the absolute best work product in the most efficient manner, but manage to remain casual and to find time to laugh." Similarly, one first-year reports that everyone, "from senior partners to first-year associates," is "very professional when it comes to dealing with clients and the work we do. That being said, breaking into the social relationships here is not at all difficult, and I actually do spend time outside of work with my office mates." Specifically, lawyers at Barnes & Thornburg "routinely eat lunch together, attend social functions together and volunteer as a group for community service activities." Adds one insider, "Partners care about you as a person, your well-being and your family's well-being."

The firm's "strong reputation in the region" makes for a steady stream of "interesting clients and projects." And while sources appreciate the experience and responsibility they receive early on, the flip side is a "sink-or-swim attitude." A junior lawyer says, "They expect you to learn by example and by actually performing the tasks assigned to you." Nevertheless, plenty of associates have found higher-ups to lend them some sage advice along the way. A litigator boasts, "I have been provided with excellent opportunities to learn valuable skills at every level of my practice, from the drafting of the complaint to the development of clients." In terms of formal training, some departments have "presentations on aspects of our practice and the firm from time to time," and the firm encourages associates "to attend useful training seminars regardless of the cost."

The firm has set a minimum requirement of 1,850 billable-hours. One source remarks, "The work is available and the expectations are acceptable. I am having no trouble meeting my billing expectations with interesting work." One associate, while acknowledging the sometimes long hours, appreciates the exchange of office "face time" for at-home family time: "The reward of a job well done and a seemingly insurmountable project completed somewhat justifies the late nights and early mornings. With today's technology, many assignments are capable of being completed at home. This option does permit you to spend a little more 'face time' with your wife, which is always greatly appreciated."

No one seems to voice any objections to Barnes & Thornburg's salary structure. "The firm's compensation system is geared to reasonably reward those that accomplish what is expected and to substantially increase compensation for those that exceed expectations," says a transactional associate. Another lawyer agrees: "Compensation seems fair and comparable to other firms in other cities, adjusted for the cost of living."

Associates of color appreciate that the firm "is striving to create a diverse environment and retain its minority employees." A female insider also observes that "there are women at all levels in the firm, and the most senior women take mentoring the newer arrivals very seriously." Still, says one litigator, "The firm, like most, is struggling to accommodate women who want both a family and a career." It undoubtedly helps that "the firm is very flexible in permitting part-time and work from home."

"Partners care about you as a person, your well-being and your family's well-being."

- Barnes & Thornburg associate

Bell, Boyd & Lloyd LLC

70 West Madison, Suite 3300
Chicago, IL 60602
Phone: (312) 372-1121
www.bellboyd.com

LOCATIONS

Chicago, IL (HQ)
Washington, DC

MAJOR DEPARTMENTS & PRACTICES

Antitrust (including FDA)
Bankruptcy
Corporate
Environmental
Estate Planning
Health Care
Intellectual Property
Labor
Litigation
Real Estate
Tax (including ERISA)

THE STATS

No. of attorneys:
  firm-wide: 230
  Chicago: 208
No. of offices: 2
Summer associate offers:
  firm-wide: 9 out of 11 (2004)
  Chicago: 9 out of 11 (2004)
Chairman: John T. ("Jack") McCarthy
Chief Operating Officer: Nancy E. Bertoglio
Hiring Partner: Randy Bridgeman

UPPERS
- Family-oriented firm with great people
- High level of responsibility

DOWNERS
- The "grid" salary system
- Monthly billing reports sent to entire firm

NOTABLE PERKS
- Luxury box at Wrigley Field and United Center
- Dinner and cab rides home when working late

BASE SALARY

Chicago, IL (2005)
1st year: $125,000
2nd year: $135,000
3rd year: $145,000
4th year: $155,000
5th year: $165,000
6th year: $175,000
7th year: $180,000
8th year: $185,000
Summer associate: $2,604/week

EMPLOYMENT CONTACT

Ms. Celeste Herrera
Recruiting Coordinator
Phone: (312) 372-1121
Fax: (312) 372-2098
E-mail: cherrera@bellboyd.com

THE SCOOP

The firm that would ultimately become Bell, Boyd & Lloyd started out in 1888 as Matz & Fisher. Its practice was built upon a foundation of business clients such as Deere & Company, the country's largest manufacturer of farm equipment. In the 1920s, Bell, Boyd & Lloyd represented *The Chicago Daily News* in the construction of its new building, which involved negotiating the first air rights deal in the city and reaching an agreement with the city and two railroads to build the pedestrian bridge between the newspaper's building and the Chicago and Northwestern Railroad building across the street. Throughout its history, the firm had an eye to public service; name partner Laird Bell was honored for his service to the University of Chicago when the school named its law complex the Laird Bell Law Quadrangle in 1966.

Bell Boyd's representation of the Idaho-based Boise Cascade Corporation is one example of the firm's long-standing client relationships. The firm has represented Boise Cascade Corp. since 1957 when it helped organize the company and it continues to represent the company in its new incarnation as OfficeMax, Inc. Over the last two years, Bell Boyd attorneys have helped Boise shift its business from the lumber and paper industry to the world of office supplies. In 2003 a team of Bell Boyd corporate lawyers represented Boise in its $1.2 billion acquisition of OfficeMax, Inc. and in the related $500 million senior notes offering. The next year, firm lawyers were on hand to assist in the sale of Boise's paper, forest products and timber operations to Madison Dearborn Partners, a Chicago-based private equity firm, for $3.7 billion. Bell Boyd also represented the company in the remarketing of senior debentures issued in connection with its adjustable conversion-rate equity securities. On November 1, 2004, Boise Cascade Corp. officially changed its company and trade name to OfficeMax, Inc.

GETTING HIRED

Bell, Boyd & Lloyd is looking for candidates with a lot more to offer than a stellar GPA. A corporate associate advises, "It is not enough to have good grades and be on a journal. We want personality. Client contact is something associates experience early in their career at BBL, so being an extrovert is always a plus." Agrees a junior lawyer, "The firm looks not just at numbers; I believe a premium is put on the interview results and not just the resume. The hiring process asks not just whether you will be a competent lawyer but also whether you will fit in as a member of the team and a good person to work with side by side."

Pedigree still matters, however: "The firm is looking for bright students from top schools," says a midlevel associate. "It's more competitive for students from local schools." Although the process for entry-level hires is similar to that of other firms, one insider notes that "lateral hiring is rare and a very lengthy process; laterals usually have to interview with more or less their entire department before an offer is extended."

OUR SURVEY SAYS

Unlike associates at many law firms, those at Bell, Boyd & Lloyd find their hours to be eminently agreeable. "The firm is active in making sure that associates do not spend too much time in the office. The firm is oriented to the fact that people have families and social lives outside the office as well," says an inside source. A litigator concurs: "Bell Boyd does not view its associates as cogs in a billing machine. The firm understands that associates are people and then attorneys, not the other way around. While hours are a necessary evil in any firm, Bell Boyd treats its attorneys with respect and understanding of personal obligations, [which] makes the hours obligations palatable."

Beyond the relaxed attitude regarding hours, the firm also provides a warm and supportive atmosphere. A midlevel reports that "the firm is in general very laid-back and casual, both in social interactions, dress and pressure. Lawyers often socialize together and the firm is good about having firm-wide events from time to time so that different departments interact." According to another source, "The people make the firm. Beyond being intelligent and knowledgeable, the attorneys at Bell Boyd are practical, ordinary people who work together to achieve results for the client without pretense or politics. It is truly a team-oriented law firm where everyone's voice is heard."

Bell Boyd provides its attorneys with "at least semi-annual training sessions open to all associates, and most departments hold monthly training sessions for its associates." One insider says that the training program "could be improved by making training more specific to certain practices and more regular, but it is sufficient." Associates get even more out of their day-to-day interactions with more experienced attorneys in the firm. A litigator says, "Partners seem to put the 'constructive' in constructive criticism. If what you do needs improvement, you'll know it, but it's usually put to you in a way geared to improving future performance."

The one bone associates have to pick with the firm regards compensation. Bell Boyd determines associate raises according to a rigid formula, and those who don't make the calculated minimums don't get a larger salary the next year. "The system here is unique in that hours billed determines salary for the following year, not bonus, and bonus is an entirely separate, mostly qualitative, determination," explains a corporate associate. "Thus, you can actually decrease your salary from year to year, but you can also 'choose' how much you want to work." Another source adds that there is "not enough of a jump for each hundred hours to make it worthwhile (most increments are in the $5–10,000 range)." (The firm reports that its compensation system was restructured in December 2004 and the pay differentials are now based on 50-hour increments.) The economy can also play a role in the "matrix," say insiders: "Salaries don't increase between first and second years if you don't hit your hours (which has been tough for the last few years, including this one), so you are effectively taking a pay cut."

Bollinger, Ruberry & Garvey

500 West Madison Street
23rd Floor
Chicago, IL 60606
Phone: (312) 466-8000
www.brg-law.com

LOCATION
Chicago, IL

MAJOR DEPARTMENTS & PRACTICES
Commercial Litigation
Construction
Environmental Law
Insurance Coverage Analysis
Litigation
Product Liability
Transportation

THE STATS
No. of attorneys: 86
No. of offices: 1
Hiring Partner: Amy Miner

EMPLOYMENT CONTACT
Amy Miner, Esq.
Hiring Partner
Phone: (312) 466-8000
Fax: (312) 466-8001

THE SCOOP

At the tender age of 19, the Chicago firm of Bollinger, Ruberry & Garvey may be young, but this nearly 90-lawyer shop still manages to snag more than its share of major league cases. The boutique firm focuses exclusively on litigation, handling a wide range of matters from toxic tort defense to medical malpractice to rental car industry disputes.

The firm was founded in 1986 by trial attorneys from Wildman, Harrold, Allen & Dixon (rumor has it that they originally hailed from the trial department of Kirkland & Ellis). Even though the firm started with only a handful of attorneys, according to statistics maintained by the *Cook County Jury Verdict Reporter*, Bollinger, Ruberry & Garvey is now one of the most active Chicago firms in trials. In fact, the firm has so many cases that associates are given their fair share – both partners and associates find themselves in a courtroom on a daily basis (some even have experience before the U.S. Supreme Court). The firm is doing so well that it renovated its office space last year and now occupies approximately 60,000 square feet on the 23rd and 24th floors of the Citicorp Center, the tallest all-glass building in Chicago with beautiful views overlooking the Chicago skyline.

In one recent case, a team of Bollinger Ruberry lawyers successfully represented client Coregis Insurance Company in an appellate matter before the 1st U.S. Circuit Court of Appeals. Coregis had been sued by the Center for Blood Research, a nonprofit organization. The Center held an insurance policy issued by Coregis and had submitted a claim for reimbursement of attorneys' fees it incurred in responding to a subpoena served on the organization by the U.S. attorney's office in an investigation of federal health care offenses. Coregis declined to cover the fees based upon an exemption in an endorsement to the Center's insurance policy. Early on in the case, Bollinger Ruberry won summary judgment for Coregis, and the Center brought the matter up on appeal. Ultimately, the 1st Circuit ruled in favor of Coregis, interpreting the language of the insurance policy to find that, since the investigation did not result in any criminal charges or civil claims against the Center for Blood Research, Coregis was not required to remunerate the Center's attorneys' fees relating to its response to a government subpoena.

Despite the high-profile cases and crowded docket, most Bollinger Ruberry attorneys are able to experience a full life outside the firm. Take for example Scott Hiller, the head coach of the Boston Cannons (Boston's Major League Lacrosse team). According to news reports, Hiller isn't quite sure if he's moonlighting as a lawyer or as a coach. Regardless, he spends much of his time air-shuttling between Boston (coaching his favorite sports team) and Chicago (coaching his favorite legal team). When asked how he manages to pursue both demanding and time-consuming careers, he answered, "furiously."

GETTING HIRED

It's no secret that Bollinger, Ruberry & Garvey looks for candidates with good research and writing skills, strong academic credentials and impressive extracurricular activities. And most of the firm's attorneys hail from local law schools, so you'll probably be able to find a friend if you're also from Illinois. But the firm does like to keep quiet about its interview process. One piece of advice: let the firm know about your interest and experience in litigation – it's all this firm does.

Brinks Hofer Gilson & Lione

NBC Tower, Suite 3600
455 North Cityfront Plaza Drive
Chicago, IL 60611
Phone: (312) 321-4200
www.usebrinks.com

LOCATIONS

Chicago, IL (HQ)
Ann Arbor, MI
Arlington, VA
Indianapolis, IN

MAJOR DEPARTMENTS & PRACTICES

Appellate
Biotechnology & Pharmaceutical
Chemical
Copyright
Electrical & Computer
Intellectual Asset Management
Interference
International Patents & Trademarks
Internet/E-Commerce
Licensing
Litigation
Mechanical
Nanotechnology
Patent Prosecution
Trademarks & Unfair Competition

THE STATS

No. of attorneys:
   firm-wide: 141
   Chicago: 122
No. of offices: 4
Summer associate offers:
   firm-wide: 8 out of 10 (2004)
   Chicago: 7 out of 9 (2004)
President: Jerold A. Jacover

NOTABLE PERKS

- Profit-sharing plan
- Moving expenses up to $4,000
- "House-hunting trip"
- Bar exam and review fees

BASE SALARY

Chicago, IL (2005)
1st year: $130,000
Summer associate: $2,400/week

EMPLOYMENT CONTACT

Ms. Kathleen E. Mallin
Director of Recruitment
Phone: (312) 321-4200
Fax: (312) 321-4299
E-mail: kmallin@usebrinks.com

THE SCOOP

In the summer of 2004, a litigation team from Brinks Hofer won a jury award of $3.95 million for client Aero Products International, makers of the popular AeroBed® inflatable mattress. A federal judge in the Northern District of Illinois then nearly *doubled* the jury award for trademark and patent infringement and attorney's fees against Intex Recreation Corporation. In doing so, the judge affirmed the jury's finding that Intex had willfully infringed upon the Aero's patented technology for the quick inflation and easy firmness adjustment of its air mattresses. Subsequently, in September, the court granted Aero's motion for a permanent injunction against Intex, awarded Aero prejudgment interest and ordered Intex to provide Aero with an accounting of its sales over the past nine months. In another news-making case, the firm is currently representing the British holder of the trademark for the Rubik's Cube in a dispute against a New York toy company for trademark infringement, among other claims.

Chicago-based Brinks Hofer Gilson & Lione has been providing learned counsel in all manner of intellectual property matters since 1917, and has served clients such as The Coca-Cola Company, Tri-Seal International, Amway, United Air Lines and Bayer AG. With nearly 150 lawyers, Brinks Hofer stands as the largest IP firm in the Windy City, and for the past two years it has been ranked by *Chambers USA* as the No.-1 firm in the state of Illinois for intellectual property law. As the sole IP counsel relied on by Fortune 250 companies Visteon Corp. and UAL Corp., Brinks Hofer was featured in the 2004 NLJ Client List, *The National Law Journal*'s annual survey of "Who Represents Corporate America."

Headquartered at the top of Chicago's NBC Tower, the firm also has offices in Indianapolis, Ann Arbor and Arlington, Va. The firm offers legal services in areas as broad as appellate litigation and as narrow as nanotechnology, and employs numerous attorneys who hold advanced degrees in the sciences. Despite the array of industries it serves, the firm remains focused on intellectual property law and has stayed "small" in that respect. In contrast with firms that have taken the route of mergers and diversification, Brinks Hofer holds to a business model of excellence within a single field. According to the firm's president, Jerold A. Jacover, the firm has been approached a number of times with invitations to merge, but has "never seen the benefit."

The firm is dedicated not only to providing "premium IP services" to paying clients, but also to serving the wider community, including those who cannot otherwise afford legal services. Brinks Hofer has a pro bono program with a formally organized committee and a written policy. Recent successes include preventing a mother of four from being deported, stopping the eviction of a low-income tenant from substandard housing and securing Veterans Administration benefits for the widow of a World War II veteran. Other community service initiatives include "Letters to Santa," a program through which the firm gives holiday gifts to inner-city preschool and kindergarten children; participation in the Corporate Internship Program at Christo Rey Jesuit High School, through which high school students intern at the firm once a week in order to learn about the working world; and involvement with Chicago Cares, an organization that coordinates service projects throughout Chicago.

GETTING HIRED

Brinks Hofer considers applications from first-, second- and third-year law students as well as experienced attorneys. Candidates must, of course, want to practice intellectual property law, and should have top grades. In addition, those interested in patent practice (which constitutes the majority of the firm's hiring) must have an undergraduate degree in a technical or scientific field, such as engineering, computer science, chemistry, physics or biotechnology. For trademark and related areas, the requirements are less technical: the firm seeks applicants with a strong interest in the area and a background in liberal arts or business.

In addition to a higher-than-average starting salary ($130,000), those lucky enough to join the firm as first-year associates will receive a signing bonus of $9,000. Thereafter, the firm's bonus program is based on work production and/or client origination. According to the firm, 2003 bonuses climbed as high as $58,000.

Get the BUZZ on Top Schools

Read what STUDENTS and ALUMNI have to say about:

- Admissions
- Academics
- Career Opportunities
- Quality of Life
- Social Life

Surveys on thousands of top programs
College • MBA • Law School • Grad School

VAULT
> the most trusted name in career information™

Go to www.vault.com

Bryan Cave LLP

One Metropolitan Square
211 North Broadway, Suite 3600
St. Louis, MO 63102
Phone: (314) 259-2000
www.bryancave.com

LOCATIONS

Chicago, IL
Irvine, CA
Jefferson City, MO
Kansas City, MO
Los Angeles, CA
New York, NY
Phoenix, AZ
St. Louis, MO
Washington, DC
Dubai
Hong Kong
Kuwait City
London
Riyadh
Shanghai

MAJOR DEPARTMENTS & PRACTICES

Business & Transactional Counseling
Litigation & Dispute Resolution
Regulatory & Tax

THE STATS

No. of attorneys:
  firm-wide: 775
  St. Louis: 250
  Chicago: 24
  Kansas City: 76
No. of offices: 15
Summer associate offers:
  firm-wide: 42 out of 42 (2004)
  St. Louis: 12 out of 12 (2004)
  Chicago: 1 out of 1 (2004)
  Kansas City: 4 out of 4 (2004)
Chairman: Don G. Lents
Hiring Attorneys:
  St. Louis: John R. Haug
  Chicago: Monica A. Carroll
  Kansas City: Robert M. Thompson

Bryan Cave LLP

UPPERS
- Reputation in the community
- Sophisticated work among talented, friendly lawyers

DOWNERS
- Understaffing in some departments
- Need for more open communication with firm management

NOTABLE PERKS
- Fee-sharing program
- Laptop, cell phone and BlackBerry service provided
- "Take a New Lawyer to Lunch" program
- Free parking (in St. Louis and Kansas City; subsidized parking in Chicago)

BASE SALARY

St. Louis, MO (2005)
1st year: $90,000
Summer associate: $1,600/week

Chicago, IL (2005)
1st year: $125,000
Summer associate: $2,400/week

Kansas City, MO (2005)
1st year: $85,000
Summer associate: $1,600/week

EMPLOYMENT CONTACTS

St. Louis
Ms. Jennifer Guirl
Legal Recruiter
Phone: (314) 259-2615
Fax: (314) 552-8615
E-mail: jguirl@bryancave.com

Chicago
Ms. Willow Esenther
Administrative Services Coordinator
Phone: (312) 602-5031
Fax: (312) 602-5050
E-mail: willow.esenther@bryancave.com

Kansas City
Ms. Cristy M. Johnson
Recruiting & Professional Development Manager
Phone: (816) 374-3362
Fax: (816) 374-3300
E-mail: cmjohnson@bryancave.com

THE SCOOP

In October 2004, a team of Bryan Cave litigators won a defense verdict for Ford Motor Company in a class-action suit that sought nearly $800 million in damages from the automotive giant. The lawsuit alleged that the Ford Crown Victoria Police Interceptor, the No.-1 police cruiser in the country, contains a design flaw that makes the cars vulnerable to catching fire in rear-end collisions. Bryan Cave, which represented Ford along with co-counsel Dykema Gossett of Detroit, presented evidence and testimony over the course of the five-week trial that ultimately persuaded the jury to conclude that the cars are safe and that plaintiffs were not entitled to any money. The verdict was an especially sweet victory in that the trial was held in Southern Illinois, an area that has made headlines with its tremendous damages awards to plaintiffs.

Bryan Cave traces its roots back to 1873, when its predecessor firm, King, Phillips & Stewart, opened in St. Louis just across the street from the firm's modern-day headquarters. In 1939, Bryan Cave scored a client that continues to rely upon the firm's counsel today: a Scotsman's little aviation concern, the McDonnell Aircraft Company, which is today known as The Boeing Company. Other high-profile clients of the 775-lawyer international firm include Wachovia, Bob Costas and the government of Kuwait.

GETTING HIRED

Associates consider Bryan Cave to be fairly selective in choosing new hires. "Bryan Cave is considered the most prestigious firm in town and has a competitive applicant pool," opines one inside source. Another says that "the firm generally hires law students with top grades or laterals from comparable firms in other cities." Echoes one associate in the know, "It's pretty competitive to get hired from one of the local schools. If you have great grades, you'll get an offer pretty quickly. They're looking for bright people that others enjoy working with." Having a connection to St. Louis helps: "Our firm would prefer to hire academically well-performing associates from national or regional law schools, with ties to the region and possibly work experience."

OUR SURVEY SAYS

Bryan Cave's size allows the firm to be very diverse, which means that associates can make a niche for themselves just about anywhere. As one senior associate puts it, "Due to the size, we have all kinds here. I don't think you have to fit a mold to make it here." Generally speaking, the lawyers at Bryan Cave "are exceptionally bright, and the associates in particular are very fun to work with on a daily basis." The firm does have a more serious side, though. One insider notes, "I would characterize it as a generally friendly and supportive environment. However, I believe sometimes the firm characterizes itself as more laid-back than it truly is." Another reports that "there are some who take themselves overly seriously, but they are the minority. Associates tend to socialize in small groups based on common interests."

With the cyclical nature of the firm's practice, the amount of time associates spend at the office varies. A corporate associate observes, "There are times I spend way more time here than I would like, but a lot of it is the nature of the practice. We have weeks that are crazy, followed by some that are quite manageable. You have to take advantage of the quiet times." A junior lawyer finds that "the firm is very flexible with respect to working hours. It's not a problem to take off early or come in late due to other obligations as long as you don't make a habit out of it and you regularly meet your project deadlines." Several respondents take advantage of a reduced schedule. However, cautions one insider, "The part-time program is gaining steam, but still has yet to demonstrate that it is a viable path to partnership." The numbers reflect this delayed "Mommy track." As one source puts it, "Although the firm has great flex-time and maternity leave policies, for years and years the percentage of women in each partner class is always 17 percent. It has not increased even with the increased number of women associates."

Money-wise, most Bryan Cave attorneys report that they are doing as well as, if not better than, their peers in the St. Louis market. One source states that "Bryan Cave sets the scale in this market," while a senior associate boasts, "I make more than my colleagues who are partners at other firms in St. Louis, including other big firms." Another insider reports that the "bonus program is excellent and very fair." However, one less enthusiastic source remarks, "The salary is certainly more than adequate to provide a good living in the Midwest; but, given that many associates are billing 'New York' hours, sometimes it seems inadequate to receive 'Midwest' pay."

Junior associates receive a generous amount of training upon their arrival at Bryan Cave, but many senior associates feel they are left high and dry in this area. Says one seasoned source, "The firm is dismal at training. It is sink-or-swim in the worst way. If you suck at something, they will not try to improve you, they will simply not give you that type of work again." But other insiders report that the firm offers a "terrific mentoring program" through which younger attorneys learn from their higher-ups. One beneficiary of the system raves, "I have had a wonderful experience learning from a partner in a similar family situation who has been successful here. It helps me keep my priorities straight."

Butzel Long

150 West Jefferson, Suite 100
Detroit, MI 48226-4430
Phone: (313) 225-7000
www.butzel.com

LOCATIONS
Detroit, MI (HQ)
Ann Arbor, MI
Bloomfield Hills, MI
Boca Raton, FL
Holland, MI
Lansing, MI
Naples, FL

MAJOR DEPARTMENTS & PRACTICES
Business Transactions & Finance
Environmental & Natural Resources
Family Law
Government Relations
International, Immigration & Global Trade
Labor, Employment & Benefits
Litigation
Media & Intellectual Property
Probate & Estate Planning
Real Estate

THE STATS
No. of attorneys:
  firm-wide: 303
  Detroit: 201
  Ann Arbor: 19
  Bloomfield Hills: 65
No. of offices: 7
Summer associate offers:
  Detroit: 5 out of 5 (2003)
Chairman and CEO: Richard E. Rassel

NOTABLE PERKS
- Paid parking in building
- Reimbursement of bar exam and review course fees
- Payment of professional bar dues

BASE SALARY
Detroit, MI (2003)
1st year: $90,000
Summer associate: $1,750/week

EMPLOYMENT CONTACT
Ms. Christine A. Scurto
Recruiting Coordinator
Phone: (313) 225-7084
Fax: (313) 225-7080
E-mail: scurto@butzel.com

THE SCOOP

Founded in 1854, Butzel Long has grown to become one of Michigan's leading law firms. With offices in Michigan and Florida, and over 200 attorneys, the firm covers a wide range of practice areas, including admiralty, marine and waterfront development (the specialty of the firm's founding senior partner, William Austin Moore), condemnation and zoning law, family law, global automotive industry, higher education law, labor and employment law, nonprofit organizations, real estate law and tax law, to name just a few.

Last March, the Detroit-based firm won the reversal of a federal court ruling that would have required the firm's client Twentieth Century Fox to pay $1.5 million in damages for an alleged copyright infringement. The lawsuit arose when Murray Hill Publications sued the motion picture company, claiming that the screenplay for Fox's 1996 holiday comedy, *Jingle All the Way*, violated Murray Hill's copyright on a script it had purchased from a Detroit-based school teacher and budding screenwriter. After the initial trial, a jury awarded Murray Hill $19 million in damages, although the district court subsequently reduced the amount to $1.5 million. On appeal, the 6th U.S. Circuit Court of Appeals reversed the finding of infringement and overturned the damages award.

Among Butzel Long's 8,000 clients are the University of Michigan, Exxon-Mobil, *The Detroit News*, CBS, Wal-Mart Stores and Infinity Broadcasting. Butzel Long assisted with the creation of the Michigan Bell Telephone Company (now part of SBC), and served as counsel for the acquisition of the Jos. Schlitz Brewing Company by the Stroh Brewing Company. A key area of the firm is its global automotive practice; Butzel Long has been involved with clients in this industry since it incorporated General Motors and represented the Dodge Brothers and Henry Ford.

A growing sector of the 300-lawyer firm's diverse practice is its China group, which assists clients from the United States, Europe and Japan in launching business operations in China. To that end, Butzel Long is a member, with three other law firms, of the China Alliance, which allows members to exchange information about the burgeoning importance of China in the global economy and to share resources such as office space in Asia. In January 2005, Butzel Long attorney and shareholder Peter Theut was elected to the Detroit Chinese Business Association (DCBA) Advisory Board.

The firm also has a Mexico trade and transactions practice, through which it assists both U.S. and Mexican clients with trade treaties and other matters. In fact, Butzel Long enjoys a long tradition of international service; one of its attorneys served as U.S. ambassador to Japan in the early 1900s, and the firm has provided legal counsel for numerous international trade disputes. A founding member of Lex Mundi, one of the oldest and largest international associations of independent law firms, Butzel Long maintains a high profile in international law. Recently, the firm's president, Philip J. Kessler, was named to *The International Who's Who of Commercial Litigators 2004*.

Butzel Long offers onsite seminars in specific areas of law and business, such as contract administration for architects and engineers; labor and employment law for administrators and supervisors; and professional responsibility and risk management for in-house law departments. In addition, the firm has launched several special initiatives, including a Global Automotive Practice Initiative, a Sarbanes-Oxley Information Center and a Wage and Hour Information Center.

On top of base salaries, Butzel Long provides performance-based bonuses to associates. First-years also receive a one-time signing bonus of $5,000 on graduation from law school. The partnership track is fairly standard: associates typically are eligible for shareholder status after eight years of employment with the firm. In addition, the firm has recently created a new "supervisory status" for associates who have performed well on a consistent basis. Associates with six years of admission to the bar may be considered for this status, which carries mentoring and administrative responsibilities, as well as enhanced benefits.

GETTING HIRED

Butzel Long hires both starting associates and seasoned attorneys. For summer associates, the firm conducts on-campus interviews at top-tier law schools as well as local favorites, including Harvard, Georgetown, Michigan, University of Chicago, University of Detroit, Michigan State, Wayne State University, Notre Dame and Northwestern. In an effort to recruit more diverse lawyers, the firm also participates in the BLSA Midwest Minority Recruitment Conference and the Wolverine Bar Association's summer associate program.

Summer associates gain hands-on experience and exposure to different areas of law. Each summer associate is assigned a mentor team (consisting of a shareholder and associate) and spends most of the summer in the firm's Detroit office, with a week in the Oakland County and Ann Arbor offices.

Calfee, Halter & Griswold LLP

1400 McDonald Investment Center
800 Superior Avenue
Cleveland, OH 44114
Phone: (216) 622-8200
www.calfee.com

LOCATIONS

Cleveland, OH (HQ)
Columbus, OH

MAJOR DEPARTMENTS & PRACTICES

Commercial Business & Finance
Employee Benefits & Executive Compensation
Environmental
General Corporate
Information Technology
Intellectual Property
International
Labor & Employment
Litigation
Partnerships, LLCs & Joint Ventures
Private Investment
Public Law & Finance
Real Estate
Securities & Capital Markets
Tax

THE STATS

No. of attorneys:
  firm-wide: 196
  Cleveland: 171
  Columbus: 25
No. of offices: 2
Managing Partner: Brent Ballard
Hiring Partner: Philip M. Dawson

NOTABLE PERKS

- Up to six months maternity leave (with three months paid)
- Paid memberships in athletic/dining clubs after two years
- $6,000 bar exam stipend
- Reimbursement of bar association dues

BASE SALARY

Cleveland, OH (2005)
1st year: $100,000
Summer associate: $1,875/week

EMPLOYMENT CONTACT

Stephanie E Haggerty, Esq.
Director of Legal Recruiting
Phone: (216) 622-8382
Fax: (216) 241-0816
E-mail: shaggerty@calfee.com

THE SCOOP

From its home base in Cleveland, Calfee, Halter & Griswold has evolved into a national and international legal service provider. Most of the firm's departments, from litigation to antitrust to mergers and acquisitions, have been engaged in matters on a global scale, and the firm is a founding member of Lex Mundi, a leading network of independent law firms with 15,000 attorneys in 155 countries. Recently, Calfee litigators represented a company based in France in a dispute that involved claims of breach of contract and fraud against British and American parties. The firm has also been retained by the Industrial Development Board of Northern Ireland to structure financing facilities for several development projects and has acted as a liaison on behalf of Swedish clients interested in making business contacts with bioscience companies in northeastern Ohio. Domestically, Calfee Halter has developed an impressive public law and finance group, which has advised the city of Cleveland and the Ohio Department of Development, among others, on bond issuances.

In 1903, Robert M. Calfee and two other lawyers set up shop in Cleveland as the law firm of Bemis, Zigelman & Calfee with offices on Euclid Avenue. Over the years, the firm has included in its members the son of a United States Supreme Court justice, a president of the Cleveland Bar Association and a U.S. senator. Just past its 100th birthday, the firm now employs nearly 200 lawyers in its two offices (the Columbus office opened in 1987 and currently has 25 attorneys). In December 2004, senior attorney Brent Ballard was elected managing partner, replacing Dale LaPorte, who stepped down at 62 (because of the firm's age policy) after five years as chairman of the firm's executive committee.

Calfee Halter attorneys have won recognition both locally and nationwide. Calfee earned 19 spots in the 2005–2006 edition of *The Best Lawyers in America*; eight of the 19 attorneys have been listed in *Best Lawyers* for 10 years. Moreover, two Calfee partners were named among Northeast Ohio's leading lawyers in the December 2004 issue of *Inside Business* magazine. The firm has recently brought more influential attorneys on board. In January 2005, Calfee hired Christopher Jones, director of the Ohio EPA, and Peter A. Carfagna, chief legal officer and general counsel of the Cleveland-based sports management and marketing company, International Management Group.

The firm has also set up a wholly-owned subsidiary, Thomas Green & Associates, which works together with the lawyers in the government relations practice to provide lobbying and consulting services to clients such as AETNA, Columbia Gas of Ohio, Morgan Stanley, the National Safety Council and Sprint. Consisting of two attorneys, Thomas Green and Kristen Brinkman, the firm considers itself "street lobbyists" because of its hands-on approach. Brinkman provides government relations representation on issues such as public utility, health care, liquor regulation, the business and shopping center industry, private prisons and public safety legislation. Green (in close collaboration with Calfee's government relations and legislation group) assists clients with issues involving the executive and legislative branches of government, as well as commissioners, authorities and other special-purpose entities.

Like other firms participating in the corporate work-study model, Calfee offers internships to high school students enrolled at St. Martin de Porres School in Cleveland. The interns perform entry-level work at the firm one day a week and attend school on the other days The internship not only helps students afford tuition (their pay goes directly to the school), but also offers a window into the professional working world. According to an article in the *Cleveland Free Times*, interns are treated to "a full month of training before starting work," including "ice breakers, team building and the school's own corporate boot camp." They learn about "making first impressions, business ethics, hygiene, phone etiquette and even how to chat in the way people in offices seem to be required to do."

GETTING HIRED

Most new associates are hired through the firm's summer program. Calfee conducts on-campus interviews at schools in the Midwest, Southeast and along the East Coast, including Case Western, Duke, Georgetown, Notre Dame, Michigan, Ohio State and Emory University. In addition to real work assignments, summer associates enjoy a full social calendar, whose highlights include an annual "Icebreaker" dinner party, tickets to Cleveland Indians games and an opportunity to strike out seasoned lawyers in the "Associates vs. Partners" softball game.

Wondering what it's like to work at a specific employer?

Read what EMPLOYEES have to say about:
- Workplace culture
- Compensation
- Hours
- Diversity
- Hiring process

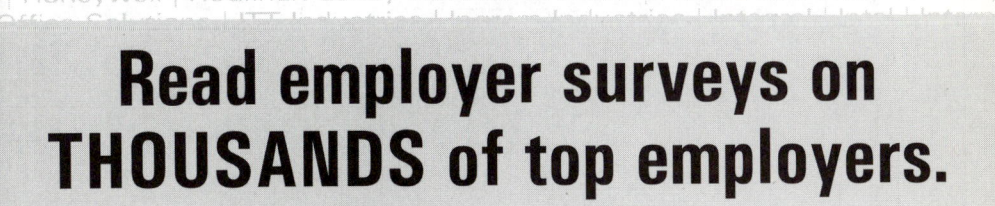

Read employer surveys on THOUSANDS of top employers.

VAULT
> the most trusted name in career information™

Go to www.vault.com

Chapman and Cutler LLP

111 West Monroe Street
Chicago, IL 60603-4080
Phone: (312) 845-3000
www.chapman.com

LOCATIONS

Chicago, IL (HQ)
Salt Lake City, UT
San Francisco, CA

MAJOR DEPARTMENTS & PRACTICES

Banking
Bankruptcy & Creditors' Rights
Corporate Finance
Corporate Securities
ERISA
Intellectual Property
Litigation
Public Finance
Tax
Trusts & Estates

THE STATS

No. of attorneys:
   firm-wide: 195
   Chicago: 176
No. of offices: 3
Summer associate offers:
   firm-wide: 10 out of 11 (2004)
   Chicago: 9 out of 10 (2004)
Chief Executive Partner: Richard A. Cosgrove
Hiring Partner: Carol Thompson

UPPERS
- Challenging work
- Family-oriented firm with great people

DOWNERS
- Long partnership track
- "Undrinkable coffee" and outdated office space

NOTABLE PERKS
- Emergency day care
- Flexible schedules
- Free or discounted technology
- Free cab rides and dinner on late nights

BASE SALARY

Chicago, IL (2005)
1st year: $125,000
2nd year: $130,000
3rd year: $135,000
4th year: $145,000
5th year: $155,000
6th year: $167,500
7th year: $180,000
8th year: $190,000
Summer associate: $2,400/week

EMPLOYMENT CONTACT

Ms. Kimberly Torvik
Legal Recruitment Coordinator
Phone: (312) 845-3488
E-mail: legalresumes@chapman.com

THE SCOOP

Founded in Chicago in 1913, the ampersand-free Chapman and Cutler has cultivated a sophisticated financial services-based practice, with a particular emphasis on banking, securities, corporate and public finance. The firm offers specialized practice groups, including cross-border institutional private placement transactions, municipal asset securitization and lease finance, to name a few, and houses growing departments in litigation, intellectual property, and trust and estates.

Chapman and Cutler has a long history of involvement in the financing of airport construction and development projects. The firm played a substantial role in the overhaul of Chicago O'Hare Airport in the 1980s and 1990s, acting as bond counsel and underwriter's counsel on financing efforts worth almost $2 billion. The airport finance group also served as bond counsel for the issuance by the city of Chicago of $250 million in Passenger Facility Charge Revenue Bonds for O'Hare. This landmark deal was the first of its kind, creating a new form of "stand alone" revenue bonds which are drawn from the facility charges paid by airline customers. Attorneys from this group have also assisted with bond issuances for airport improvements in Phoenix, Salt Lake City, Dallas-Ft. Worth, New York (JFK and LaGuardia), Newark, Los Angeles (LAX), Atlanta and Minneapolis-St.Paul. Meanwhile, Chapman and Cutler's aircraft financing group has counseled clients on structuring deals such as secured and leveraged lease financings, synthetic lease financings, lease portfolio securitizations and enhanced equipment trust certificates. The firm's bankruptcy department has handled matters relating to the insolvency proceedings of major airlines including United Air Lines, TWA, Eastern Airlines and America West, as well as the insolvency proceedings of major corporations such as Pacific Gas and Electric.

GETTING HIRED

Like most other firms, Chapman "looks to hire lawyers who have performed extremely well in law school and have a good work ethic." Of course you should be "well-rounded" and have "good interpersonal skills," too. A finance or business background doesn't hurt either, since the firm's business "is chiefly finance-related." But don't let your great grades and experience give you a swelled head. Insiders say that even though the firm looks for "high-quality candidates," it won't hire people who "exude a sense of arrogance or self-importance as a result of their law school and undergraduate success. There are plenty of other law firms that will hire attorneys like that."

OUR SURVEY SAYS

Relative to other firms that are comparable in size, "the overall package can't be beat" at Chapman and Cutler. By and large, "a friendly atmosphere" pervades the firm and "partners are easy to talk with and generally have an open door." One associate gushes that the firm is "very family-friendly and lifestyle-oriented" and adds that "the firm has done an amazing job of recruiting lawyers and other personnel that are very pleasant to work with." But other insiders say that firm culture varies according to department. "Depending on the group, the culture ranges from laid-back to formal," says one associate. Fortunately, "the litigation group is pretty laid-back," he notes. Some attorneys socialize together outside the office, but it isn't the norm.

Lawyers at the firm are "most impressed with the respect Chapman shows their associates and the flexibility they are willing to give associates." As long as you get your work done, sources say, the firm is "not too particular" about where you do it (i.e., at home or at work) and "face time" isn't important. "They truly understand that associates can balance their work and home life successfully with the right support system," says a midlevel associate. Even better: the firm is not a sweatshop and billable-hour expectations are "very reasonable." Nevertheless, the firm does provide "ample opportunities for associates to earn billable time."

Most attorneys at Chapman and Cutler feel that the pay is "on par" with similar law firms in the area. The firm recently restructured its compensation structure to "increase salaries across the board." At the same time, however, "bonus amounts were reduced." According to one seasoned associate, "The pay is fair for the hourly requirements. The bonus structure is poor because there is a 200-hour gap between hourly requirements and the first bonus level," offering "no incentive to work extra and fall into that gap."

Opinions about the firm's training program vary. "Training is hit and miss," says one insider. Other associates note that "the firm has recently started more formal training sessions across departments that are open to all associates. Within each department, hands-on training prevails much more than actual formalized training." According to one insider, "Associates don't care" about formal training anyway. "We want real-world training," he says.

And the firm delivers. As a midlevel associate says, "The firm definitely subscribes to the 'learn-by-doing' theory, which may be difficult at first but provides very good knowledge-based learning." The good news is that most of the partners are very helpful and quick to offer advice when asked.

Associates appreciate the firm's growing commitment to pro bono work but seem uncertain whether time spent on pro bono projects counts toward billable-hours targets or bonuses or neither. While few insiders consider office space a factor in choosing a law firm ("The emphasis here is on the work, not the image," sniffs one associate), several note that the "décor varies from floor to floor" and many offices "could use an upgrade."

Clark Hill PLC

500 Woodward Avenue, Suite 3500
Detroit, MI 48226-3435
Phone: (313) 965-8300
www.clarkhill.com

LOCATIONS

Detroit, MI (HQ)
Birmingham, MI
Lansing, MI

MAJOR DEPARTMENTS & PRACTICES

Business & Transactional
Communications, Energy & Regulatory
Family Law
Government Policy & Practice
Immigration
Intellectual Property
Labor & Employment
Litigation & Alternative Dispute Resolution
Tax Law
Trusts & Estates

THE STATS

No. of attorneys:
 firm-wide: 141
 Detroit: 108
 Birmingham: 25
No. of offices: 3
Summer associate offers:
 firm-wide: 4 out of 4 (2004)
Chief Executive Officer: John J. Hern
Hiring Partner: John T. Clappison

NOTABLE PERKS

- Parental leave
- Reimbursement of bar review and exam expenses
- Payment of professional seminars and dues
- Onsite parking

BASE SALARY

Detroit, MI (2005)
1st year: $95,000
Summer associate: $1,730/week

EMPLOYMENT CONTACT

Ms. Elizabeth A. Claes
Professional Recruiting and Development Coordinator
Phone: (313) 965-8253
Fax: (313) 965-8252
E-mail: eclaes@clarkhill.com

THE SCOOP

Clark Hill owes its origins to Joseph Clark and Levi Griffin, who hung out their shingle in Detroit in the 1890s. The firm was ideally situated to provide legal services to the burgeoning automobile companies in the early 20th century, and as the population and industry of Detroit exploded, the early lawyers of what is now Clark Hill established themselves as leaders in the fields of automotive, business and transportation law. The firm's oldest client, the Michigan Manufacturers Association, has been with Clark Hill for more than 100 years. The firm now has 100 attorneys in three offices in Michigan (Detroit, Birmingham and Lansing). In December 2004, 15 Clark Hill attorneys appeared in the 2005 – 2006 edition of *The Best Lawyers in America*. Also that month, Clark Hill attorney Daniel J. Scully became one of six Michigan lawyers inducted as a fellow in the American College of Trial Lawyers.

Clark Hill has been engaged in an ambitious project of Midwest expansion. According to CEO John Hern, the firm has grown by 35 percent in the last two years. In 2004 alone, the firm brought on board nearly 20 seasoned attorneys, adding to the firm's depth in its litigation, real estate, construction, business and government relations practices. In addition, in fall 2004, the firm relocated its Lansing office to a 17,000-square-foot historic building in the city's Old Town district, a commercial district that is also home to a growing art and cultural community. The newly refurbished building, which dates back to 1846, sits on the bank of the Grand River and will soon house some 60 lawyers and other employees.

Along with its automotive practices, Clark Hill has developed a strong construction law group. The firm has represented contractors, subcontractors, architects and other major players in construction projects, including the Detroit Renaissance Center, the Midland Nuclear Power Plant, the University of Michigan Hospital, the Pontiac Silverdome and the DaimlerChrysler Technology Center. This practice group also provides litigation services to clients in the construction industry, including one case in which the firm won summary judgment dismissing a $30 million claim brought against an engineering design firm in a major tunnel project.

In other litigation matters, Clark Hill lawyers provide learned counsel on matters as diverse as securities, divorce and family law, immigration, employment discrimination, and director and officer liability. During the Cold War, they helped a hockey player get relieved of his contract with the Red Army Team in order to join the National Hockey League (according to the firm, the unnamed athlete has been an NHL All-Star ever since). In 2000, Clark Hill attorneys recovered several million for clients in a condemnation case and the next year successfully defended R.J. Reynolds Tobacco Company against a wrongful death claim. Beyond Michigan, the firm has represented foreign clients doing business in the United States, including Daimler Chrysler Corporation, Thyssen Krupp AG, Sumitomo Corporation and BMW, as well as domestic clients securing footholds abroad, such as McLaren Performance Technologies and Fabri-Kal Corporation. Clark Hill is a member of both Legal Network International, an association of independent law firms throughout the world, and the International Business Law Consortium, which is affiliated with the Center for International Legal Studies in Salzburg, Austria.

The firm's attorneys devote an average of 30 hours per year to pro bono work. For instance, Detroit partner Thomas Nowinski provides legal counsel for Community Legal Resources, a joint project of Michigan Legal Services and the Pro Bono Committee of the Business Law Section of the American Bar Association working in conjunction with the Michigan Litigation Assistance Partnership Program. Through his work for Community Legal Resources, Nowinski advises nonprofits on a range of tax matters; for example, he assisted Mothers Observing Mothers, a second-chance home for teen mothers in Detroit, in applying for tax-exempt status with the IRS.

Attorneys at Clark Hill have authored a number of articles on specific cases of interest and on topics such as sexual harassment in the workplace, contaminated property, litigation, community foundations and tax law. The firm releases the biweekly *Michigan Telecommunications Report* and hosts seminars and conferences periodically, including an Annual Employment Law Conference. The subject of the 2004 conference was "Avoiding Tomorrow's Problems Today."

GETTING HIRED

Summer classes at Clark Hill are fairly small, perhaps because associates are hired with the expectation that they will stay with the firm for the long haul. Hiring criteria include academic performance, participation in moot court, journals and other extracurricular activities, as well as prior work experience. While paper credentials are certainly valued, Clark Hill also wants "independent thinkers and hard workers," the ideal candidate being "well-rounded both in the law and in life." Through a program with the Detroit Legal Services Clinic, the firm offers summer associates the opportunity to intern at the clinic for one week during their summer with the firm.

Clausen Miller, P.C.

10 South LaSalle Street
Chicago, IL 60603-1098
Phone: (312) 855-1010
www.clausen.com

LOCATIONS

Chicago, IL (HQ)
Irvine, CA
New York, NY
Parsippany, NJ
Wheaton, IL
London

MAJOR DEPARTMENTS & PRACTICES

Business Litigation
Insurance
Insurance Litigation

THE STATS

No. of attorneys:
  firm-wide: 160
  Chicago: 110
No. of offices: 6
Hiring Partners: David M. Heilmann and James F. Smith

NOTABLE PERKS

- Matching 401(k) plan
- Qualified profit-sharing plan
- Flexible spending accounts

EMPLOYMENT CONTACTS

David M. Heilmann, Esq.
Recruitment and Retention Co-Chair
Phone: (312) 606-7705
Fax: (312) 606-7777
E-mail: dheilmann@clausen.com

James F. Smith, Esq.
Recruitment and Retention Co-Chair
Phone: (312) 606-7709
Fax: (312) 606-7777
E-mail: jsmith@clausen.com

THE SCOOP

In 1936, Donald Clausen and Norman Miller opened the doors of their eponymous firm on LaSalle Street in Chicago. From the outset, Clausen Miller has concentrated on insurance litigation, although over time the firm's practice has broadened to include such areas as admiralty law, corporate law, intellectual property and unfair competition, professional liability, tax and transportation law. Today, Clausen Miller's roster is over 150 attorneys strong, with five offices around the United States and one branch in London. Also across the pond, the firm has formed alliances with legal practitioners in Rome and Paris through a related entity known as Clausen Miller Europe.

Within its three major practice areas, Clausen Miller subdivides into more than 34 specialty sections. The firm boasts expertise in some fairly obscure areas – how many lawyers do you know with vast stores of knowledge on crane law? At Clausen Miller, the firm has over 25 years of crane law experience under its proverbial belt, representing an array of clients in the construction and carrier and rigging industries. Similarly, the firm has made its presence known in the toxic tort area, acting as counsel to insurance companies, insureds and third parties in asbestos, mercury, lead and toxic mold cases (some of Clausen Miller's ads feature the slogan "We Are Mold Zappers"!). In the field of subrogation law, Clausen Miller has led the charge in obtaining recoveries arising out of major fires, including those at One Meridian Plaza in Philadelphia, the First Interstate high-rise in Los Angeles, the McCormick Place convention hall in Chicago and the Milani Foods warehouse in Chicago.

In current litigation, the firm is seeking review by the Illinois Supreme Court of what it describes as an "absurd result" in a personal injury lawsuit recently tried before a Cook County jury. The motion for direct appeal to the state's highest court seeks to bypass the intermediate appellate court because, Clausen attorneys say, of the issue's wide impact. The underlying lawsuit, in which Clausen Miller represents defendant Romar Transportation Inc., resulted from a multi-vehicle pile-up on I-90 in 1999. Driver Scott Yoder collided with a Romar-owned truck, killing Yoder's four-year-old daughter and causing permanent brain damage to his two-year-old son. Yoder filed claims against other owners and drivers involved in the accident, but the jury ruled against him. Meanwhile, Yoder's wife Jerelyn also brought suit against her husband, Romar Transportation and a Romar employee. Because husband and wife settled before trial, Scott Yoder's name did not appear on the list of defendants to which the jurors were to assign liability for the accident. The jury divvied up 100 percent of the liability for the $38.3 million verdict among the four remaining defendants, including Clausen's clients. Romar and its employee were declared 30 percent at fault, making them jointly liable for the entire award. However, as Clausen attorneys pointed out, in effect, the jury assigned more than 100 percent blame among the parties since, by having ruled against Scott Yoder, they implicitly found him at least 51 percent at fault. Clausen Miller's motion for high court review is still pending.

Clausen attorneys' expertise has earned them a reputation as the go-to lawyers among their peers. In 2004, partner Jim Barber was recognized by *Crain's Chicago Business* as a "Leading Lawyer in Employment Law" in Illinois. The selection was the result of a survey of employment lawyers who were asked, "If a family member or friend needed legal help and you couldn't take the case, to whom would you refer them?"

Despite the firm's high-stakes litigation and "strong work ethic," Clausen Miller prides itself on maintaining "a congenial atmosphere." Through firm-sponsored summer and holiday parties, as well as informal get-togethers, the firm encourages the building of "personal camaraderie" among attorneys. Teamwork, it seems, is desired as much as talent.

Psst...
Need a Change in Venue?

Use the Internet's most targeted job search tools for law professionals.

Vault Law Job Board
The most comprehensive and convenient job board for law professionals. Target your search by area of law, function, and experience level, and find the job openings that you want. No surfing required.

VaultMatch Resume Database
Vault takes match-making to the next level: post your resume and customize your search by area of law, experience and more. We'll match job listings with your interests and criteria and e-mail them directly to your inbox.

VAULT
> the most trusted name in career information™

Dickinson Wright PLLC

500 Woodward Avenue
Suite 4000
Detroit, MI 48226-3425
Phone: (313) 223-3500
www.dickinsonwright.com

LOCATIONS

Detroit, MI (HQ)
Ann Arbor, MI
Bloomfield Hills, MI
Grand Rapids, MI
Lansing, MI
Washington, DC

MAJOR DEPARTMENTS & PRACTICES

Banking
Bankruptcy
Commercial Litigation
Corporate & Securities
Employment
Environmental
Product Liability
Real Estate

THE STATS

No. of attorneys:
  firm-wide: 215
  Detroit: 86
  Ann Arbor: 15
  Bloomfield Hills: 71
  Grand Rapids: 16
  Lansing: 22
No. of offices: 6
Summer associate offers:
  firm-wide: 9 out of 12 (2004)
  Detroit: 7 out of 10 (2004)
  Grand Rapids: 1 out of 1 (2004)
  Lansing: 1 out of 1 (2004)
Chairman: Dennis W. Archer
Hiring Partner: Louis Theros

UPPERS
- Friendly, supportive atmosphere
- Challenging work, with lots of responsibility from the outset

DOWNERS
- Salaries could be higher
- Sometimes long hours

NOTABLE PERKS
- Offices are "some of the nicest in Detroit"

BASE SALARY

Detroit, MI (2005)
1st year: $95,000
Summer associate: $1,735/week

EMPLOYMENT CONTACTS

Detroit, Ann Arbor, Bloomfield Hills and Grand Rapids
Ms. Patricia A. Diefenbacher
Director of Legal Recruitment
Phone: (313) 223-3639
Fax: (313) 223-3598
E-mail: pdiefenbacher@dickinsonwright.com

Lansing
Ms. Sue A. Talarico
Lansing Office Recruitment Coordinator
Phone: (517) 487-4737
Fax: (517) 487-4700
E-mail: stalarico@dickinsonwright.com

THE SCOOP

With deep roots in Motor City dating back to 1878, Dickinson Wright has built a solid, diverse practice with particular strengths in the automotive industry – Ford and DaimlerChrysler are clients – and the telecommunications and education law fields. Litigators at Dickinson frequently argue before the Michigan Court of Appeals and the Michigan Supreme Court as well as in federal courts, including the U.S. Court of Appeals for the 6th Circuit. Transactional attorneys at the firm participate in high-powered mergers and acquisitions, corporate finance deals and asset securitization projects.

As one of the leading law firms in Detroit, according to *Corporate Board Member* magazine in 2004, Dickinson Wright has gained renown in the international sphere in recent years. A London publication, *Global Counsel 3000*, named Dickinson one of its highly recommended firms and gave the firm the highest rating among Michigan legal service providers. *IP Worldwide* also ranked the firm among the best trademark counsel in the United States and one of the top 50 patent counsel in the nation. In large part, Dickinson has earned this recognition due to the firm's highly impressive attorney roster, which includes the former mayor of Detroit and recent president of the American Bar Association, Dennis W. Archer. Archer, who has also served as an associate justice of the Michigan Supreme Court, a member of the Michigan House of Delegates and a professor at area law schools, has been the chairman of Dickinson Wright since 2002.

GETTING HIRED

The hiring process at Dickinson Wright is considered highly competitive. According to an insider, Dickinson seeks those who will help shape the profession, not just perform well: "My firm looks for people that love the law and will challenge the ideas of others – including partners – when called for." Another associate believes that the firm seeks "people who will fit in, be great lawyers and bring business into the firm."

Once hired, associates receive a fair amount of training. "We are required to attend three in-house seminars each year," says an experienced associate. The informal mentoring is even stronger than the formal training; according to a source, "Partners recognize talent, encourage its development and use it. They don't let it expire in useless attorney work."

OUR SURVEY SAYS

Job satisfaction at Dickinson Wright ranges from above average to very high. "It's the best firm that I've worked in – great people and great work," says a senior associate. A litigator shares this sentiment: "I'm surrounded by the state's best attorneys and they rely on me and give me significant responsibility on important and publicly visible cases." One associate boasts that the firm has the "best clients and practice in Michigan." The only drawback to such a stellar reputation, says the source, is sometimes fierce competition from rival firms: "Other firms are shooting to bring you down. It's like playing the Super Bowl champs when you're up against us."

For some, the hours are excessive; for others, they are fair. Survey respondents in the litigation department report billing on average between 176 and 200 hours per month, whereas respondents in other departments report billing fewer hours (151 to 175 per month). One midlevel associate complains about the billable-hour requirement: "The number of hours at the office far exceeds the hours billed. I think 1,950 [hours] is too high for a Detroit firm (but they are all this way)." Another associate takes the hours in stride: "There is little pressure to bill at the firm, but there is pressure to become a great attorney. Having responsibility placed in your hands sometimes requires long hours, but not always. Partners work just as hard as associates."

Attorneys agree that excellence and congeniality coexist at the firm. As one lawyer puts it, "While there is an emphasis on doing good work, the culture is laid-back. Associates generally get along and there is not a competitive environment. Lawyers do tend to socialize together on a regular basis." "The associates do not compete for jobs," agrees another source. "We work together." One associate describes the Dickinson atmosphere as "informal and friendly, but still professional," while a litigator says the firm is "formal in the sense of the pursuit of excellence, but otherwise simply friendly." Relations between partners and associates are very good overall, though they can vary, according to sources. "If you earn the respect, you get it," declares one insider. Another says, "For the most part, the associates are treated with respect by the partners."

Reports on salary are mixed. "We're on the low end of the scale as associates become more senior," says one insider. Another concurs that the salaries are "perhaps just a bit below other similar firms in the city." Yet a third attorney, by contrast, describes the salaries as "tops for a Michigan firm, with the exception of that one top-five sweatshop firm in Michigan." According to one source, the greatest perk of the job is "the opportunity to get early responsibility on significant cases. No internal politicking; if you earn it, you'll get it."

DLA Piper Rudnick Gray Cary US LLP

203 North LaSalle Street
Suite 1900
Chicago, IL 60601-1293
Phone: (312) 368-4000
www.dlapiper.com

LOCATIONS

Austin, TX • Baltimore, MD (2 offices) • Boston, MA • Chicago, IL • Dallas, TX • East Palo Alto, CA • Los Angeles, CA (2 offices) • New York, NY • Philadelphia, PA • Reston, VA • Sacramento, CA • San Diego, CA (2 offices) • San Francisco, CA (2 offices) • Seattle, WA • Tampa, FL Washington, DC • Amsterdam • Antwerp • Bangkok • Bergen • Birmingham • Bradford • Bratislava • Brussels • Budapest • Cologne • Copenhagen • Edinburgh • Glasgow • Hamburg • Hong Kong • Leeds • Liverpool • London • Madrid • Manchester • Milan • Moscow • Oslo • Paris • Prague • Rome • Rotterdam • Salzburg • Sarajevo • Shanghai • Sheffield • Singapore • Stockholm • Vienna • Warsaw • Zagreb

MAJOR DEPARTMENTS & PRACTICES

Corporate & Securities • Employee Benefits & Executive Compensation • Finance, Financial Services & Bankruptcy • Franchise & Distribution Government Affairs • Intellectual Property • Litigation • Real Estate • Tax • Trusts & Estates

THE STATS

No. of attorneys:
 firm-wide: 2,800
 Chicago: 277
No. of offices: 49
Summer associate offers:
 firm-wide: 48 out of 50 (2004)
 Chicago: 11 out of 11 (2004)
Firm-wide CEOs: Frank Burch, Nigel Knowles and Lee Miller
Chicago Managing Partner: Allen J. Ginsburg
Chicago Hiring Partner: Christina L. Martini

UPPERS
- Sophisticated work and "superb" hands-on training
- Strong pro bono program

DOWNERS
- Big-firm politics and increasing bureaucracy
- Heavy workload

NOTABLE PERKS
- Emergency child care
- Bar expenses
- Free dinners
- MBA scholarship

BASE SALARY

Chicago, IL (2005)
1st year: $125,000
Summer associate: $2,400/week

EMPLOYMENT CONTACT

Ms. Marguerite E. Durston
Legal Recruiting Manager
Phone: (312) 368-8928
Fax: (312) 236-7516
E-mail: marguerite.durston@dlapiper.com

THE SCOOP

In January 2005, Piper Rudnick Gray Cary LLP merged with U.K.-based DLA. The world's largest law firm merger has produced the world's third-largest law firm, with 2,800 lawyers in 18 countries and revenues of more than $1 billion. Although a union of this size is especially significant, mergers in general are nothing new to the former Piper Rudnick, which was itself the product of a 1999 merger between Baltimore's Piper & Marbury and Chicago's Rudnick & Wolfe. Only a few months before the merger with DLA, Piper Rudnick agreed to merge with Silicon Valley-based Gray Cary Ware & Freidenrich LLP. The California firm added its impressive technology practice to Piper Rudnick's national practices in commercial litigation, corporate and securities, real estate and government affairs. Now, with the DLA merger, the combined new firm has gained significant worldwide presence.

DLA Piper Rudnick Gray Cary has already been honored as the 2005 "Law Firm of the Year" by the U.K.-based monthly, *Legal Business*. This is only the most recent of many honors awarded to Piper Rudnick attorneys. In 2004 *Chambers USA* named 40 Piper Rudnick attorneys to its list of *America's Leading Lawyers for Business*, with two of those receiving the prestigious rating of "Exceptional" and one earning the rarified title of "Senior Statesman." Also in 2004, 70 Piper Rudnick lawyers in Chicago were dubbed "Leading Lawyers in Illinois" by the Leading Lawyers Network, an organization that asks legal professionals to nominate outstanding lawyers based upon their achievement and esteem in their chosen field of practice.

While the mammoth new firm will share a firm-wide vision, firm management has announced that local offices will retain autonomy over such things as compensation and culture. Approximately 10 percent of DLA Piper's attorneys work in Chicago, which is the firm's largest office. The Second City office focuses on practices including finance, bankruptcy, real estate, corporate and securities, international transactions, litigation, intellectual property, labor and employment, and tax.

GETTING HIRED

Insiders report that it's getting "harder all the time" to get a foot in the door of DLA Piper's Chicago office. The firm is "becoming more and more selective," says a senior associate in the Windy City. DLA Piper as a whole focuses on Ivy League and other top-tier law schools, looking for candidates "with impressive academic backgrounds and experience." Nevertheless, insiders say that "a surprising amount of weight" is put on "personality and how the candidate would 'fit' in the office culture." Says one associate: "We've had no problem rejecting candidates from top-three law schools whose personalities didn't seem to mesh with the firm."

OUR SURVEY SAYS

No one knows for sure what the latest mega-merger will mean for the culture at DLA Piper, but if anyone can guess, it's the associates who came aboard as a byproduct of past mergers. Unfortunately, insiders disagree about the firm's success when it comes to integrating. "As a junior associate coming over in the last merger, I have not found the attorneys here particularly welcoming," complains one attorney. "As the firm has increased in size, the collegiality and sense of being a firm has decreased," says another. But life in the Chicago office, which most describe as "friendly and collegial," isn't expected to change much – although associates might welcome change in one aspect. If the office culture is "not as laid-back as in years past," its décor reportedly dates back to the 1970s. Associates grumble about "grungy" furnishings and "cramped," windowless offices for all but the most senior associates and partners. Maybe as the firm prepares for a global future, it will consider a facelift for the Chicago office.

One thing that's not likely to change is the workload. Insiders say that associates are expected to bill at least 1,900 hours, "but the real requirement is a minimum of 2,000 hours." And productivity bonuses "only kick in at 2,200 hours." Nevertheless, some associates consider the hours "very reasonable" and insist that "the firm is not a sweatshop." Others who consider the demand for billable-hours high acknowledge, "That's part of the deal when you begin as an associate ... so is the salary." On the plus side, the firm does allow flex-time and has a number of part-time associates (primarily women). Luckily, "face time" isn't required and the firm gives "billable credit for up to 100 hours of pro bono work." In fact, associates report, "Pro bono is a major focal point of the firm."

DLA Piper associates tend to consider themselves "very well-compensated," at least when it comes to base salary levels. A Chicago source says that the "firm has done well in keeping up with prevailing rates," although the bonus levels are "perhaps a bit low." Others agree that the firm rewards attorneys who put in long hours, but is lean on bonuses for exceptional work product. "I am thrilled with my base salary," declares a senior associate, "but I feel that I have been treated unfairly where my bonus is concerned."

DLA Piper has "a very good formal training program" with "retreats in various practice areas" that are "especially helpful." In fact, associates "are offered and expected to participate in extensive training throughout the year." As for informal training, associates say that the level of "day-to-day mentoring" is "hit or miss." In Chicago, most agree that it's up to you to make mentoring happen – go to the right people and ask the right questions, and you'll get what you need. However, for several sources, the limited feedback suggests that "little attention is paid to personal development," with the consequence that some associates feel that they are "working in a vacuum."

Note: As of the time of the associate survey, neither the Gray Cary nor the DLA merger had been completed; the comments in Getting Hired and Our Survey Says reflect pre-merger views of associates at the former Piper Rudnick.

"Because of the steady stream of large deals, exposure and 'hands-on' training as a young associate is superb."

– *DLA Piper associate*

Dykema Gossett PLLC

400 Renaissance Center
Detroit, MI 48243
Phone: (313) 568-6800
www.dykema.com

LOCATIONS

Detroit, MI (HQ)
Ann Arbor, MI
Bloomfield Hills, MI
Chicago, IL
Grand Rapids, MI
Joliet, IL
Lansing, MI
Lisle, IL
Pasadena, CA
Washington, DC

MAJOR DEPARTMENTS & PRACTICES

Bankruptcy
Corporate & Finance
Employee Benefits
Employment & Labor
Environmental
Government
Health Care
Intellectual Property
Litigation
Real Estate
Tax & Estates

THE STATS

No. of attorneys:
  firm-wide: approx. 360
  Detroit: 105
  Ann Arbor: 32
  Bloomfield Hills: 68
  Chicago area: approx. 100
  Grand Rapids: 13
  Lansing: 23
No. of offices: 10
Summer associate offers:
  firm-wide: 13 out of 20 (2004)
  Detroit: 8 out of 11 (2004)
  Ann Arbor: 0 out of 1 (2004)
  Bloomfield Hills: 3 out of 4 (2004)
  Chicago area: N/A (no summer associates in 2004)
  Grand Rapids: N/A (no 2Ls in 2004)
  Lansing: 1 out of 3 (2004)
Chairman and CEO: Rex E. Schlaybaugh Jr.
Hiring Partner: Brendan J. Cahill

NOTABLE PERKS

- Health and dependent care reimbursement programs
- Parking
- Flexible work arrangements
- Firm-sponsored social events

BASE SALARY

Detroit, MI (2005)
1st year: $95,000
Summer associate: $1,800/week (Michigan offices)

Chicago, IL (2005)
1st year: $115,000
Summer associate: $2,100/week

EMPLOYMENT CONTACT

Ms. Sarah K. Staup
Professional Personnel Specialist
Phone: (313) 568-6831
Fax: (313) 568-6691
E-mail: sstaup@dykema.com

THE SCOOP

In February 2004, Dykema Gossett announced that it would be merging with Chicago-based firm Rooks Pitts, effective April 1. The addition of Rooks Pitts expanded Dykema Gossett's presence in Chicagoland, where the combined firm now employs more than 100 attorneys in the Windy City and maintains three offices in the surrounding 'burbs. This expansionist move was just one among several this year by the Detroit-based firm: in March, Dykema Gossett joined forces with Jones & Blouch in Washington, D.C., enhancing its corporate finance practice; and in February, Dykema also welcomed a high-profile group of real estate lawyers from the Motor City firm Howard & Howard. A Los Angeles office was added in August 2003, when Dykema brought in 14 lawyers from the litigation firm of Feeney Kellet Wienner & Bush P.C.

The firm has touted these steps as "advancing the strategic plan" for Dykema Gossett to become the preeminent law firm in the Midwest (it is already among the largest). Having won the No.-1 ranking in *Corporate Board Member*'s assessment of Motown law firms, Dykema is already well on its way to achieving its goal and more. With nearly 400 attorneys and professionals, and seven offices that stretch from coast to coast, the firm is expanding beyond the region and into the national and international arenas. In September 2004 the firm announced that it was linking up with Fahmy Hudome International and the Haveman Group, two consulting firms with connections in the Middle East, thereby strengthening its government relations and international practice areas. The firm already has a strong base of relations with clients from Arab-American communities in the Midwest and hopes to grow its client base abroad as well. One of the firm's attorneys, Richard D. McLellan, recently represented Iraq's Ministry of Health in litigation resulting from the sale of HIV-tainted blood under Saddam Hussein's regime to several Middle Eastern countries.

The firm has six broad departments – business services, employment, government policy, litigation, real estate and environmental, and tax and estates – within which lawyers practice in nearly 50 specialties, ranging from intellectual property and employment law to casino gaming law and medical malpractice litigation. Dykema Gossett's diverse client base includes publicly held corporations, privately held companies, individuals, partnerships and associations in industries ranging from retail to finance to managed care. The firm recently scored a big victory for client Ford Motor Company. Working with co-counsel Bryan Cave, firm litigators successfully defended Ford against a class-action lawsuit filed by St. Clair County and the city of Centerville on behalf of municipalities and other Illinois entities using the Ford Crown Victoria Police Interceptors. The suit, which sought nearly $800 million in damages, claimed that Ford failed to disclose that a design flaw made the car vulnerable to catching fire in rear-end collisions. After a five-week trial, in October 2004 the jury returned a unanimous defense verdict.

Even while fulfilling the firm's manifest destiny, the lawyers of Dykema Gossett manage to find the time to serve their communities. The firm donates over $200,000 annually to community organizations and programs such as the Detroit Medical Center, Detroit Symphony, Anti-Defamation League and Gleaners Community Food Bank. Dykema attorneys assist the elderly through membership in Focus Hope (a nationally recognized civil and human rights organization based in Detroit) and have provided mentorship for programs such as the Detroit Compact (a scholarship incentive program for high school students). In recognition of its record of public service, the firm has received the prestigious American Bar Association's National Public Service Award. Dykema's pro bono program primarily assists victims of domestic violence and provides housing-related legal services to indigent clients, although recent projects have also included the representation of two Georgia inmates on death row.

GETTING HIRED

According to the firm, its extensive recruiting efforts include the review of more than 2,500 applications each year. These come from mail-in candidates as well as those participating in the on-campus interview process. From this symbolic mass of humanity, the firm eventually winnows down the applicant pool to hire between 20 and 30 associates per year. Candidates called in for an interview would be wise to make nice with any junior attorneys they meet, since the firm gives "substantial weight" to associates' evaluations. Prospective associates should also take note that the firm has one of the largest law firm libraries in Michigan.

Foley & Lardner LLP

Firstar Center
777 East Wisconsin Avenue
Milwaukee, WI 53202-5306
Phone: (414) 271-2400
www.foley.com

LOCATIONS
Milwaukee, WI (HQ)
Boston, MA
Chicago, IL
Del Mar, CA
Detroit, MI
Jacksonville, FL
Los Angeles, CA
Madison, WI
New York, NY
Orlando, FL
Sacramento, CA
San Diego, CA
San Francisco, CA
Silicon Valley, CA
Tallahassee, FL
Tampa, FL
Washington, DC
West Palm Beach, FL
Brussels
Tokyo

MAJOR DEPARTMENTS & PRACTICES
Business Law
Health Law
Intellectual Property
Litigation
Regulatory
Tax & Individual Planning

THE STATS
No. of attorneys:
  firm-wide: 937
  Milwaukee: 224
  Chicago: 148
  Detroit: 38
  Madison: 66
No. of offices: 20
Summer associate offers:
  firm-wide: 54 out of 60 (2004)
  Milwaukee: 17 out of 18 (2004)
  Chicago: 8 out of 9 (2004)
  Detroit: 3 out of 3 (2004)
  Madison: 8 out of 8 (2004)
Chief Executive Officer: Ralf Böer
Hiring Partners:
  Milwaukee: Daniel M. Hess
  Chicago: Michael J. Small
  Detroit: John Birmingham Jr.
  Madison: Daniel A. Kaplan

EMPLOYMENT CONTACTS

Milwaukee and Madison
Ms. Kerri A. Sell
Regional Legal Recruiting Coordinator
Phone: (414) 297-4968
Fax: (414) 297-4900
E-mail: ksell@foley.com

Chicago and Detroit
Ms. Elaine F. Miller
Regional Legal Recruiting Coordinator
Phone: (312) 832-4556
Fax: (312) 832-4700
E-mail: emiller@foley.com

UPPERS
- Midwestern mentality with national practice
- High level of responsibility

DOWNERS
- Difficulty in making partner
- Pressure to bill

NOTABLE PERKS
- Loan assistance for first-time homebuyers
- Free Wednesday night dinners
- Four weeks paid child-care leave for men and women (plus eight weeks leave for women giving birth)
- Spirit Week events

BASE SALARY

Milwaukee, WI, and Detroit, MI (2005)
1st year: $115,000
2nd year: $125,000
3rd year: $130,000
4th year: $140,000
5th year: $150,000
6th year: $165,000
7th year: $175,000
Summer associate: $2,100/week

Chicago, IL (2005)
1st year: $125,000
2nd year: $135,000
3rd year: $150,000
4th year: $165,000
5th year: $180,000
6th year: $190,000
7th year: $200,000
Summer associate: $2,400/week

Madison, WI (2005)
1st year: $105,000
2nd year: $115,000
3rd year: $120,000
4th year: $130,000
5th year: $140,000
6th year: $150,000
7th year: $160,000
Summer associate: $2,000/week

THE SCOOP

Headquartered in Milwaukee, with sizeable offices in Madison, Detroit and Chicago, Foley & Lardner has long been a major player in America's heartland. Over the past few years, however, the firm has implemented a steady strategic expansion plan that has solidified its presence from coast to coast and beyond. In the first half of 2004 alone, Foley opened up two new offices: In March, the firm established a Silicon Valley presence, offering practice areas in intellectual property and biotechnology, and in late June, the firm acquired its first toehold in New York, bringing on board the lawyers of the litigation boutique formerly known as Friedman, Wang & Bleiberg, P.C. Most recently, the firm acquired the entire Boston office of Epstein, Becker & Green, P.C. With nearly 950 lawyers, Foley & Lardner stands as the 11th-largest law firm in the United States, and with branches in Brussels and Tokyo, global domination is just a few continents away.

For two years running, Foley & Lardner has won a spot on *CIO* magazine's "CIO 100" list. The prestigious ranking recognizes companies around the world that seamlessly integrate technology into their business and find innovative ways to incorporate technology to achieve greater efficiency. Foley & Lardner was singled out for its unique training programs aimed at educating firm staff on new technologies, its advanced client extranet intended to expedite client access to files and information at the firm and its rapid entry into new markets.

GETTING HIRED

Foley doesn't kid around when it comes to hiring; it's looking for "the best-of-the-best from big-name law schools." This "highly competitive" approach to hiring leads some associates to think that the "minimum requirements for associates are artificially, excessively high." A senior attorney notes that the firm is "pretty strict on the numbers." One associate believes that the process "differs among the offices despite attempts to make [it] uniform." It's also important to be a team player, as Foley is looking for "candidates who are not only bright, but will fit into a friendly atmosphere." Callback interviews "are scheduled for a half-day in the office, with each candidate meeting about two or three partners and two or three associates," reports a junior associate.

OUR SURVEY SAYS

Foley & Lardner combines big-firm expectations with a "'Midwest' feel." Associates vary in their assessments of the firm's atmosphere, even within the same office. Where one attorney describes the firm's home office as "collegial," "supportive" and with a "strong sense of teamwork," another claims that the "culture is formal and somewhat uptight," and a third grumbles that "the entire place seems to be lacking a sense of humor." Several Milwaukee associates express concern over "a perceived lack of job security," referring to recent layoffs and budget cuts. A Chicago lawyer describes the culture as "half laid-back, half uptight and worried." The firm's smaller offices seem to fare better. "Overall," says one associate, "the Detroit office is a fairly laid-back, friendly place to work." Similarly, "the Madison office is more friendly and laid-back than other offices," according to an inside source.

If insiders aren't uniformly ecstatic about their jobs, many praise the caliber of the work and their colleagues. Most associates seem to enjoy "a good variety of complex legal work with smart colleagues and good clients." Others wish the "stress level" weren't so high. Despite "challenging work with some great opportunities," some associates find it "hard to maintain a balanced life and meet the firm's hour expectations." Foley officially requires 1,850 billable-hours, but one midlevel associate claims that "simply billing the minimum will guarantee that you will never make partner." Another lawyer agrees that "the expectations regarding the 'real' minimum are rising." "Twelve-hour days (plus both weekend days)" are not uncommon, sighs a litigator in Wisconsin. On top of billable expectations, the 150-hour non-billable requirement often keeps associates "working later than [they'd] like." As for including pro bono projects in billable-hours, a third-year responds: "Pro bono counting as billable? What universe are you in?"

Still, some attorneys look on the bright side: "The hours are not bad given the pay," declares one young litigator. Indeed, associates perk up noticeably when discussing compensation. Foley has a two-tier system, with salary levels set at 1,850 and 1,950 billable-hours, which one midlevel attorney calls "a major benefit, particularly when work is slow." The pay is considered "very generous for the Milwaukee market." But, while the firm provides "great compensation for young associates," one Chicago attorney believes that it is "probably not up to market for senior associates." A fourth-year suggests that "discretionary bonuses for quality of work (not just quantity) would improve the incentive system." Another insider complains that the "firm has recently experienced record partner profits without adjusting set pay increases for the associates."

One of Foley's strongest areas is associate training. "I think the firm does a very good job with formal training of associates," reports a source. There are "constant training opportunities for lawyers at all levels, including formal multi-day seminars, lunch seminars, afternoon training sessions, online training opportunities and outside training." At least one lawyer even finds that the training "borders on excessive." More informally, mentoring can be "a crap shoot," but a senior litigator notes that "if the associate takes the initiative, most partners will take the time." That said, "Partners never take the initiative," and the best mentoring comes from senior associates "who still seem to remember what one actually knows (or doesn't know) as a junior associate)."

Freeborn & Peters LLP

311 South Wacker Drive
Suite 3000
Chicago, IL 60606-6677
Phone: (312) 360-6000
www.freebornpeters.com

LOCATIONS
Chicago, IL (HQ)
Springfield, IL

MAJOR DEPARTMENTS & PRACTICES
Banking & Bond
Bankruptcy & Creditors' Rights
Corporate
Employment & Benefits
Estate Planning & Tax
Government Relations
Intellectual Property & Technology
Litigation
Product Liability
Real Estate, Zoning & Land Use

THE STATS
No. of attorneys:
    firm-wide: approx. 120
    Chicago: 114
No. of offices: 2
Summer associate offers:
    Chicago: 5 out of 5 (2003)
Managing Partner: Michael J. Kelly
Hiring Partner: William N. Howard

UPPERS
- Congenial atmosphere
- Comfortable office space

DOWNERS
- Minimal raises
- Little support for working mothers

NOTABLE PERKS
- At-home DSL
- Frequent parties and other social events

BASE SALARY
Chicago, IL (2003)
1st year: $125,000
Summer associate: $2,604/week

EMPLOYMENT CONTACT
Ms. Julie Yedinak
Recruiting Coordinator
Phone: (312) 360-6532
Fax: (312) 360-6595
E-mail: jyedinak@freebornpeters.com

THE SCOOP

At the tender age of 21, Freeborn & Peters employs almost 120 lawyers in its two Illinois offices. The firm houses four major practice areas – bankruptcy, business law, government relations and litigation – which break down into more than 35 specialty groups, with a China practice, M&A and antitrust among them.

This past June, a group of Freeborn & Peters associates learned that document review, the bane of most junior lawyers' existence, can be an outcome-determinative task in litigation. The firm was representing a plaintiff who had filed suit against a technology company, claiming that the defendant had committed fraud in the sale and delivery of a software package. After mediation early on in the case, the defendant demanded a payment of $2 million based upon its counterclaim for unpaid licensing fees. Things were not looking promising for Freeborn's client, until the team discovered some damaging e-mails in the defendant's document production. Largely on the strength of those documents, the firm negotiated a $3.4 million settlement in favor of its client.

Freeborn & Peters associates get plenty of experience beyond due diligence and document review, however. Also in 2004, a flock of litigators achieved a major victory in a hearing loss class-action lawsuit that had been pending for three years. After filing flurries of briefs and delivering intense oral arguments on behalf of client Burlington Northern Santa Fe, the Freeborn team's efforts resulted in summary judgment, a denial of class certification and complete dismissal of the case.

GETTING HIRED

Getting hired at Freeborn & Peters is pretty tough, according to insiders, due to the value placed on personality fit. "It might seem easier to get in here than at a bigger firm," says a source, "but personality counts for a lot. Many great resumes get rejected because they wouldn't fit in with the culture." Basically, the firm is "looking for smart, hardworking people with whom you wouldn't mind working long hours."

OUR SURVEY SAYS

Overall job satisfaction ranges among our sources, although respondents appear to be rating the legal profession as much as their own firm. "Any dissatisfaction I feel is with the practice of law, not the firm," says one insider. Another comments, "While at times I encounter the challenges that are common to large law firms, I am confident that there is not another firm at which I would be as comfortable." Although long hours are generally part of the law firm package, Freeborn associates voice few complaints about their hours. One associate reports, "While at times the hours can get heavy, overall, I find that I have enough time to pursue as many outside interests as I choose." Although "there is some pressure to bill," acknowledges another attorney, "there is definitely no pressure to bill more than the required 2,000 hours."

The atmosphere at Freeborn is congenial, "almost strangely so," an associate remarks. There are "tons of parties," according to a source, and people are "always willing to help each other out." For the most part, lawyers are positive about partner-associate relations. One experienced associate says, "There are a handful of partners I'd rather not work with, but compared to a big law firm I used to work at, it's *de minimus*. More importantly," the attorney adds, "you know who is difficult in advance, and associates and other partners are great at helping you navigate the waters." In fact, insiders are generally happier with the informal guidance they receive than with the firm's formal training programs.

Compensation, according to an insider, is better than average, but "below market for large law firms." Another associate complains that the salary structure is "highly punitive to midlevel and senior associates," arguing that in order to offer first-years a starting salary of $125,000 the firm compresses the salary scale for subsequent classes. Moreover, this attorney continues, bonuses are "insignificant." Outside compensation, other perks include at-home DSL for attorneys and lots of social events, which, according to one source, are "unusual because everyone actually has a good time." However, one less party-happy associate wishes the firm would spend more money on bonuses instead of "frequent, wasteful parties that feel like extended work when you attend them." Insiders appear to be very happy with the office space, which was recently remodeled. "Great big windows!" exclaims one source.

Associates express some criticism of the firm's efforts to promote and retain women. While the firm does have "a large number of young female associates," there are no female equity partners and "only a couple [of] income partners." One insider claims that the firm does little to accommodate working mothers: "Women who have had children are quickly written off, and the firm is very reluctant to allow anyone to work on a part-time schedule and will only do so if the attorney agrees to be paid by the hour instead of a reduced salary." Another associate acknowledges that "the numbers don't look great," but believes the firm is supportive of women: "I am female and feel the firm is extremely receptive to hiring and promoting women. To my knowledge, only one partner is known to be difficult for women to work with, and that's a very low percentage in my experience." Sources also think the firm could diversify in other ways; insiders say there are only two minority partners and no openly gay or lesbian employees at the firm.

"Great big windows!"

– *Freeborn & Peters associate*

Frost Brown Todd LLC

2200 PNC Center
201 East Fifth Street
Cincinnati, OH 45202
Phone: (513) 651-6800
www.frostbrowntodd.com

LOCATIONS

Cincinnati, OH (HQ)
Columbus, OH
Lexington, KY
Louisville, KY
Middletown, OH
Nashville, TN
New Albany, IN

MAJOR DEPARTMENTS & PRACTICES

Bankruptcy
Commercial & Real Estate
Corporate & Securities
E-Business
Environmental
ERISA
Health Care
Intellectual Property
International
Labor, Immigration & Workers' Compensation
Litigation
Tax & Estate Planning

THE STATS

No. of attorneys:
 firm-wide: 354
 Cincinnati: 149
 Columbus: 15
No. of offices: 7
Summer associate offers:
 firm-wide: 22 out of 23 (2004)
 Cincinnati: 11 out of 11 (2004)
Co-Managing Partners: Richard J. Erickson and C. Edward Glasscock
Hiring Partner: Theresa A. Canaday

UPPERS
- Substantial early responsibility and interesting work
- Flexible schedule and family-friendly environment

DOWNERS
- Compensation could be higher
- Parking

NOTABLE PERKS
- Profit-sharing plan
- Firm-provided BlackBerry service
- Client development/entertainment opportunities

BASE SALARY

Cincinnati, OH (2005)
1st year: $85,000
Summer associate: $1,500/week

Columbus, OH
1st year: $89,000
Summer associate: $1,600/week

EMPLOYMENT CONTACT

Ms. Karen Laymance
Director of Attorney Recruitment & Development
Phone: (513) 651-6800
Fax: (513) 651-6981
E-mail: klaymance@fbtlaw.com

THE SCOOP

Frost Brown Todd was created by the November 2000 merger of the Louisville-based Brown, Todd & Heyburn and the Cincinnati shop, Frost & Jacobs. The combined entity now stands as the largest law firm in the region between Chicago and Atlanta. Today, Frost Brown Todd comprises almost 350 lawyers, with seven offices across Indiana, Ohio, Kentucky and Tennessee. As a member of both the United States Law Firm Group and Multilaw, the firm reaches clients around the United States and abroad.

Frost Brown Todd houses more than 40 practice areas, from traditional departments such as litigation, government relations, and mergers and acquisitions, to more unusual specialties in between (equine law!). The intellectual property department has created licensing agreements for such famed brands as Pokemon, Care Bears, Star Wars and Jurassic Park, and acts as counsel to Minor League Baseball. Meanwhile, Frost Brown Todd's product liability group has served as national coordinating defense counsel for massive serial liability litigation on Fen-Phen, tobacco, breast implants and lead paint.

Another of the firm's key departments is its labor and employment group, which declares its focus to be "staying union-free." To that end, Frost Brown Todd counsels clients on how to develop personnel strategies and policies that will provide their workers with an environment that does not foster a need to unionize. The firm has also defended hundreds of clients against employment discrimination claims before the EEOC and other state agencies.

GETTING HIRED

Due to the "large number of highly skilled and talented candidates" whom Frost Brown Todd interviews, "the competition is tough during the interview process." Nevertheless, this firm is "more willing than most large firms to look at candidates from lower-tier schools" and "doesn't seem to have strict grade cutoffs or journal requirements." Instead, it "looks at the entire applicant" and "individual qualities." More good news: Once you're hired as a summer associate, you will find "very little competition" to receive an offer upon graduation. Sources say that's because "the recruiting team makes every effort to estimate how many associates they will need when recruiting summer associates."

OUR SURVEY SAYS

Insiders describe the culture at Frost Brown Todd as "friendly" and "very laid-back." "People do socialize together and generally get along very well," says one associate. According to another, "From the partner level down, there is a camaraderie between the associates and the partners that I don't think exists at other firms." One senior associate best summarizes the consensus by saying, "We work hard and enjoy each other's company. I have great respect for my colleagues and genuinely like the majority of associates and members in the firm."

The great feelings about Frost Brown Todd's culture are partly due to the firm's reasonable billable requirements. Most associates feel that, compared to other law firms, "billable-hour expectations here are quite low" at 1,800 hours per year. And if you miss the target, says an insider, "it is no big deal. The hours can be distributed as the attorney sees fit." Says one second-year, "I've never worked on a weekend, yet I am well ahead of pace for the goal." "The pressure to bill is not a great one," agrees another new attorney. "However," he cautions, "when the work comes, it needs to be completed, usually right away."

With lower billable expectations come lower salary expectations. But even though the firm's salary structure "might be lower than many comparable large law firms," at least one associate doesn't complain: "I have friends working at Jones Day and Vorys Sater who have to bill 2,000+ hours, and they don't make that much more." On the other hand, insiders describe the firm's bonus structure as "a little weak." According to one senior associate, "In order to be considered for an objective bonus, one needs to bill 125 hours over goal. The amount of money awarded for that additional amount of work is too low to make it worthwhile – unless your practice/workload is so busy that it justifies putting in the hours."

Contrary to the bonus program, the firm's training program can't be beat. As for formal training, insiders say that each department trains its own associates and the firm has "monthly lunch trainings" so that associates can "learn how the firm operates." Insiders say that the firm's informal training is even better. "Each department has a system of informal training that includes working in a variety of areas within the practice group to get a full sense of what the practice group entails," explains one lawyer. Every associate is assigned two mentors (one senior associate and one partner) and each month, "two associates and partners are randomly paired to go to lunch together." "The mentoring I have received is phenomenal," gushes one first-year, who says that his mentor "goes out of his way to teach me everything he knows about law practice and client relations."

The firm also randomly pairs female associates and partners for monthly lunch dates. In fact, the firm's Women's Project, "which was created to address women's issues in the legal field," is called "superb." Frost Brown "allows associates to move to a flex-time schedule and the individual can stay on partner track; the track is just delayed according to the cut in hours." Moreover, adds one source, "Associates are still respected if they choose to follow a flex schedule." Similarly, lawyers appreciate that "great emphasis is placed on [diversity] in our annual recruiting efforts."

Gardner Carton & Douglas LLP

191 North Wacker Drive
Suite 3700
Chicago, IL 60606-1698
Phone: (312) 569-1000
www.gcd.com

LOCATIONS

Chicago, IL (HQ)
Albany, NY
Milwaukee, WI
Washington, DC

MAJOR DEPARTMENTS & PRACTICES

Corporate & Securities
Corporate Restructuring & Financial Institutions
Environmental Law
Health Law
Human Resources Law
Intellectual Property
International Law
Litigation
Real Estate
Tech Ventures
Telecommunications
Wealth Planning & Philanthropy

THE STATS

No. of attorneys:
  firm-wide: 251
  Chicago: 215
No. of offices: 4
Summer associate offers:
  firm-wide: 11 out of 11 (2004)
  Chicago: 11 out of 11 (2004)
Chairman: Harold L. Kaplan
Hiring Partner: Jennifer Breuer

UPPERS

- Great work culture
- Flexible schedules

DOWNERS

- Some growing pains
- Client demands and pressure to bill ("things which are inherent to the practice of law")

NOTABLE PERKS

- Attorney lunches every Thursday
- Annual Associates Dinner
- "Free pie for Thanksgiving!"
- Nice offices

BASE SALARY

Chicago, IL (2005)
1st year: $125,000
Summer associate: $2,400/week

EMPLOYMENT CONTACT

Ms. Nancy M. Berry
Director of Recruitment and Career Development
Phone: (312) 569-1902
Fax: (312) 569-3902
E-mail: nberry@gcd.com

THE SCOOP

Gardner Carton & Douglas is currently implementing a policy of aggressive expansion, and it shows: In the past year alone, GCD has added two new offices (one in Milwaukee and another in Albany) and has dramatically expanded its health care practice. In May 2004, the firm announced that it had acquired all five attorneys comprising the Chicago health care labor and employment shop, Stickler & Nelson, P.C. Just a week later, GCD's Washington and Albany offices brought on board a group of 13 lawyers from Akin Gump's D.C.-based health care transactions department. These additions will add several prestigious medical center clients to GCD's health care practice, which offers subspecialties in transactional, labor, regulatory and reimbursement law.

The Second City-based Gardner Carton & Douglas frequently handles cases and deals at the intersection of health care and other disciplines. In one recent example, the firm successfully defended client Riveredge Hospital against a reverse discrimination suit in federal court. GCD lawyers won summary judgment in the Title VII case, which was filed by a former male employee of the hospital who had worked in an adolescent psychiatric unit. The plaintiff claimed he had been terminated and not rehired on the basis of his gender. In spite of some sticky issues, such as the statements of a hospital administrator about concerns regarding the male-to-female ratio in the unit, GCD persuaded the court that no material issues of fact existed, and the case was dismissed.

GETTING HIRED

To land a job at this firm, you need the right personality. According to one associate involved in hiring, the firm is "very concerned about whether a person is a good fit for us in terms of personality, and we are very careful in making that determination." Arrogance is a no-no. One insider describes the ideal candidate as "smart and well rounded," with a "good personality." He or she should also be "able to connect with people." An experienced associate opines, "Because we have been in a growth mode, it has probably been easier to get hired in the last year. Most of the hiring, however, has been laterals rather than first-year hires."

The hiring process may be competitive, but, says one source, "the actual interviews are laid-back." Moreover, "GCD is great about letting you know where you stand during the hiring process. They are quick to respond and this makes you feel wanted."

OUR SURVEY SAYS

"I don't think there is another law firm in Chicago I'd be happier at," declares a Gardner Carton associate. A seasoned attorney offers this perspective: "GCD offers a great variety of high-quality work, opportunities to serve the community through pro bono work and colleagues who are both professionally and personally excellent." Hours, according to most survey respondents, are fair, especially in light of the salaries. "I think you would be hard-pressed to find another firm that matched GCD's associate salaries without demanding more billable-hours in return," says one source. Not everyone agrees; a junior associate complains about "face time" and says, "GCD is no longer [a] family-friendly and laid-back firm."

Some GCD attorneys believe the atmosphere is changing as the firm grows, although most associates still find it congenial. A senior associate says that GCD "began as fairly laid-back but is becoming increasingly more formal." On the other hand, a litigation associate describes the culture as "definitely laid-back and friendly" and says that "people tend to socialize at work but have lives of their own outside the office." Women are a strong presence within the firm, according to sources, and several partners are openly gay. The firm is also working on hiring more minority associates; according to a source, "This is a very important issue to me and I feel that my concerns [and] questions have been well received. The firm is very responsive."

Nearly all responding attorneys describe partner-associate relations positively and praise the firm's cooperative atmosphere. "Partners seem to value associate effort and input on projects," says an insider. Another concurs: "I think that the partners value my input on client matters, and I have even had partners ask me to be a second set of eyes on materials they have prepared." "Partners in this firm," says one insider, "with the notable exception of two or three, treat associates as equals and really have a team mentality." They also make themselves available to offer guidance to associates. A corporate attorney reports that "it is very typical for an associate to find an informal mentor and learn a great deal from that person."

That's a good thing, because aside from the initial orientation, formal training has tended to be irregular. "We learn a lot on our feet – trial by fire, if you will," says one associate. Another sees progress underway: "This is an area in which GCD has historically been lacking. However, a recent reorganization of the recruiting and development department offers an opportunity to address these issues." The firm notes that this reorganization includes the addition of a new chief career development officer and internal career counseling. Respondents praise the firm's strong support for pro bono work, noting that up to 75 hours of pro bono activity count toward billable-hours.

Sources report varying degrees of satisfaction with salary. "The compensation is a bit below market," says one lawyer, "but then again so is the billables requirement (1,900 [hours])." "Generally," says a transactional attorney, "I think the compensation I receive adequately reflects the amount of time and energy I am expected to put in." However, according to another associate, the balance between hours and salary is no longer as satisfying as it once was: "As the culture continues to change to being more like other larger firms, the salary should change to reflect the same." The firm seems to have taken associates' concerns to heart: GCD reports that a shift to market-level compensation is underway, and toward that end the firm has recently made "meaningful" salary adjustments across the board.

Godfrey & Kahn, S.C.

780 North Water Street
Milwaukee, WI 53202
Phone: (414) 273-3500
www.gklaw.com

LOCATIONS
Milwaukee, WI (HQ)
Appleton, WI
Green Bay, WI
Madison, WI
Waukesha, WI

MAJOR DEPARTMENTS & PRACTICES
Banking & Financial Institutions
Business Litigation
Corporate & Business
Environment & Land Use
Estate Planning & Business Succession
Food, Drug, Medical Devices & Agriculture
Human Resources & Employment Law
Insurance & Reinsurance
Mergers & Acquisitions
Real Estate
Taxation
Technology & Intellectual Property

THE STATS
No. of attorneys:
  firm-wide: 185
  Milwaukee: 106
  Madison: 47
No. of offices: 5
Summer associate offers:
  firm-wide: 12 out of 12 (2004)
  Milwaukee: 8 out of 8 (2004)
  Madison: 4 out of 4 (2004)
Managing Partner: Richard J. Bliss
Hiring Partners: Patricia Falb and Mark Witt

NOTABLE PERKS
- Social club dues
- Home loan assistance
- Moving expenses
- Reserved parking

BASE SALARY
Milwaukee, WI (2005)
1st year: $105,000
Summer associate: $1,825/week

Madison, WI (2005)
1st year: $100,000
Summer associate: $1,725/week

EMPLOYMENT CONTACT
Mrs. Kelly S. Conrardy
Manager of Attorney Recruiting
Phone: (414) 273-3500
Fax: (414) 273-5198
E-mail: kconrardy@gklaw.com

THE SCOOP

Godfrey & Kahn started out in 1957 as a two-man tax and estate planning firm in Milwaukee. Today, the firm is one of Wisconsin's largest law firms, with more than 180 attorneys in five offices around the state. Godfrey & Kahn expanded in 2000, when it joined forces with Madison's LaFollette Sinykin. (In Madison the firm is known as LaFollette Godfrey & Kahn.)

Godfrey & Kahn's practice has diversified a great deal since the early days of the firm; now, lawyers work in more than 35 specialty areas on matters ranging from mergers and acquisitions to immigration to trademarks and advertising. Although Godfrey & Kahn's practice is predominantly business-oriented, the firm has achieved notable success in other areas. In March 2004, the *Wisconsin Law Journal* dubbed two shareholders in the environmental law group, Arthur Harrington and John Clancy, "Leaders in the Law." For three and a half years, the duo oversaw a legal effort opposing the construction of the Crandon Mine in northeastern Wisconsin and assisted in the buyout of the mine's property by the Forest County Potawatomi Community for $16.5 million. The deal marked the end of a controversy that had spanned more than two decades. This resolution has been lauded as a major victory for the Native American population of the state as well as for the preservation of local natural resources.

In 2003, the firm was one of only 15 Midwest law firms (and the only firm in Wisconsin) selected for a nationwide "who-to-call" list for bank managers published by *Bank Director* magazine. Godfrey & Kahn attorneys regularly receive attention for their involvement in high-profile business transactions and settlements. Recently, the firm assisted multiple banking clients during Wisconsin's crackdown on banks with Nevada tax shelters. Instead of consuming bank revenues with costly litigation expenses, Godfrey & Kahn attorneys helped its clients reach a settlement agreement. In total, over 100 banks were involved in the crackdown, which generated approximately $24 million in back taxes for the state of Wisconsin.

Not only does the firm represent several Wisconsin banks, but Godfrey & Kahn attorneys also serve as counsel for the Community Bankers of Wisconsin, a trade group representing over 220 Wisconsin community banks. Additional clients include Manpower Inc., Marshall & Ilsley Corporation, American Family Insurance, Kohl's Department Stores, Schneider National and KI.

The firm employs an impressive collection of attorneys, including the former assistant attorney general in charge of antitrust enforcement, a former associate chief counsel for the FDA, a former federal prosecutor in the Justice Department, a former chief scientist at the Wisconsin Center for Space Automation and a former Dane County Circuit Court judge. Many of the firm's attorneys are listed in publications such as *The Best Lawyers in America*, *Who's Who in America*, *Who's Who in American Law*, *Who's Who in the World*, *Who's Who of Emerging Leaders in America* and *Who's Who in Finance and Industry*. Most recently, the firm's corporate/mergers and acquisitions, real estate, and litigation practices were ranked among the top statewide, according to the listing of *America's Leading Business Lawyers 2004 – 2005* compiled by Chambers & Partners.

The firm was also chosen to be Wisconsin's exclusive member of TerraLex, a network of independent law firms throughout the world. This worldwide network isn't the only evidence of Godfrey & Kahn's international ties. Late last year, a Godfrey & Kahn attorney was chosen as one of only 25 observers of the most recent election in the Ukraine to help ensure that the widespread voting irregularities seen during the country's last election didn't happen again.

Godfrey & Kahn's associates generally work with the firm for at least eight years before being elected to shareholder status. Some are considered earlier or later, depending on personal and work-related factors such as alternative work arrangements (the firm allows flexible and part-time schedules), different work experiences and individual development of skill sets.

GETTING HIRED

To land a job at Godfrey & Kahn, you must have an "entrepreneurial spirit" and demonstrate strong leadership skills. The firm seeks "talented attorneys from top law schools across the country whose academic achievements and personal skills mark them as future leaders in the firm and the community." Godfrey & Kahn prefers candidates who are in the top 20 to 25 percent of their class. Experience on law review, journals or moot court is a plus.

Goldberg Kohn Bell Black Rosenbloom & Moritz, Ltd.

55 East Monroe Street, Suite 3700
Chicago, IL 60603
Phone: (312) 201-4000
www.goldbergkohn.com

LOCATION

Chicago, IL

MAJOR DEPARTMENTS & PRACTICES

Bankruptcy
Corporate
Employment
Finance
Intellectual Property
Litigation
Real Estate
Tax

THE STATS

No. of attorneys: 84
No. of offices: 1
Summer associate offers: 4 out of 4 (2004)
Hiring Partner: David E. Morrison

UPPERS

- Sophisticated practice
- Warm, genuinely congenial culture

DOWNERS

- Only one office
- Not much formal training

NOTABLE PERKS

- BlackBerries, laptops and high-speed Internet access at home
- Assistance with personal real estate closings
- Monthly associate lunches
- "Spacious" offices with "outstanding views"

BASE SALARY

Chicago, IL (2005)
1st year: $125,000
Summer associate: $2,400/week

EMPLOYMENT CONTACT

Ms. Sherry L. Gini
Director of Human Resources
Phone: (312) 201-3952
Fax: (312) 863-7452
E-mail: sherry.gini@goldbergkohn.com

THE SCOOP

The 80-plus lawyers at Chicago-based Goldberg Kohn may not party like rock stars, but the firm does get to rub elbows with bigwig music industry types, given its long-running representation of the premier manufacturer of electric guitars and amplifiers, Fender Musical Instruments Corporation. The firm regularly handles intellectual property and litigation matters for Fender, from prosecuting trademark infringement disputes involving the company's Stratocaster® and Telecaster® guitars, to bringing claims against "gray market" sellers of knock-off products. Goldberg Kohn lawyers also get to engage in child's play through the firm's substantial work for clients in the toy industry. Partner Frederick R. Cohen chairs the toy and musical instruments industry group, which engages in licensing, copyright, patent and trademark matters. Meanwhile, litigators work on major toxic tort, product liability and class-action cases; the firm has even developed a web site, www.classactiondefense.com, which features legal developments and commentaries for clients in the ever-expanding area of class-action defense.

On the transactional side, the real estate group at Goldberg Kohn has established a visible presence in the hotel industry, frequently counseling lenders on financing issues related to hospitality projects. The firm has advised clients on financial issues relating to Chicagoland accommodations providers, including the Omni Hotel, the Days Inn and the Doubletree Club Hotel. Corporate attorneys at Goldberg Kohn also have plenty to keep themselves busy, acting as counsel on mergers and acquisitions, securities law, stockholders agreements and other commercial matters to clients such as ABN-AMRO, Obayashi Corporation and Allied Capital.

GETTING HIRED

Goldberg Kohn is very selective in its hiring, according to insiders. The firm recruits from only a handful of law schools, including Harvard, Northwestern, Chicago, Michigan and Georgetown. The firm prefers to hire slowly, "adding one new person at a time in order to maintain the existing culture," according to a source. The process is especially competitive for lateral candidates. "The callback process for laterals is intense," says one insider. "I had interviews with over 18 attorneys before getting hired," says another. "GK is dedicated to finding associates with the right 'fit' and takes the hiring process very seriously," explains a seasoned associate.

OUR SURVEY SAYS

Goldberg Kohn is a "wonderful place to work," according to insiders. A senior associate describes it as "a great combination of sophisticated work but reasonable work expectations and friendly environment." Another attorney declares, "No firm in the country has a more perfect balance of prestige, quality of work, quality of life and [collegial] atmosphere." One experienced associate offers this perspective: "The firm is very entrepreneurial and associates are encouraged, at a young age, to get involved in marketing and client development activities in a low-stress way. Lawyers tend to socialize together and everyone (partners and associates alike) respects that we all have interests other than the law."

"The people in the firm are what make it such a great place," says one source. Other respondents seem to agree. "The culture is very friendly and warm," says one attorney, "and people have very good friendships with each other. They also respect one another tremendously." "Attorneys seem to genuinely like each other and enjoy being attorneys," remarks another inside source. The firm is, according to a newcomer, very "family-oriented (is anyone not married?)."

Such congeniality and respect for personal lives contribute to the firm's "excellent perspective on work-life issues." When it comes to work, "there is no 'face time,'" says one lawyer. Hours are generally reasonable, although some seem to feel the crunch more than others. "The work flow is steady and predictable," says a corporate associate; meanwhile, a real estate attorney acknowledges, "I would like to work slightly less, but business is booming and keeping everyone in my department this busy."

Another big plus in the eyes of insiders is the absence of hierarchy. "Partners mentor young associates and work alongside them in the trenches," says a source. At the same time, "expectations are very high," and, according to one lawyer, some partners "have no consideration for an associate's workload, and one or two can be especially difficult for women to work for." Even so, says a seasoned attorney, "You do not hear of the occurrences here where partners scream at associates, provide busy work for the sake of ruining associates' weekends or demean associates in front of clients (all of which I have seen firsthand at large firms)." Formal training exists, but it tends to take a back seat to informal training and mentorship which, according to several insiders, "is an area where GK really excels." The pro bono program is also very strong, according to sources who note that the firm "just won a huge case against the state of Illinois relating to Medicare benefits for children."

Associates are generally happy with their compensation. Even if the pay is "slightly less than larger Chicago firms," it is "very competitive when all factors [are] taken together." Such factors include different billable expectations and "very fair" bonuses "designed to compensate associates that have gone above and beyond." In addition, the firm provides those little extras that make associates feel welcome, such as "wicked good cookies at just about every meeting" and "beautiful, roomy" offices with "incredible artwork." "All associates have their own offices," reports an insider, "and all have windows."

Greenberg Traurig, LLP

77 West Wacker Drive, Suite 2500
Chicago, IL 60601
Phone: (312) 456-8400
www.gtlaw.com

LOCATIONS

Albany, NY • Atlanta, GA • Boca Raton, FL • Boston, MA • Chicago, IL • Dallas, TX • Denver, CO • Florham Park, NJ • Fort Lauderdale, FL • Los Angeles, CA • Miami, FL • New York, NY • Orange County, CA • Orlando, FL • Palo Alto, CA • Philadelphia, PA • Phoenix, AZ • Tallahassee, FL • Tysons Corner, VA • Washington, DC • West Palm Beach, FL • Wilmington, DE • Amsterdam • Zurich

MAJOR DEPARTMENTS & PRACTICES

Bankruptcy
Corporate & Securities
Environmental
Government
Information Technology
Intellectual Property
Land Development
Litigation
Public Finance
Real Estate
Tax

THE STATS

No. of attorneys:
  firm-wide: 1,300
  Chicago: 88
No. of offices: 24
Summer associate offers:
  firm-wide: 39 out of 43 (2004)
  Chicago: 3 out of 3 (2004)
President and CEO: Cesar L. Alvarez
Co-Managing Shareholders: Paul T. Fox and Keith J. Shapiro
Hiring Shareholder: Rita M. Alliss Powers

UPPERS
- Growing office with high-quality work
- Good relations among different levels of attorneys

DOWNERS
- Lack of formal training
- Often intense hours

NOTABLE PERKS
- Free a la carte breakfast on Fridays
- Bar expenses paid
- "Excellent health benefits"
- Associate profit-sharing program

BASE SALARY

Chicago, IL (2005)
1st year: $125,000*
Summer associate: $2,403/week

*Plus discretionary bonus at year-end

EMPLOYMENT CONTACT

Ms. Nancy Verheyen
Recruiting Coordinator
Phone: (312) 476-5074
Fax: (312) 456-8435
E-mail: verheyenn@gtlaw.com

THE SCOOP

The Chicago office of Greenberg Traurig, LLP is a tyro in the law firm big leagues, having opened for business in 1999. Nevertheless, this office has ballooned from a mere three lawyers at its inception to about 88 today, earning it the distinction of having the highest percentage growth among Chi-town law firms, as measured by *The Chicago Lawyer* in 2004. This office has built its roster solely by self-styled "cherry-picking," carefully selecting lateral hires and resisting the urge to merge. Despite its conservative hiring process and its lack of a summer associate program for the first five years of its existence (the firm plans to host its first formal summer program in 2005), Greenberg Traurig-Chicago has more than doubled its size in the last two years and added another 26 attorneys in 2003.

Along with talented lawyers, Greenberg has picked up plenty of blue-chip clients during its brief tenure in the Windy City. The firm has acted as national coordinating counsel for Lockheed Martin in various litigation matters. In one case, a team of Greenberg attorneys helped defeat a lawsuit against the aerospace titan in which a plaintiff sought damages for allegedly harmful exposure to industrial sand. Meanwhile, the real estate group recently assisted in a high-profile environmental remediation. There, a former jet fuel storage site was acquired by a major airline for use as a pilot training facility. The parcel of land, close to Midway Airport, had previously been used by the U.S. Air Force, and the jet fuel clean-up, spearheaded by a Greenberg team, is being overseen by the EPA, the Army Corps of Engineers and the city of Chicago.

GETTING HIRED

The Chicago office hasn't yet begun its summer program, but with regard to hiring in general, it's "very tough to get a job here." Greenberg Traurig seeks "top-notch candidates," and, according to several insiders, "grades mean a lot." Despite a "trend towards hiring from the more prestigious firms," a senior associate contends that the firm is "much more focused on the person than the statistics on the resume." Another attorney agrees: "The firm looks to hire a well-rounded candidate who is an entrepreneur. Grades are important, but so is the individual." A few insiders suggest that the firm aims "for the cream [of the crop], but will not pay for it." But other sources believe that fitting into the firm's "laid-back and friendly" culture is the key. "An impressive resume is not enough," explains one lawyer: "It all boils down to personality and drive."

OUR SURVEY SAYS

Although the vibe at Greenberg Traurig "varies significantly from department to department and office to office," most associates agree that the atmosphere is generally congenial. A midlevel associate reports that people are "very friendly, cooperative and collegial." Attorneys wear "business attire when needed or appropriate," but otherwise the culture is "laid-back and informal." The "level of socializing outside the office varies widely from attorney to attorney," reports a litigator, but inside the office, there is an "unspoken 'open-door' policy." A Chicago attorney reports that "there is dramatically less emphasis upon the shareholder-associate hierarchy here than at many other firms of comparable size and sophistication of practice." Despite a "few bad apples," insiders agree that "respect permeates this place from top to bottom."

Many attorneys describe the firm as "entrepreneurial." A junior associate claims that the firm "rewards diligence and professionalism." According to another, this means that "associates get a lot of responsibility up front." One happy insider concludes, "I think Greenberg is a great place to work."

If associates are pleased by the quality of work and opportunity to grow, their views on salary are less uniformly sanguine. The Chicago office, however, fares notably better than the firm's other offices. According to the firm, the Chicago compensation structure is at the top of the legal market. And indeed, few Chicagoland contacts complain, although a number of associates outside the Midwest voice money-related gripes. "We are a national firm with national clients paying its associates less than market," complains a Florida litigator. A New Yorker declares that salary is "the absolute biggest issue at the firm and the reason why some associates have left for top firms paying top dollar." Other sources criticize the bonus structure. "If you bill a lot," explains a midlevel associate, "you will get a bonus. If not, you will not get a raise or a bonus, no matter how stellar your work is." The silver lining to the compensation cloud, at least for one Big Apple lawyer, is that a lower salary "means that associates can maintain reasonable hours."

Generally, associates say their firm is a "hard-working shop, but not a sweat shop." "The number of hours varies sharply," says an experienced lawyer, "but the hours are often intense (and long)." Another senior associate accepts that long hours simply go with the job: "I understand that the job requires many hours, and that is the career I chose." Moreover, according to several insiders in different departments, "The hours flow from workload," rather than from "pressure to meet billable goals." However, one attorney disagrees: "Work billable-hours or get fired is the motto here."

Outside "numerous CLE opportunities," Greenberg doesn't offer "much formal training." The firm, however, "acknowledges that this is an area that needs to be made more comprehensive," and a litigator notes that "the firm is very receptive to associates' ideas and needs for training programs." The degree and quality of mentoring can vary "from group to group." A second-year associate reports, "I am very happy with the training and mentoring I am receiving, but I do think this varies depending on who you work with." In the end, insiders agree that most training is "on the job."

Hinshaw & Culbertson LLP

222 North LaSalle Street
Suite 300
Chicago, IL 60601
Phone: (312) 704-3000
www.hinshawlaw.com

LOCATIONS

Chicago, IL (HQ)
Appleton, WI • Belleville, IL • Champaign, IL • Crystal Lake, IL • Edwardsville, IL • Ft. Lauderdale, FL • Jacksonville, FL • Joliet, IL • Lisle, IL • Los Angeles, CA • Miami, FL • Milwaukee, WI • Minneapolis, MN • New York, NY • Peoria, IL • Phoenix, AZ • Portland, OR • Rockford, IL • San Francisco, CA • Schererville, IN • Springfield, IL • St. Louis, MO • Tampa, FL • Waukegan, IL

MAJOR DEPARTMENTS & PRACTICES

Construction Law
Corporate & Business Law
Environmental
Government
Health Care
Insurance Services
Labor & Employment
Litigation
Professional Liability
School Law

THE STATS

No. of attorneys:
  firm-wide: 419
  Chicago: 147
  Rockford: 35
  Minneapolis: 25
No. of offices: 25
Summer associate offers:
  firm-wide: 9 out of 13 (2004)
  Chicago: 4 out of 5 (2004)
Chairman: Donald L. Mrozek
Managing Partner: J. William Roberts
Hiring Partner: David R. Creagh

NOTABLE PERKS

- Business development program in which associates receive a percentage of business they bring to the firm
- Half-pay for associates studying for the bar exam
- Free dinners after 7 pm
- Extensive entry-level training

BASE SALARY

Chicago, IL (2005)
1st year: $90,000

EMPLOYMENT CONTACT

Ms. Paula A. Goldberg
Legal Recruitment and Development Manager
Phone: (312) 704-3000
Fax: (312) 704-3001
E-mail: pgoldberg@hinshawlaw.com

THE SCOOP

Now in its 70th year of practice, Hinshaw & Culbertson LLP has 25 offices in 10 states and employs over 400 attorneys. The firm's four broad, nationwide practice areas – business transactions, business litigation, lawyers for professionals and defense litigation – subdivide into specialty groups including toxic tort defense, securities and not-for-profit tax. Hinshaw is the 11th-largest law firm in the state of Illinois and one of the 100 largest firms in the country. With nearly 150 attorneys, the Chicago office is the firm's biggest as well as its oldest, dating back to 1934.

In July 2004, the firm landed a key interdisciplinary representation when the city of St. Charles, Ill., selected the firm to oversee the two-year, three-phase construction of a long-awaited bridge in the town. The Red Gate Road Bridge Project, as it is known, will combine the efforts of environmental, construction and transactional lawyers at Hinshaw. Also this past summer, the firm successfully represented a public defender in a legal malpractice lawsuit, thought to be the first action of its kind to be brought against a public defender in Illinois. The case arose out of Michael Halloran's representation of Richard Johnson, who was ultimately convicted of several crimes and sentenced to over 30 years in prison. Johnson sued his attorney for alleged negligence in excluding serology evidence from his defense in the criminal trial. Halloran had moved to exclude the evidence, which had produced conflicting lab reports that could have harmed his client's defense. After eight years of litigation, the Hinshaw team emerged victorious at the civil trial when the jury agreed that the public defender had acted properly.

In December 2004 Hinshaw & Culbertson was retained to represent the owners of LaSalle Bank Building in Chicago after a fire damaged the 45-story building and injured dozens of people, including 22 firefighters. In fact, Hinshaw partner Dan Boho is one of Chicago's most prominent litigators and frequently represents owners or managers of buildings involved in high-profile disasters. Clients have included the managers of the Cook County Administration Building where six workers died in a fatal fire in 2003, and the management of the John Hancock Center in connection with a 2002 accident in which three people were killed by falling scaffolding.

The firm recently brought more talent on board when three veteran attorneys joined the firm's main office. In December 2004, trial lawyer Jude Quinn moved to the Second City office from the Philly-based firm, German, Gallagher & Murtagh, and the next month John Sebastian and Robert Konop came on board as partners in the surety and construction law and business litigation practices, respectively. Sebastian defected from the Chicago law firm Leo & Weber, while Konop gave up his long-held position as general counsel to CUNA Mutual Group in Madison, Wis.

In order to help preserve its stable of skilled practitioners, the firm provides extensive formal training. Every fall new associates attend "Hinshaw University," a four-day training program in Chicago that brings together lawyers from all firm offices for guidance in the day-to-day skills of practicing law as well as specific, practice-oriented training. Graduates then have the opportunity to participate in the firm's Trial Advocacy Program. These off-site seminars include three days of seminars on trial and appellate practice, as well as two weekend clinics at which attorneys exercise their courtroom skills and work one-on-one with members of the "Hinshaw U" faculty. As the program's final exam, attorneys participate in a videotaped trial presided over by active and retired trial judges.

GETTING HIRED

Hinshaw is in the market for "bright and highly motivated law students and attorneys." Students in the summer program rotate through each of the firm's four departments, with an attorney mentor, a counselor and a summer associate coordinator to help them maneuver the ins-and-outs of law firm life. Lest candidates worry that the summer will be all work and no play, the firm arranges a variety of social activities for summer associates to get to know each other and the rest of the firm.

Holland & Knight LLP

131 South Dearborn Street
30th Floor
Chicago, IL 60603
Phone: (312) 263-3600
www.hklaw.com

LOCATIONS
Annapolis, MD • Atlanta, GA • Bethesda, MD • Boston, MA • Bradenton, FL • Chicago, IL • Chicago-Oakbrook, IL • Fort Lauderdale, FL • Jacksonville, FL • Lakeland, FL • Los Angeles, CA • McLean, VA • Miami, FL • New York, NY • Orlando, FL • Portland, OR • Providence, RI • Rancho Santa Fe, CA • Sacramento, CA • St. Petersburg, FL • San Antonio, TX • San Francisco, CA • Seattle, WA • Tallahassee, FL • Tampa, FL • Washington, DC • West Palm Beach, FL • Beijing • Caracas* • Helsinki* • Mexico City • Rio de Janeiro** • São Paulo** • Tel Aviv* • Tokyo

*Representative offices
**Strategic alliance

MAJOR DEPARTMENTS & PRACTICES
Business (Banking & Finance, Corporate/Mergers & Acquisitions, Public Companies & Securities)
Government (Public Policy & Regulation)
Litigation (Commercial Litigation, Intellectual Property, Labor & Employment, Product Liability)
Private Wealth Services (Dispute Resolution, Estate Planning & Administration, Family Business & Exempt Organizations)
Real Estate (Land Use & Local Government, Transactions)

THE STATS
No. of attorneys:
  firm-wide: 1,250+
  Chicago: 160
No. of offices: 33
Summer associate offers:
  firm-wide: 61 out of 66 (2004)
  Chicago: 6 out of 7 (2004)
Managing Partner: Howell W. Melton Jr.
Hiring Partner: Michele Sibley Gonzales (Chicago)

UPPERS
- Interesting, challenging work
- Partner feedback and support from colleagues

DOWNERS
- Sometimes long hours
- Few traditional big-firm perks

NOTABLE PERKS
- Domestic partner benefits for same- and opposite-sex partners
- Monthly attorney beer socials
- 401(k) matching plan
- Brand new office space is "very stylish"

BASE SALARY
Chicago, IL (2005)
1st year: $125,000*
2nd year: $130,000
3rd year: $135,000 – 165,000
4th year: $140,000 – 175,000
5th year: $150,000 – 190,000
6th year: $160,000 – 200,000
7th year: $170,000 – 210,000
8th year: $180,000 – 220,000
Summer associate: $2,400/week

*Plus reimbursement for bar review and registration fees

EMPLOYMENT CONTACT
Ms. Julie Garcia
Attorney Recruitment Coordinator
Phone: (312) 578-6599
Fax: (312) 578-6666
E-mail: julie.garcia@hklaw.com

THE SCOOP

In February 2000, Holland & Knight's Chicago branch opened when the firm acquired the 30-plus lawyers of Burke, Weaver & Prell. This was just one in a long series of national and global mergers and acquisitions on the part of Holland & Knight, which was established by a single practitioner in Tampa, Fla., in 1889. Now, after years of careful but swift expansion, the firm is one of the country's largest, employing over 1,250 attorneys in 33 offices. The Chicago location alone houses approximately 160 lawyers, making it the firm's second-largest outpost.

Most recently, the Second City office has added some heft to its real estate, land use and government practices. In 2004, five real estate attorneys jumped ship from Piper Rudnick and landed at Holland & Knight, which boasts the largest real estate practice in the country. In addition, Jack Siegel, a prominent attorney who has been dubbed the "Dean of Illinois Municipal Law," brought his practice to Holland & Knight last year, augmenting the firm's already substantial list of local government clients with major suburban townships including Arlington Heights, Evanston, Northbrook, Glencoe, Lake Forest and Highland Park.

GETTING HIRED

Holland & Knight is selective when it comes to hiring new associates, but many attorneys think the firm's strategy needs work. "For our summer associate program," a seasoned associate explains, "the Chicago office of our firm will only interview candidates at the University of Michigan, Northwestern, University of Illinois and University of Chicago. Candidates also need to be on law review and at the top of their class." "They do not interview on campus at local Chicago schools, which is a mistake," agrees a third-year associate. Many sources feel that this "elitist approach" is "just absurd." Although the firm "is trying to hire all these Ivy Leaguers," it ends up with "mid-range people from top-shelf law schools or top-range people from mid-range law schools." As one lawyer concludes, "The firm would be much better off if it were honest with itself about who its target audience is." (The firm reports that five of the seven summer associates in Chicago in 2004 were from local law schools and that in 2005 the office will interview at several local schools, including DePaul University and Loyola University.)

OUR SURVEY SAYS

The Chicago office of Holland & Knight "has a relatively laid-back atmosphere, especially for a larger firm." One lawyer describes the culture as "disjointed, but generally friendly." Apparently, the vibe "varies from group to group." Litigators say their group is "very friendly and social," although "pretty high intensity." According to a transactional attorney, "The real estate transactional section is filled with great people with great attitudes. Other sections tend to be filled with uptight and arrogant people." One lawyer concludes, "We seem to have all personality types."

Most attorneys are satisfied with their starting salaries, since the firm "pays almost market for starting associates." However, some feel that the firm "lags more substantially in subsequent years." A major complaint is the amount of time it takes to determine compensation; one attorney observes that "it should not take over two months to determine associates' salaries." Sources also complained that bonuses for 2003 were still not awarded as of March 2004. The firm's "tier system" also comes under fire. As an associate explains, "You can supposedly make more in salary based on a series of criteria, including one being billing 2,150 [hours]." However, "There isn't enough work to bill those kinds of hours here," the source complains, "and I know of no one who was able to be in the higher tier." On the other hand, a colleague appreciates the opportunity such a system offers: "The tier levels allow higher-performing associates to benefit with a higher salary."

Some insiders believe the firm skimps in other ways. H&K, says a Chicago associate, has a "pretty perk-free environment." "We are not supplied with, or even reimbursed for, dinner when working late," complains one attorney. The firm as a whole offers "little to no training," although, according to one Chicagoan, "this is an area that is improving." Associates cite firm plans to have "lawyers lecture via teleconference." "You have to create your own training opportunities," shrugs one midlevel lawyer. Another finds that "the only effective training here is hands-on," but at least "a lot of partners give very good off-the-record feedback." The firm reports that a chief professional development officer was appointed in August 2004 to address the training, mentoring and evaluation process.

Hours at Holland & Knight are typically long, but many associates find them "manageable." If some insiders consider the 2,150 billable-hour requirement too high, others claim that "billing 2,000 or 2,010 hours here is just fine." And, adds an associate, "You don't see that many people here late at night or on the weekends, except when necessary." (In 2005, the firm reduced the minimum billable-hour guideline from 2,000 hours to 1,900.) One problem seems to be the issue of non-billable work which, according to one source, can result in "hundreds of hours per year." Another attorney agrees, explaining that while he spends "between 10 and 12 hours a day" at work, it can be "difficult to bill much of this time."

One area in which the firm as a whole excels is pro bono, although a few Windy City lawyers worry that their office's commitment "has slipped." Nevertheless, other Chicago associates cite "the opportunity to perform very worthwhile pro bono work" as one of the best things about their firm. Holland & Knight has hired full-time pro bono attorneys, say insiders, and "100 hours of pro bono go toward the billable-hour requirement."

Honigman Miller Schwartz and Cohn LLP

2290 First National Building
660 Woodward Avenue
Detroit, MI 48226-3506
Phone: (313) 465-7000
www.honigman.com

LOCATIONS

Detroit, MI (HQ)
Bingham Farms, MI
Lansing, MI

MAJOR DEPARTMENTS & PRACTICES

Antitrust & Trade Regulation
Bankruptcy, Reorganization & Commercial
Corporate, Securities, Intellectual Property & Immigration
Employee Benefits
Environmental
Health Care
Labor & Employment
Litigation
Real Estate & Land Use
Real Estate Tax Appeals
Regulatory
Tax, Estate Planning & Probate

THE STATS

No. of attorneys:
   firm-wide: 218
   Detroit: 147
No. of offices: 3
Summer associate offers:
   firm-wide: 8 out of 9 (2004)
   Detroit: 8 out of 9 (2004)
Chief Executive Officer: Alan S. Schwartz
Hiring Partner: Linda S. Ross

NOTABLE PERKS

- Automatic $5,000 bonus for new associates
- Interest-free home loan
- Paid indoor parking
- Friday afternoon cocktail parties

BASE SALARY

All offices (2005)
1st year: $110,000*
Summer associate: $1,850/week

*Exclusive of starting and year-end bonuses. Salary ranges for associates in their first through fourth years with the firm are posted on the firm's web site.

EMPLOYMENT CONTACT

Ms. Jan Baggett
Legal Recruitment Coordinator
Phone: (313) 465-7812
Fax: (313) 465-8213
E-mail: JBaggett@honigman.com

THE SCOOP

Honigman Miller Schwartz and Cohn LLP had a banner year in 2004, earning lauds from several trade publications for the firm's outstanding contributions to the legal field in Honigman's home state of Michigan. In May, *ChambersUSA* ranked Honigman Miller No. 1 on its lists of the best real estate and corporate practices in Michigan. Then, in October, the firm landed a spot on the Michigan Business & Professional Association's list of "Metropolitan Detroit's 101 Best & Brightest Companies to Work For." More recently, Honigman attorneys dominated the 2005 – 2006 edition of *The Best Lawyers in America*, with one quarter of its attorneys receiving this distinction – more than any other law firm in Michigan.

The firm also scored a coup this past year when it poached nine attorneys, including a founding partner, from the Detroit-based intellectual property firm of Rader Fishman & Grauer, PLLC, in May 2004. Honigman Miller had previously lacked a full-fledged IP department, and now the firm employs nine highly regarded patent lawyers in addition to the Honigman attorneys who work on trademark, copyright and licensing as part of their existing practices. In November 2004, Honigman Miller boosted its masthead again by scooping up several partners (including another founding partner) from now-dissolved Miro, Weiner, & Kramer P.C.

Established in 1948 with only six attorneys, the Detroit-based law firm now has 218 attorneys working across a diverse field of practice areas. The firm opened its Lansing office in 1985 to serve clients with interests in the state's capital. Honigman Miller also has offices in Oakland County which focus on real estate, intellectual property, litigation, family law and estate planning. Michigan attorneys have described the full-service law firm as a "large general firm with a first-rate reputation." Representative clients include Michigan big-wigs such as Compuware Corporation, General Motors Corp., Pulte Homes, Inc., The Taubman Company and major Detroit retailers. The firm also serves as general counsel for Delta Dental Plan of Michigan, *The Detroit Free Press*, Forbes/Cohen Properties and W. W. Group, Inc. (Weight Watchers), among others.

The firm encourages pro bono work and counts pro bono hours toward billable requirements. Over the past five years, Honigman attorneys have donated more than $250,000 worth of free legal services to Habitat for Humanity Detroit, working on a variety of real property matters, including finance transactions to help the Habitat fund more home-building, and legal issues related to property donation and mortgage delinquencies. Firm attorneys have also received rewards for participating in a community land trust project with Community Legal Resources and for pro bono work with the Coalition on Temporary Shelter's affordable housing program.

Unlike many other large law firms, salaries and bonuses at Honigman Miller are based primarily on merit rather than seniority. The firm has two stages of partnership: non-percentage (usually achievable after four to six years) and percentage (generally attained by most non-percentage partners after eight to 10 full years of legal practice). Roughly three-fourths of the firm's 218 attorneys (154) are partners.

In a recent setback, one of the firm's partners filed a discrimination lawsuit against Honigman Miller. In the complaint, the partner claims that the firm denied her job opportunities and compensation because of her gender. Honigman has denied these allegations, and the lawsuit is unlikely to have much effect on the firm's bottom line or its reputation.

GETTING HIRED

Getting into this top-notch Detroit firm can be a challenge. Honigman Miller recruiters look for "superior law school achievement," "demonstrated capabilities and motivation," "excellent interpersonal skills" and "extracurricular activities." They will also take prior work experience into account. The firm expects candidates to have a strong presence and partnership potential. Looking to recruit "the best and brightest," the firm conducts on-campus interviews at law schools all over the country, including Harvard, Notre Dame and, naturally, the University of Michigan.

If you're selected for an interview, check out the extensive list of interviewing tips on the firm's web site before you walk through the door. For example, you should strive to be "personable," "articulate" and "direct." And, while you are encouraged to "relax," that doesn't mean you should "slump in your chair." Finally, you'll receive the practical, though perhaps surprising, advice to "act like you want the job, even if you do not want it."

Husch & Eppenberger, LLC

190 Carondelet Plaza, Suite 600
St. Louis, MO 63105
Phone: (314) 480-1500
www.husch.com

LOCATIONS

St. Louis, MO (HQ)
Chattanooga, TN • Jefferson City, MO • Kansas City, MO • Downtown Memphis, TN • East Memphis, TN • Nashville, TN • Peoria, IL • Springfield, MO

MAJOR DEPARTMENTS & PRACTICES

Antitrust
Appellate & Complex Litigation
Benefits Litigation
Class Actions
Commercial Finance
Construction
Corporate
E-Business
Employee Benefits
Environmental & Regulatory
Family Law
Franchise Law
General Litigation
Health Law
Immigration
Insolvency
Intellectual Property & Technology
International
Labor & Employment
Land Use Development & Financing
Levee & Drainage
Mergers, Acquisitions & Securities
Product Liability & Toxic Torts
Tax & Estate Planning

THE STATS

No. of attorneys:
  firm-wide: 313
  St. Louis: 152
  Jefferson City: 10
  Kansas City: 67
  Peoria: 14
  Springfield: 13
No. of offices: 9
Summer associate offers:
  firm-wide: 27 out of 38 (2004)
  St. Louis: 14 out of 18 (2004)
  Kansas City: 2 out of 3 (2004)
  Springfield: 3 out of 3 (2004)
Chairman: Joseph P. Conran
Hiring Partners:
  St. Louis: Dutro "Bruce" Campbell
  Jefferson City: Barbara L. Miltenberger
  Kansas City: Bruce A. Moothart
  Peoria: Kenneth Eathington
  Springfield: Charles R. Greene

NOTABLE PERKS
- Associate fee-sharing program
- Matching 401(k) plan
- Paid parking
- Bar dues and expenses

BASE SALARY

St. Louis, MO (2005)
1st year: $90,000
Summer associate: $1,500/week

Jefferson City and Springfield, MO (2005)
1st year: $72,000
Summer associate: $1,200/week

Kansas City, MO, and Peoria, IL (2005)
1st year: $80,000
Summer associate: $1,346/week

EMPLOYMENT CONTACT

Ms. Ciana LaGrone
Recruiting Coordinator
Phone: (314) 480-1620
Fax: (314) 480-1505
E-mail: ciana.lagrone@husch.com

THE SCOOP

Established in 1922, Husch & Eppenberger, LLC employs 300 attorneys in nine offices in Missouri, Illinois and Tennessee. With an extensive variety of business and litigation practice groups, Husch represents clients at the local, regional, national and even international levels. Among those on the firm's client roster are Arch Chemicals, DaimlerChrysler, Emerson Electric, General Electric Capital Corp., Olin, Monsanto, Siemens and Sprint.

The firm's litigation group, which has nearly 150 attorneys, handles a broad range of matters, from class actions, product liability and toxic tort cases, to disputes involving lender liability, construction law, insurance coverage, health law, intellectual property and real estate. On the transactional side, the firm's practice focuses on closely held businesses, entrepreneurs and private clients.

Husch won a recent victory for client Sprint/United Management Company in an age discrimination suit. The plaintiff, a former Sprint employee, claimed that Sprint's decision to lay her off during a workforce reduction was based on her age, in violation of the Age Discrimination in Employment Act. After an eight-day trial in Kansas federal court, the jury rejected the plaintiff's claims and returned a unanimous verdict in favor of Sprint. In another recent defense verdict, Husch persuaded a jury to rule in favor of Heartland Regional Medical Center in a medical malpractice case seeking $1 million in damages from the St. Joseph, Mo., hospital.

In the last few years, the firm has made a steady climb up the list of the nation's top 200 firms. Husch made its first appearance in *The American Lawyer*'s Top 200 list in 2003, coming in at No. 195. Last year, it rose to No. 169. The firm's total revenue ($104 million) rose by 24.6 percent in 2004, the biggest jump of any of the firms ranked between 100 and 200 by *AmLaw*. In November 2004, *The National Law Journal* ranked Husch the 132nd-largest firm in terms of number of lawyers. On a more local level, *Corporate Board Member*, in its "Special Legal Issue 2004," ranked Husch as the fifth-best law firm in St. Louis, the same position it held in the previous year's rankings.

GETTING HIRED

The summer program at Husch & Eppenberger is, according to the firm, somewhat atypical in that the number of summer associates it hires matches the number of openings for permanent associates. This promotes a cooperative spirit rather than a competitive one, since summer clerks aren't vying for the same full-time spot.

The firm hires both 1Ls and 2Ls, all of whom are eligible for permanent offers after finishing their summer with the firm. Husch looks for students who rank among the top 15 to 20 percent of their law school class. But more important than mere book smarts are solid personal qualities such as "integrity," "good judgment," "creativity" and a "sense of humor." The firm seeks "dynamic, bright, mature, innovative" people "willing to take on significant responsibilities." Although law review and moot court are certainly pluses, Husch & Eppenberger also values other experiences and diverse backgrounds; the firm notes that many of its attorneys have come to law as a second career.

Ice Miller®

One American Square, Box 82001
Indianapolis, IN 46282-0002
Phone: (317) 236-2100
www.icemiller.com

LOCATIONS
Indianapolis, IN (HQ)
Chicago, IL
Washington, DC

MAJOR DEPARTMENTS & PRACTICES
Business
Labor
Litigation
Municipal Finance
Real Estate

THE STATS

No. of attorneys:
   firm-wide: 215
   Indianapolis: 214
No. of offices: 3
Summer associate offers:
   firm-wide: 10 out of 10 (2004)
   Indianapolis: 10 out of 10 (2004)
Co-Managing Partners: David M. Mattingly, Melissa Proffitt Reese and Phillip L. Bayt
Hiring Partner: Mark W. Ford

NOTABLE PERKS

- Pre-tax parking program
- Casual dress policy
- Reimbursed moving expenses and bar dues
- Associate bonus program

BASE SALARY

Indianapolis, IN (2005)
1st year: $85,000
2nd year: $87,000
3rd year: $92,000
4th year: $96,000
5th year: $99,000
6th year: $105,000
7th year: $120,000
Summer associate: $1,500/week

EMPLOYMENT CONTACT

Ms. Lisa M. Watson
Director of Legal Personnel
Phone: (317) 236-5871
Fax: (317) 236-4280
E-mail: lisa.watson@icemiller.com

THE SCOOP

Despite its keg-friendly name, Ice Miller® is a serious law firm with more than 90 years of distinguished experience to back up its memorable masthead. The Indianapolis-based firm, which employs more than 200 attorneys in its three offices, represents banner-name clients including DaimlerChrysler Motors Corporation, Eli Lilly & Co., Pfizer and The Coca-Cola Company. Ice Miller boasts expertise in industries from education to gaming to transportation. But don't expect to see any diplomas on the wall. According to the philosophy of the firm's late name partner, Harry Ice, "It does not matter where you went to law school, now you are an Ice Miller lawyer."

Among its many specialties, Ice Miller has developed a strong practice in sports and entertainment. The firm has acted as counsel to more than 35 colleges and universities, including Midwestern football powers Purdue, Notre Dame and Michigan, on matters relating to NCAA sports, and it has represented entertainment clients including James Dean, Inc. and TNT Media on licensing, corporate and intellectual property matters. Meanwhile, Ice Miller's financing strategies group regularly advises clients on innovative funding initiatives like employee stock option plans, initial public offerings and venture capital finance. For its part, the litigation practice has become highly diversified, having provided dispute resolution services on everything from asbestos cases to toxic mold. In addition to serving major multinational corporations, Ice Miller litigators also represent individual plaintiffs who have been the victims of catastrophic injury or wrongful death, whether through a defective product or auto accident.

The Indiana-based firm was originally founded as a general practice firm in 1910 as Henley Matson and Gates. Harry Ice came aboard in 1929 and encouraged the firm's attorneys to "specialize, specialize, specialize," believing that clients needed experts instead of generalists. He was right. Over the past century, the firm has represented some of the most respected corporations in America and grown to become the largest law firm in Indianapolis, with over 210 attorneys working in 30 practice areas. Major areas of concentration include business, employment and labor law, litigation, municipal finance and real estate. After no less than seven name changes, the Hoosier law firm finally settled on its current moniker in 2000.

In the early 1950s, two attorneys in the firm helped found the then-controversial Indiana affiliate of the American Civil Liberties Union. One of the firm's most famous cases came 10 years later after a fire in the Fairgrounds Coliseum killed 74 people and injured 350. Recognizing the injustice of high pay-outs to early-filing plaintiffs and zero sums to those who filed later, Ice Miller obtained approval to join all claimants in a single action, setting the standard for all similar lawsuits in the future.

The firm has appeared on The Am Law 200, *The American Lawyer*'s list of the nation's 200 top-grossing law firms, with annual revenues of $88 million in 2003. Ice Miller also had the fifth-highest percentage of female partners in the country in 2001, according to *The National Law Journal*'s survey of the top 250 law firms in the United States. Since then, even more women have joined the partnership ranks, and last year Ice Miller added the first woman to its list of managing partners.

Perhaps most importantly from a new associate standpoint, Ice Miller combines reasonable billable-hour expectations with a better-than-average partnership track. Even though there is "no specific period to partnership," most candidates are considered during a window of six and one-half to eight and one-half years of service.

GETTING HIRED

Although Ice Miller says that it "individually considers each applicant" by "taking into consideration law school performance, experience, needs of the firm" and "special skills," don't be fooled into thinking that grades and law school don't matter. The firm's recruitment efforts focus on "leading graduates of the top law schools." You should also have a "can-do" attitude and be eager to help out on whatever needs to be done.

If you're selected for an interview, expect to meet with associates and partners from a variety of practice groups. The firm assigns each interviewer a "target area" for discussion, such as interpersonal skills, communication skills, problem solving and organizational skills. Most interviews last 30 minutes and end with lunch or dinner.

VAULT

THE MOST TRUSTED NAME IN CAREER INFORMATION

"With reviews and profiles of firms that one associate calls 'spot on,' [Vault's] guide has become a key reference for those who want to know what it takes to get hired by a law firm and what to expect once they get there."

– New York Law Journal

"To get the unvarnished scoop, check out Vault."

– SmartMoney magazine

VAULT

"Vault is indispensable for locating insider information."
- Metropolitan Corporate Counsel

Jenkens & Gilchrist, a Professional Corporation

225 West Washington, Suite 2600
Chicago, IL 60606
Phone: (312) 425-3900
www.jenkens.com

LOCATIONS

Dallas, TX (HQ)
Austin, TX
Chicago, IL
Houston, TX
Los Angeles, CA
New York, NY
Pasadena, CA
San Antonio, TX
Washington, DC

MAJOR DEPARTMENTS & PRACTICES

Construction
Corporate & Securities
Intellectual Property
Litigation
Tax

THE STATS

No. of attorneys:
　firm-wide: 412
　Chicago: 35
No. of offices: 9
Summer associate offers:
　firm-wide: 28 out of 47 (2004)
　Chicago: 2 out of 2 (2004)
Chairman and President: Thomas H Cantrill
Hiring Partner: John C. Gatz

UPPERS
- High level of responsibility
- Reasonable hours

DOWNERS
- Lack of transparency about partnership prospects
- Recent negative publicity over tax-shelter issues

NOTABLE PERKS
- Shuffleboard table
- Bar expenses and association dues
- Moving expenses

BASE SALARY

Chicago, IL (2005)
1st year: $125,000
Summer associate: $2,400/week

EMPLOYMENT CONTACT

Ms. Dawn Dykshorn
Recruiting Coordinator
Phone: (312) 425-8573
Fax: (312) 425-8699
E-mail: ddykshorn@jenkens.com

THE SCOOP

Jenkens & Gilchrist may call Dallas home, but its Chicago office, with just one-tenth of the firm's attorneys, still manages to pack a Texas-sized wallop. The Midwestern contingent of Jenkens is particularly well known for its robust intellectual property practice. A substantial portion of the 46 attorneys have backgrounds in science or engineering, and many have had technical careers prior to their transition into the law. With this specialized knowledge and experience, backed by the reputation and resources of a national firm, Jenkens & Gilchrist-Chicago has landed some clutch clients and matters. In recent months, the firm has handled patent infringement cases involving everything from integrated circuit chips to synthetic rubber to currency counting equipment. Copyright and trademark matters have included one case involving the unauthorized use by a building contractor of protected home decor designs.

Unfortunately, Jenkens-Chicago has recently made headlines for less desirable reasons. Thanks to controversial tax-shelter advice given by three Chicago lawyers in 1999, the firm faced a class-action lawsuit, IRS summonses and a slew of negative publicity. When the Internal Revenue Service went after the firm's clients for millions of dollars in back taxes, the clients went after their advisors for bad advice. Others pursued by the angry advisees include Sidley Austin Brown & Wood and accounting firms Ernst & Young and BDO Seidman. Jenkens & Gilchrist undoubtedly breathed a heavy sigh of relief when it reached an $81.55 million settlement with the majority of the plaintiffs early in 2005.

In other litigation matters, the firm's Windy City attorneys counsel corporations and individuals in Asia, Europe and the Caribbean. The litigation group's client roster includes Siemens Westinghouse Power Corporation and Mitsui Babcock Energy Limited. In one local case, Jenkens litigators recently acted as counsel to the Chicago Park District in a dispute that successfully challenged the proposed renovation of Soldier Field and the closing of the Meigs Field airport.

GETTING HIRED

Jenkens & Gilchrist's Chicago office conducts on-campus interviews at top-ranked national law schools around the country – Harvard, Columbia, Boalt

Hall, Duke and Michigan among them – and at local institutions such as University of Chicago, Loyola, John Marshall Law School, Chicago-Kent College of Law, Northwestern and the University of Illinois. According to the firm, hiring criteria are established "on a school-by-school basis." Generally speaking, however, "candidates must have a strong undergraduate and law school academic record, demonstrated leadership abilities, good interpersonal skills and strong writing skills." As one associate sums up the firm's standards, "We look to hire qualified candidates who will fit in with our work atmosphere."

OUR SURVEY SAYS

Although Jenkens & Gilchrist associates are enthusiastic about the work they do, the highlight of the work day comes during the lunch hour, when lawyers at the firm gather for a few heated rounds of mini-shuffleboard. As one insider reports, "Not a day goes by without hearing the roar of the crowd (or trash-talking) around the shuffleboard table." A little friendly rivalry contributes to the overall atmosphere of collegiality at Jenkens. "Lawyers routinely meet for lunch, events and outings at each others' homes," reports a junior associate. "We have a very friendly, laid-back environment and it is extremely easy to talk to upper-level partners."

The lawyers in this office benefit from a supportive environment, fostered by informal mentoring and the "open-door policy" of the firm. One source notes, "As a first-year, I am pleasantly surprised at how many senior associates are providing me with daily mentoring and support." However, a high-level associate comments that most partners "are quite busy, so there is not a lot of time for 'training' other than the process of feedback that arises from actual work product." On a more structured basis, the firm is making strides in associate training. First- and second-years receive "eight-week NITA litigation training," and the firm is "developing a formal associate development program to help in associate training and career development" for all levels of seniority. In addition, Jenkens "recently appointed a partner to devote a percentage of his practice to associate and shareholder training activities."

Associates find that the hours "are not unreasonable, and there are plenty of weekends that aren't filled with office work." A senior lawyer remarks that "the shareholders in the Chicago office want everyone to have balanced lives and not to live in the office. I have never felt pressure to bill 2,000+ hours."

For those who need to balance work with a family life, the firm "is willing to accommodate alternate work arrangements while maintaining a realistic expectation that such individuals will still be promoted." Jenkens also offers "three months paid maternity leave with pro-rated billable credit, with an additional three months unpaid and no adverse effect on class advancement."

Compensation at Jenkens, according to associates, is "at least market and, if you are good and work hard, you get compensated for it." A senior associate notes that the firm does not impose an "'artificial' minimum hour requirement" for bonuses and advancement; but another experienced attorney cautions that bonuses are "entirely based upon meeting minimum hours targets. It is no longer worth working harder for a bonus." The firm awards performance-based bonuses in November and hands out nominal "bonuses" at the end of the year for the holidays.

"Not a day goes by without hearing the roar of the crowd (or trash-talking) around the shuffleboard table."

— Jenkens & Gilchrist associate

Jenner & Block LLP

One IBM Plaza
Chicago, IL 60611
Phone: (312) 222-9350
www.jenner.com

LOCATIONS
Chicago, IL (HQ)
Dallas, TX • Washington, DC

MAJOR DEPARTMENTS & PRACTICES
Antitrust & Trade Regulation • Appellate & Supreme Court Practice • Arbitration: Domestic & International Association Practice • Bankruptcy, Workout & Corporate Reorganization Action Litigation • Commercial Law & Uniform Commercial Code • Construction Law • Corporate • Corporate Finance • Defense & Aerospace • Employee Benefits & Executive Compensation • Entertainment & New Media • Environmental, Energy & Natural Resources Law • ERISA Litigation • Estate Planning & Administration • Family Law • Government Contracts Health Care Law • Insurance Litigation & Counseling • Intellectual Property • Labor & Employment • Litigation • Media & First Amendment Practice • Mergers & Acquisitions • Private Equity & Emerging Companies Products Liability & Mass Tort Defense • Professional Liability Litigation • Public Policy • Real Estate Reinsurance Practice • Securities • Securities Litigation • Tax Controversy Practice • Tax Practice • Telecommunications • Trade Secrets & Unfair Competition • White-Collar Criminal Defense & Counseling

THE STATS
No. of attorneys:
firm-wide: 437
Chicago: 368
No. of offices: 3
Summer associate offers:
firm-wide: 48 out of 51 (2004)
Chicago: 33 out of 34 (2004)
Managing Partner: Gregory S. Gallopoulos
Hiring Partners: Reginald J. Hill, Mark D. Schneider and Charlotte L. Wager

UPPERS
- High-profile litigation and complex corporate work
- Strong commitment to pro bono

DOWNERS
- Bonuses are tied to billable-hours
- Firm doesn't pay bar association fees

NOTABLE PERKS
- Weekly visits from massage therapist
- Free dinner buffet four nights/week
- Friday happy hours
- BlackBerry devices and laptop/desktop computers

BASE SALARY
Chicago, IL (2005)
1st year: $125,000
Summer associate: $2,403/week

EMPLOYMENT CONTACT
Ms. Shannon Christopher
Manager of Legal Recruiting
Phone: (312) 923-2617
Fax: (312) 840-7616
E-mail: schristopher@jenner.com

THE SCOOP

Jenner & Block opened its doors in 1914 under the masthead Newman, Poppenhusen & Stern. Initially, the firm focused its practice on transactional work for financial institutions and industrial corporations; but within a few years several star trial attorneys came on board, and in 1925 the firm won its first case before the United States Supreme Court.

Today, Jenner & Block is no less ambitious. In September 2004, a group of attorneys in the firm's environmental practice won a federal appeal that will allow two clients, the Lake Michigan Federation and the Friends of Milwaukee's Rivers, to continue pursuing a claim that seeks to halt the discharge of raw sewage into Lake Michigan by the Milwaukee Metropolitan Sewerage District. The firm has been representing the organizations since 2002, when they commenced the lawsuit; this ruling by the U.S. Court of Appeals for the 7th Circuit reverses a decision last year that dismissed the case.

On the corporate side, the firm has handled multiple deals on behalf of client General Dynamics, such as the company's acquisition of several information systems segments of GTE for $1 billion and its purchase of a division of Motorola for $825 million. For its work as lead bankruptcy counsel for Archibald Candy Corporation, Jenner & Block was honored in December 2004 by *M&A Advisor* magazine, which selected the company's post-bankruptcy sale as the "U.S. Middle Market Deal of the Year." The sale was also named "Transaction of the Year" by the Chicago Chapter of the Turnaround Management Association.

Jenner & Block has a highly active pro bono program, which regularly provides legal services to incarcerated persons and writes amicus briefs for public interest organizations. Thanks in part to the firm's commitment in this area, Jenner & Block has made *The American Lawyer*'s "A-List" of elite law firms for the last two years. The magazine's ranking of the top 20 law firms in the nation is based on revenue, associate satisfaction, diversity and pro bono service.

GETTING HIRED

According to associates, the hiring process at Jenner & Block is "very competitive." "If you come from a top school," says a second-year, "your chances are great. If you are from a more local school, it is a bit harder and you probably need to be at the top of your class."

However, once you land the initial interview, personality matters as much as pedigree. "The firm looks for those who have diverse backgrounds and experiences," notes one source. While many believe that the hiring process is "too selective" and "too tied to GPA and school," some associates insist that Jenner & Block is "looking for the total package." "We are an elite law firm," says an insider, "and our hiring practices reflect that."

OUR SURVEY SAYS

Associates at Jenner & Block get to engage in "challenging and meaningful work with extraordinary attorneys." Transactional lawyers and litigators alike comment on the quality and the "variety of work," as well as the "increasing levels of responsibility and client contact" they receive. In the word of one associate, "I get the feeling that I have much more substantive and fulfilling work than fellow associates from other Chicago-area firms."

The vibe at Jenner & Block has two facets: intense, but friendly. "The firm's culture is fairly friendly and informal," says one associate, "but people are definitely here to work, not socialize." The atmosphere can get "intense at times," acknowledges another insider. Still, "nearly every lawyer has an open-door policy." When it comes to socializing outside the office, attorneys are divided. One source says, "I socialize with numerous attorneys here outside of work," while another states, "I think people work hard and like each other, but then want to go home."

Jenner & Block provides a "very extensive formal training program for junior associates," including a "number of CLE programs" and deposition training through the National Institute of Trial Advocacy. Despite "plenty of opportunities," however, it can be "difficult to find the time." The firm also has a formal mentoring program, although "some people have better luck with it than others." Certain partners are reportedly "fabulous at providing guidance." "Some partners take the time to explain and offer advice for improvement," says one source, but "many do not." In general, associates rate partner-associate relations very highly. "This is one of the strongest areas of the firm," declares a Chicago attorney.

Insiders have few complaints when it comes to money. "I think the pay here is very good and appropriate considering our billable-hours requirement," says one source. "Our compensation is generous and the benefits are outstanding," agrees a corporate colleague. Not everyone thinks the system is perfect, however. "Jenner's base salary is at market," observes an attorney, "but its bonus system seems to trail other large firms." And many associates wish billable-hours weren't the sole basis for bonuses. "Non-billable client development and department development are not really considered at all," complains one attorney. "Although the firm says it compensates for quality of work and efficiency," says another, "it really only compensates for number of billable-hours." You won't get a bonus "if you don't make your hours, even if it is through no fault of your own," gripe a couple of associates.

And those hours are no joke. The firm requires 2,000 hours to be billed annually, which is "a high requirement" but "nothing out of the ordinary." As one corporate attorney shrugs, "Unfortunately, challenging and meaningful work often necessitates meaningful time commitments." At least "there is no 'unwritten' rule that suggests you bill more than the minimum," nor do associates feel "pressured to put in 'face time' at the office."

The firm earns perhaps its highest marks for its well-known commitment to pro bono work. Jenner & Block, according to several insiders, has the "best pro bono practice in the country, hands down." But associates note that "no pro bono hours count toward the minimum billable requirement," although "up to 100 hours of pro bono work count toward an associate's bonus." Speaking of this policy, one associate says, "I'm not sure that Jenner has it right." (The firm explains that 100 pro bono hours count toward the minimum required for bonus eligibility; after that, pro bono hours constitute one of various factors that are considered.)

"Unfortunately, challenging and meaningful work often necessitates meaningful time commitments."

– Jenner & Block associate

Jones Day

North Point
901 Lakeside Avenue
Cleveland, OH 44114-1190
Phone: (216) 586-3939
www.jonesday.com

LOCATIONS

Atlanta, GA • Chicago, IL • Cleveland, OH • Columbus, OH • Dallas, TX • Houston, TX • Irvine, CA • Los Angeles, CA • Menlo Park, CA • New York, NY • Pittsburgh, PA • San Diego, CA • San Francisco, CA • Washington, DC • Beijing • Brussels • Frankfurt • Hong Kong • London • Madrid • Milan • Moscow • Munich • New Delhi* • Paris • Shanghai • Singapore • Sydney • Taipei • Tokyo

*Associate firm

MAJOR DEPARTMENTS & PRACTICES

Bankruptcy • Corporate Criminal Investigations • Corporate Finance, Lending & Structured Finance • Employee Benefits & Tax • Energy • Environmental • Intellectual Property • Labor & Employment • Litigation • Mergers & Acquisitions • Real Estate

THE STATS

No. of attorneys:
firm-wide: 2,242
Cleveland: 272
Chicago: 157
Columbus: 90
No. of offices: 30
Summer associate offers:
firm-wide: 165 out of 172 (2004)
Cleveland: 18 out of 18 (2004)
Chicago: 18 out of 20 (2004)
Columbus: 8 out of 8 (2004)
Managing Partner: Stephen J. Brogan
Hiring Partners:
Cleveland: Michelle K. Fischer
Chicago: Tina M. Tabacchi
Columbus: Jeffrey J. Jones

UPPERS
- Commitment to associate training
- Down-to-earth colleagues and appreciative clients

DOWNERS
- Lack of communication from management
- "The hours can be hard"

NOTABLE PERKS
- Annual associates' retreat
- Firm parties, including the "prom"
- Assistance with personal real estate closings
- Free dinner and cab ride home at night/on weekends

BASE SALARY

Chicago, IL (2005)
1st year: $125,000
Summer associate: $2,400/week

Cleveland and Columbus, OH (2005)
1st year: $110,000
Summer associate: $2,076.92/week

EMPLOYMENT CONTACTS

Cleveland
Ms. Paula T. Nylander
Recruiting Manager
Phone: (216) 586-1034
Fax: (216) 579-0212
E-mail: ptnylander@jonesday.com

Chicago
Ms. Jane McAvoy
Recruiting Manager
Phone: (312) 269-4163
Fax: (312) 782-8585
E-mail: jmcavoy@jonesday.com

Columbus
Ms. M. Jane Shields
Recruiting Manager
Phone: (614) 281-3982
Fax: (614) 461-4198
E-mail: mshields@jonesday.com

THE SCOOP

As the second-largest firm in the country, Jones Day boasts over 2,200 lawyers and 30 offices on four continents. In January 2005, for the fifth year in a row, both Thomson Financial and Bloomberg ranked Jones Day No. 1 for number of completed deals worldwide.

Among the more than 500 deals Jones Day completed in 2004 were several high-profile transactions, including the $46.5 billion merger between Nextel Communications and Sprint, in which Jones Day attorneys from Cleveland, New York, Atlanta and Washington worked together as counsel for Nextel. The firm also advised grocery chain Albertson's, Inc., as it acquired Shaw's Supermarkets, Inc., for $2.5 billion last spring. The transaction involved the efforts of M&A, corporate finance, tax, employee benefits, antitrust and lending lawyers in five Jones Day offices around the country, including the Chicago office. In another inter-office, inter-departmental deal, Jones Day represented The J.M. Smucker Company when it acquired International Multifoods Corporation for $840 million in March 2004. An M&A partner in Chicago co-chaired the team.

Jones Day also houses an impressive litigation practice. Recently, lawyers in several Jones Day offices, including Chicago, New York and D.C., teamed up to win a patent infringement suit for Abbott Laboratories. In 2004, the Cleveland-based head of the products liability practice led a trial team to a unanimous defense verdict for IBM in the first U.S. "toxic tort" trial involving the microelectronic industry. And in December 2004, Cleveland associate John Q. Lewis successfully argued a pro bono case before the U.S. Supreme Court on behalf of an Ohio inmate seeking to use a federal civil rights law to challenge unconstitutional parole proceedings; on March 7, 2005, the high court ruled 8-1 in the inmate's favor.

GETTING HIRED

Get your transcripts ready! At Jones Day, "Excellent grades are required to get in the door, but beyond that, the recruiting committee values normal, outgoing people who can function in a team environment," advises a veteran associate. Echoes another, "Even from the best law schools, the firm requires superior grades. Second-tier law school applicants must be at the very top of their class." Beyond pedigree, the firm is "looking for people who will fit into the cooperative and team-oriented firm culture [and] whom we'll enjoy working with." Another insider cautions would-be candidates, "Only apply if you have something to add beyond your resume, like a personality – a personality that is friendly and works well with others is preferable."

OUR SURVEY SAYS

Associates at Jones Day recognize that life in a big law firm is not all wine and roses, but they feel they are better off than many of their peers. A senior associate says, "Once you decide to go the route of BigLaw, this is an excellent place to practice. Cases are varied and always challenging. The office maintains a very free market to allow associates to seek out the type of work they want to do and work with a variety of different partners." Another source agrees: "Not only have I gotten great experience on big cases, but I also work with first-rate attorneys who know their stuff and are great people to work with, too." A midlevel attorney reports that "the culture here is friendly and just really normal. People have personal lives and other lawyers respect your outside life. Lawyers do socialize both in and outside of the office, formally and informally, and there is no pressure to do so."

Although Jones Day reportedly "does not place unreasonable hours targets on associates (the average is slightly under 2,000 hours)," many lament the sheer volatility of their workload. A third-year comments, "Naturally, I would love to work less but considering the size of the firm and the clients' needs, I have been neither shocked nor upset by the hours. At times it is difficult to plan events because the schedule is often unpredictable." Similarly, another junior lawyer observes, "The overall hours worked are not particularly high, but the problem is that I am either billing 70-hour weeks or 20-hour weeks." A longtime associate offers, "I have billed in excess of 2,300 hours a year, with the highest being 2,700. That said, I have also come in below 2,000 and nothing was said. I do not believe there is a heavy emphasis on hours."

Jones Day expends substantial time and resources on associate development. According to one inside source, the firm "makes extensive use of NITA training programs, both offering them in-house and sending associates to NITA-sponsored programs. The annual associates' meetings, held at a resort, offer a variety of training programs to choose from, as well as the chance to meet and socialize with associates from other offices." Even so, a seasoned associate opines, "We have some formal training programs, but most learning is done on the job, with partner/senior associate supervision. Frankly, most people will learn more from that anyway, by doing rather than watching/listening."

The biggest downfall at Jones Day is the compensation system. As a midlevel puts it, "I am pretty happy with my salary, but it's disheartening to know that I will never get a bonus. At least the firm is consistent in never giving bonuses except in extreme circumstances – they're the stuff of law firm lore." Says another insider, "Unlike a lot of firms, Jones Day does not do much in the way of bonuses, and certainly does not link year-end payments directly to the number of hours billed." Although "some view it as the firm being cheap," a source explains, "the firm views it as a matter of basic firm culture and not wanting to create the atmosphere where it's all about hours."

Katten Muchin Zavis Rosenman

525 West Monroe Street
Chicago, IL 60661-3693
Phone: (312) 902-5200
www.kmzr.com

LOCATIONS

Chicago, IL (HQ)
Charlotte, NC
Los Angeles, CA
New York, NY
Washington, DC

MAJOR DEPARTMENTS & PRACTICES

Bankruptcy
Corporate
Employee Benefits
Environmental
Financial Services
Health Care
Intellectual Property
International Trade
Labor
Litigation
Public Finance
Real Estate
Structured Finance
Tax
Trusts & Estates

THE STATS

No. of attorneys:
  firm-wide: 596
  Chicago: 274
No. of offices: 5
Summer associate offers:
  firm-wide: 55 out of 56 (2004)
  Chicago: 29 out of 29 (2004)
National Managing Partner: Vincent A.F. Sergi
Hiring Partners: Brian F. Richards and Andrew D. Small

UPPERS
- Sophisticated work
- Great pro bono program

DOWNERS
- Heavy work demands
- Unattractive offices (which, "thankfully," are undergoing renovation)

NOTABLE PERKS
- One-month paid sabbatical after five years with the firm
- Access to skybox for Bulls, Black Hawks and White Sox games
- Subsidized cafeteria
- "We have lots of parties"

BASE SALARY

Chicago, IL (2005)
1st year: $125,000
2nd year: $135,000
3rd year: $150,000
4th year: $165,000
5th year: $185,000
6th year: $195,000
Summer associate: $2,403/week

EMPLOYMENT CONTACT

Ms. Elizabeth E. Cibula
Director of Attorney Recruiting & Development
Phone: (312) 902-5547
Fax: (312) 577-8937
E-mail: elizabeth.cibula@kmzr.com

THE SCOOP

In 2004, Katten Muchin Zavis Rosenman debuted on *Corporate Board Member*'s ranking of the top five corporate law firms in Chicago. The list is compiled from surveys of CEOs who serve on the boards of directors of major corporations, and KMZR broke into the top tier at No. 5. The 600-lawyer firm, which is headquartered in the Windy City, earned the spot through its work on high-visibility deals such as the summer 2004 sale of client InstallShield Software Corporation to Macrovision Corporation. The technology transaction was worth $76 million in cash, and InstallShield may receive another $20 million for performance after the closing.

On the litigation side, KMZR has recently added two former assistant U.S. attorneys to its Chicago partner roster. Last spring, KMZR welcomed Stuart J. Chanen from the Chicago U.S. attorney's office. There, he focused primarily on white-collar crime cases in the Major Case Division. He also teaches at Northwestern Law School and the National Institute of Trial Advocacy. A few months later, in July 2004, Brian P. Netols joined the firm after working for the U.S. attorney's office for 14 years, handling cases including corruption, racketeering, tax and financial crimes. At KMZR, the two new partners will have the opportunity to work on litigation and dispute resolution for clients in diverse industries such as health care, securities, entertainment and media, and intellectual property.

GETTING HIRED

Of course, candidates should have excellent credentials if they want to get hired at Katten Muchin Zavis Rosenman. But insiders insist that "KMZR is not wedded to the top schools." Although the firm is "very selective," it will "look past" school for otherwise impressive prospects. KMZR "attracts people of varied personalities" and "you don't have to be one particular type to fit in." "We're looking for smart, engaged individuals who want to be good lawyers," says one source. "The screening interview is about figuring out who's 'smart enough' to work here – the callbacks are for finding out if the fit is right."

Views differ as to the firm's attitude toward bringing on more people right now. Although one associate says there have been "cutbacks in hiring" (with resulting intensification in selectivity), another assures us that "the firm is in hiring mode, looking to add to associate ranks."

OUR SURVEY SAYS

Insiders describe Katten Muchin Zavis Rosenman's Chicago office as "busy" and "hardworking" – but they also emphasize that the attorneys are "collegial and cooperative." According to one second-year, "The firm culture is pretty informal, and the associates all tend to socialize together." "Some of the partners can be stuffy" and, according to one associate, there are "pockets of 'old boys' clubs,'" but, by and large, "the firm is laid-back." You can even "wear jeans to work without any noticeable adverse consequences," says one insider. As for social activity, "some lawyers socialize together and others go straight home, and you're welcome to whichever suits you."

Despite the firm's "friendly" atmosphere, sources say that "hard work, long hours and significant responsibility are emphasized and expected." The firm expects a minimum of 2,000 billable-hours per year, and most attorneys clock in well over that. But most sources feel that's just part of the job. "The work load is comparable with any other large Chicago law firm. It is manageable, but requires a significant commitment," explains one senior associate. Another disagrees, complaining that "we fixate on hours here more than any other large firm I know." But it isn't all bad. "Working hard here is enjoyable for the most part because I like the people I work with," explains a newcomer. More good news: "There is almost no face time. Obviously work needs to get done, but no one is checking offices."

One would think that KMZR's high expectation of billable-hours would generate sufficient revenues to pay handsome salaries and bonuses. And many associates agree, considering their salaries to be among the "highest in Chicago." But there's always room for improvement. According to one attorney, "KMZR pays salaries and bonuses that are somewhat below the top-tier firm bonuses and salaries. The compensation is not unfair," he adds, "just a little below market." On the other hand, insiders should be pleased that the firm has recently eliminated the unpopular salary deferral system, in which a portion of each associate's salary is reserved and paid at the end of the year to associates who hit target hours. (The firm reports that the salary deferral has been eliminated for all associates as of January 1, 2005.)

Most attorneys at KMZR consider the firm's formal training program extensive. Insiders say that the firm "has good formal training and mentoring initiatives, including participation in-house and external programs, such as NITA." But some complain that while trainings are regularly scheduled, they're not that great. The firm's informal training and mentoring programs receive better reviews overall. Still, attorneys are expected to take some responsibility on themselves when it comes to training and mentoring. Says one midlevel associate, "Informal training is something that usually requires active participation/solicitation on the part of the associate."

KMZR's pro bono program scores among the best, according to insiders. "The firm allows attorneys to bill up to 100 pro bono hours per year, and approval for additional hours is granted when the case warrants it," says one midlevel associate. "Even more importantly," she adds, "the firm has a full-time pro bono partner, who coordinates pro bono assignments, as well as works full-time on pro bono matters himself."

"There is almost no face time. Obviously work needs to get done, but no one is checking offices."

– *Katten Muchin Zavis Rosenman associate*

Kirkland & Ellis LLP

200 East Randolph Drive
Chicago, IL 60601
Phone: (312) 861-2000
www.kirkland.com

LOCATIONS

Chicago, IL (largest office)
Los Angeles, CA
New York, NY
San Francisco, CA
Washington, DC
London
Munich

MAJOR DEPARTMENTS & PRACTICES

Bankruptcy
Corporate/Transactional
Intellectual Property
Litigation
Real Estate
Tax

THE STATS

No. of attorneys:
  firm-wide: 997
  Chicago: 490
No. of offices: 7
Summer associate offers:
  Chicago: 64 out of 64 (2004)
Management Committee Chair: Thomas D. Yannucci
Hiring Partner: Linda K. Myers (Chicago)

UPPERS
- "All the responsibility you can handle"
- Interesting work and good pay

DOWNERS
- Long hours and "intense" atmosphere
- Firm could be more generous with bonuses and benefits

NOTABLE PERKS
- Back-up child care
- Fresh fruit and pastries in the morning
- $10,000 summer stipend and payment of all bar expenses
- Cab rides home and dinner reimbursement after 7 p.m.

BASE SALARY
Chicago, IL (2005)
1st year: $125,000
2nd year: $135,000
3rd year: $150,000
4th year: $165,000
5th year: $185,000
6th year: $195,000
Summer associate: $2,404/week

EMPLOYMENT CONTACT
Ms. Kimberley J. Klein
Attorney Recruiting Specialist
Phone: (312) 861-8785
Fax: (312) 861-2200
E-mail: attorney_recruiting@kirkland.com

THE SCOOP

Kirkland & Ellis' position as a top-of-the-heap firm is clear both from its regular appearance on *The National Law Journal*'s annual survey, "Who Represents Corporate America," and from a quick glance at its list of recent cases and transactions. As just one example, a group of attorneys from the Chicago office recently won summary judgment for blue-chip client Amazon.com in a dispute brought by IPXL Holdings. The suit alleged that Amazon's "1-click®" ordering system infringed upon a patent held by IPXL for an electronic funds transfer system, and the plaintiff sought over $50 million in damages. The Kirkland & Ellis team prevailed with its argument that the Amazon feature was just a part of an electronic ordering system and did not comprise such a system itself. For its involvement in this and other major disputes, the firm was named the 2004 "Litigation Law Firm of the Year" by *Chambers USA* and was a finalist for *The American Lawyer*'s "Litigation Department of the Year" award for 2003.

Meanwhile, on the corporate side, Chambers & Partners selected Kirkland & Ellis as the "U.S. Private Equity Law Firm" of 2003 and short-listed the firm for the same award in 2004. Transactional attorneys at Kirkland & Ellis-Chicago handled a deal in the summer of 2004 that resulted in client Madison Dearborn Partners acquiring $3.7 billion in assets formerly owned by paper, forest and timberland company Boise Cascade Corporation. Also as a result of the deal, Boise Cascade has taken on the more widely known name of OfficeMax, Inc., which Boise purchased last year. In October 2004, the Midwest Chapter of the Turnaround Management Association awarded Kirkland "Transaction of the Year" honors for its representation of Conseco Inc. in what was reportedly the third-largest Chapter 11 filing in U.S. history. Thanks to the efforts of Kirkland's restructuring team, Conseco emerged from bankruptcy in September 2003.

GETTING HIRED

"Everyone says they hire 'the best of the best,'" observes a second-year associate, "but few firms mean it as much as Kirkland." Inside sources agree that "this is a tough place to get a job." One midlevel lawyer calls Kirkland "as selective as any firm in Chicago." The firm places a lot of "emphasis on law school and grades." According to one attorney, "The firm generally hires candidates from top schools with good grades. Candidates with great grades from any school are hired, and hot specialties (like IP) help, too."

In addition to pedigree, candidates should have "a lot of drive" and "self-motivation." "This is not a place for the meek," cautions one insider. A seasoned lawyer advises would-be Kirkland associates: "Be smart, personable, adaptable, a good writer and [an] incisive thinker." It also helps to have "a fertile imagination and intellectual agility."

OUR SURVEY SAYS

There are a few aspects of life at Kirkland & Ellis on which almost every contact agrees: the work is challenging, the lawyers are top-notch and it's not a good place to be a pushover. Overall, insiders describe the firm culture as "very professional," "work-oriented," and "entrepreneurial, aggressive, fun, and informal." As one associate says, "The firm is relatively informal but takes its work very seriously." According to another, "You get the quality of work that is otherwise only available in New York City, but you get the quality of life of a Chicago firm."

Kirkland employs a "free-market" work distribution system that results in too much downtime, or too many missed vacations, for the unassertive. The assignment system is "extremely informal," says a newcomer in Chicago. "It's all word-of-mouth how you get your work. People with a thick skin and initiative will do well. If you're sitting in your office waiting for work to come your way, it's tougher." But the assertive will enjoy "the chance to get lots of responsibility fast" and "the opportunity to learn from the best of the best trial lawyers in the country."

In fact, according to many insiders, the "unparalleled training" is "one of the reasons to come to Kirkland." "The partners put a lot of time, money and effort into structured training programs," says a Chicago associate, "including lectures/seminars throughout the year and a weekend intensive training program." "KITA – the Kirkland Institute for Trial Advocacy – has to be near the best formal litigation training program of any big firm," declares a litigator. According to another associate, the Kirkland Institute of Corporate Practice (KICP) "provides invaluable training in what it means to be a corporate lawyer."

Kirkland associates also rate their firm's compensation "at or near the top of the market." "After a couple of years of disappointing bonuses," sources report, "the firm has once again stepped up to provide top-of-the-market bonuses to associates that reward both merit and billable-hours." That does not mean that attorneys are without complaint, however. Several associates "still think the firm should be more generous, given the huge profits generated around here," and a few sources grumble about a "secretive" bonus policy: "nobody seems to know what level of work is expected, or what kind of compensation to expect." (The firm notes that, in response to such criticisms, in 2005 it provided associates with extensive information about its compensation policies.) In a money-related aside, associates wouldn't mind less expensive insurance plans and a few more "perks," like subsidized gym memberships and technology subsidies; according to some contacts, all attorneys have to purchase their own BlackBerry devices (although the firm pays the monthly service fees).

Insiders say the hours are rough but flexible. "Personally, I have spent more time in the office than I would have liked over the last few years," reports a midlevel associate. "However, the responsibility for that rests with me, to a certain extent. You are free here to work as much or as little as you like (within reason)." Another insider agrees: "It would be nice to be 9-to-5, but that is unrealistic. However, I have learned over the years that I am much more in control of my hours than I had initially thought. There may be difficult deadlines to meet, but I can monitor how much work I take on to make life generally better."

"You get the quality of work that is otherwise only available in New York City, but you get the quality of life of a Chicago firm."

– Kirkland & Ellis associate

Latham & Watkins Illinois LLP

Sears Tower, Suite 5800
Chicago, IL 60606
Phone: (312) 876-7700
www.lw.com

LOCATIONS

Los Angeles, CA (HQ)
Boston, MA
Chicago, IL
Costa Mesa, CA
Los Angeles, CA
Menlo Park, CA
New York, NY
Newark, NJ
Reston, VA
San Diego, CA
San Francisco, CA
Washington, DC
Brussels
Frankfurt
Hamburg
Hong Kong
London
Milan
Moscow
Paris
Singapore
Tokyo

MAJOR DEPARTMENTS & PRACTICES

Corporate
Environmental, Land & Resources
Finance
Litigation
Tax

THE STATS

No. of attorneys:
  firm-wide: 1,572
  Chicago: 136
No. of offices: 22
Summer associate offers:
  Chicago: 9 out of 10 (2003)
Chairman and Managing Partner: Robert M. Dell
Hiring Partner: Marcelo Halpern

UPPERS
- Sophisticated clients and work
- Great pro bono program

DOWNERS
- Unpredictable and sometimes long hours
- New associates could use more guidance

NOTABLE PERKS
- Friday afternoon "BID" (Beer in the Diner)
- Associate exchange program with international offices
- Donuts and pastries on Fridays
- Free dinners and cab rides for late nights

BASE SALARY
Chicago, IL (2004)
1st year: $125,000
Summer associate: $2,400/week

EMPLOYMENT CONTACT
Ms. Jennifer Boehnel
Manager of Attorney Recruitment
Phone: (312) 876-7700
Fax: (312) 993-9767
E-mail: jennifer.boehnel@lw.com

THE SCOOP

Los Angeles-based Latham & Watkins has established a strong presence in the Midwest thanks to its 135-lawyer office in the Sears Tower. The global firm's depth and breadth of experience in broad practice areas are used by Latham-Chicago's attorneys to serve clients in wide-ranging industries such as manufacturing, pharmaceutical, biotechnology, financial institutions and hospitality.

The Chicago office of Latham & Watkins has earned a particularly stellar reputation for its bankruptcy work. With 24 active insolvency cases in the first half of 2004, the firm as a whole garnered a No.-1 ranking among the "Top 10 Bankruptcy Lender Law Firms," a list compiled by *The Deal: Bankruptcy Insider* in its June 28, 2004 issue. Chicago partners David Heller and Joe Athanas came in at No. 1 and No. 4, respectively, on the list of the "Top 10 Bankruptcy Lender Lawyers" in the same article.

With the co-chair of the firm's global mergers and acquisitions group on hand, Latham's Second City corporate practice closes stellar, multibillion-dollar deals on a regular basis. For the first three quarters of 2004, the firm at large handled 19 deals with a total worth of over $4.7 billion, winning it the No.-3 spot in *Dealogic*'s Global Project Finance League Table. Clients of the Chicago office in this area have included Bally Total Fitness Corporation, Orbitz, Inc., Sears, Roebuck and Co. and Credit Suisse First Boston.

GETTING HIRED

Latham & Watkins looks for candidates in the "top 10 percent" of their law school class. However, "great grades, alone, are not enough to get an offer," say associates: "A candidate must fit with the culture and have a great personality, too." In the Chicago office, smart may be the norm, but "bookworms are the exception."

One associate sums up the firm's hiring philosophy: "Latham lawyers look for people who are engaging, self-assured (but not cocky), poised and have good judgment. While Latham wants superstars, they also want people with whom they will enjoy working. You need to have a personality to work here!"

OUR SURVEY SAYS

The culture at Latham & Watkins may be "officially laid-back," but, sources say, it is "unofficially very serious and hard-working." Most Chicago attorneys describe their office as friendly and "relatively relaxed." "As far as big firms go, I doubt you could find a better culture," says one associate. Most extra-office socializing seems to take place among junior attorneys. In-house, the firm sponsors a weekly Friday afternoon "BID" (Beer in the Diner), "where drinks and food are served for all lawyers and employees to enjoy and mingle."

One thing that sets Latham apart is the firm's "transparent" management style. "Financial information, as well as information regarding pace, bonuses and so on, is shared with the associates," says a Chicago attorney. That doesn't mean the associates always like what they hear. "For the amount of money the partners are raking in, they could throw a little more our way," mutters one midlevel. Newcomers complain that the firm replaced the summer bar stipend with a salary advance. Still, most Windy City lawyers are happy enough with their salaries, though they say "the bonus structure could be improved." "It's not quite investment banking pay," says one associate, "but it's excellent all the same."

Attorneys work hard for the money, although many associates find their hours quite manageable. "Obviously there are times when you will work long hours," explains one associate. "But thus far, there have been slow periods as well. You usually have some downtime after a deal closes or a matter ends." On the other hand, "It is not unusual to spend eight or nine hours in the office doing absolutely nothing, simply putting in face time, and then have a bit of work finally trickle down at night or over the weekend," complains one associate. Another lawyer shrugs, "It's the nature of the beast." On a positive note, all pro bono hours count toward the annual billable requirement of 1,950 hours. In the words of one insider, "It's the best pro bono program of any law firm in the country, in my opinion – no cap on hours, one-for-one credit, great opportunities."

As for learning the ropes, Latham has a "very full training schedule," but associates say that the sessions are "not always very effective or helpful." In the end, "you're pretty much thrown onto deals with little or no training and then expected to learn quickly as you go, while making few mistakes. It's basically up to midlevels to train the newer associates," explains one attorney. And this can leave some gaps, according to Chicago sources. One associate complains that "the greatest of the many flaws of this firm is the lack of a formal mentoring program. As an associate, from day one you are on your own, there is no one to talk to or learn from." "The informal mentoring and training is what you make of it," argues another Chicago attorney. "I enjoy a very comfortable relationship with my supervisors and often ask for advice and constructive criticism, which they are happy to provide. I also feel like I can ask just about anyone a question if I am uncomfortable asking my direct reports," he explains.

Latham's policy of not assigning associates to specific groups for their first two years of practice has both advantages and disadvantages. While it allows new attorneys "time to become better generalists," it also means that they don't gain "the same specific experience" as associates at firms "where specialization begins immediately."

Leydig, Voit & Mayer, Ltd.

Two Prudential Plaza
180 North Stetson, Suite 4900
Chicago, IL 60601
Phone: (312) 616-5600
www.leydig.com

LOCATIONS

Chicago, IL (HQ)
Rockford, IL
Seattle, WA
Washington, DC

MAJOR DEPARTMENTS & PRACTICES

Copyright
Intellectual Property Litigation
Licensing
Patent
Trade Secret
Trademark

THE STATS

No. of attorneys:
   firm-wide: 82
   Chicago: 66
No. of offices: 4
Summer associate offers:
   firm-wide: 4 out of 6 (2004)
   Chicago: 3 out of 4 (2004)
Managing Partner: John Kilyk Jr.
Hiring Partner: Brett A. Hesterberg

NOTABLE PERKS

- 401(k) plan
- Profit-sharing program
- Professional development account
- "Overtime" bonuses

BASE SALARY

Chicago, IL (2005)
1st year: $130,000
Summer associate: $2,250/week

EMPLOYMENT CONTACT

Ms. Beatriz Swiech
Recruiting Manager
Phone: (312) 616-5602
Fax: (312) 616-5700
E-mail: bswiech@leydig.com

THE SCOOP

Established in 1893, Leydig, Voit & Mayer owes its genesis to Luther Miller, a young lawyer who hung out his shingle and filed his first patent application just after getting admitted to the Illinois Bar. The firm was originally based in Rockford, Ill., where it still maintains an office staffed by four attorneys; but in 1898 Luther Miller moved his burgeoning practice into the big city. Now that it has more than a century of intellectual property practice under its belt, Leydig Voit numbers over 80 lawyers in four cities.

Attorneys at Leydig, Voit & Mayer specialize in all technologies, including mechanics, electronics, chemistry, computer software and genetics. Practicing at this firm is not for those who fear polysyllabic words. Among the fields covered by the firm's specialty areas are hybridoma and monoclonal antibody technologies, semiconductor polishing compositions and combinatorial chemistry. At least clients understand them: The firm was recently identified as one of the 10 "Most Wanted" intellectual property firms in *Corporate Counsel Magazine*'s review of "Who Represents America's Biggest Companies."

The firm made its mark in patent law 50 years ago when Leydig attorneys argued a patent infringement lawsuit before the U.S. Supreme Court using the "doctrine of equivalents," which allows patent owners to prove an infringement where a device or method is basically the same as (even if not identical to) the claimed invention. That doctrine remains a cornerstone of modern patent law today.

In the mid-1970s, Leydig handled an industry-wide dispute in which several major beer brands thwarted Miller Brewing Company's attempt to prohibit other brands to use the word "Lite" or "Light" in their low-alcohol beverage names. Ever since then, Leydig has been one of the chief go-to firms for trademark matters. As a result of its groundbreaking work in this area, last year the firm was honored with the Trademark Insider Award and was singled out by the industry publication as the No.-1 firm in Chicago for trademark filings.

While the firm's 11 name changes in the past century may have confused or concerned some, most of Leydig's clients have stuck with the Midwest firm through thick and thin. Two of the firm's earliest clients (Woodward Governor Company and the Barber-Colman Company, now a division of Invensys) are still with the firm after over 100 years. Leydig also appears on *The National Law Journal*'s list of "Who Represents Corporate America" for the ongoing intellectual property services it provides to AIG, Morgan Stanley and Microsoft. Additional representative clients include the National Institutes of Health (a client for more than 10 years), Johns Hopkins University, Mitsubishi Electric Corp. and American Express.

One of the most interesting things about Leydig Voit may be its bonus system. The firm recently eliminated target billable-hours in favor of an "overtime" bonus structure. Now, associates are awarded a bonus of $62.50 per hour for each hour billed above 1,900. And to encourage its "small firm" feeling, Leydig sponsors a number of social events throughout the year, including monthly lawyer luncheons, a golf and tennis outing, a summer associate reception and a holiday ball.

GETTING HIRED

Because Leydig, Voit & Mayer's practice is technology-based, the firm prefers candidates with "backgrounds in the hard sciences (e.g., chemistry or molecular biology) or engineering (preferably chemical, electrical, mechanical or computer)." But the firm will consider exceptional candidates with other technical backgrounds as well. More good news: you don't have to be in the top 10 percent of your class – top half will do. In addition to specialty and class rank, the firm places a particular emphasis on analytical and writing skills. So if you have a technical or analytical writing sample that you're especially proud of, send it in.

Lord, Bissell & Brook LLP

115 South La Salle Street
Chicago, IL 60603
Phone: (312) 443-0700
www.lordbissell.com

LOCATIONS

Chicago, IL (HQ)
Atlanta, GA
Los Angeles, CA
New York, NY
Washington, DC
London

MAJOR DEPARTMENTS & PRACTICES

Antitrust
Appellate
Bankruptcy
Business Litigation
Class Actions
Corporate
Employee Benefits
Entertainment & Media
Environmental
Financial Institutions
Insurance
Intellectual Property & Technology
Investment Services
Labor & Employment
Product Liability
Real Estate
Reinsurance

THE STATS

No. of attorneys:
   firm-wide: 310
   Chicago: 225
No. of offices: 6
Summer associate offers:
   firm-wide: 24 out of 27 (2004)
   Chicago: 16 out of 18 (2004)
Chief Executive Officer: Thomas W. Jenkins
Hiring Partner: David M. Agnew

UPPERS

- Substantial early responsibility
- Friendly environment

DOWNERS

- Poor communication regarding firm matters
- "Nebulous" compensation guidelines

NOTABLE PERKS

- Generous business development bonus (50 percent of firm profit)
- Free dinners and cab fare after 7 pm
- Regular attorney dinners

BASE SALARY

Chicago, IL (2005)
1st year: $125,000
Summer associate: $2,400/week

EMPLOYMENT CONTACT

Ms. Kerry B. Jahnsen
Recruiting Coordinator
Phone: (312) 443-0455
Fax: (312) 443-0336
E-mail: kjahnsen@lordbissell.com

THE SCOOP

For two years running, the Chicago-based firm of Lord, Bissell & Brook has been at the top of the charts. In 2003 and 2004, *Reactions* magazine, a publication for the insurance and reinsurance industry, listed Lord Bissell as the No.-1 law firm in the United States for insurance and reinsurance matters generally and for specific insurance-related areas such as litigation, insolvency, corporate and policy drafting. The firm was also dubbed the best insurance firm in Illinois in the 2004 rankings compiled by *Chambers USA*, a publication which polls corporate clients and law firm lawyers to assess the best law firms in a variety of practice areas.

Although Lord, Bissell & Brook is a clear leader in the insurance field, the firm also has strong practices in general commercial litigation and transactional matters, which encompass a variety of industries including e-commerce, entertainment and media, and financial institutions. In one recent case, the firm represented Apotex, Inc. in a lawsuit brought by pharmaceutical titan Glaxo Group Limited. Apotex had filed an FDA application to market a generic drug in the United States, and Glaxo sued for patent infringement. The action went up to the U.S. Court of Appeals for the Federal Circuit, where the Lord Bissell team won a reversal of the lower court's finding that Apotex had willfully infringed upon Glaxo's patent. The Federal Circuit opinion contained important new law, clarifying the standard for a finding of willful patent infringement on the basis of an FDA application.

GETTING HIRED

This regal-sounding firm is becoming increasingly selective, especially over the last couple of years, say insiders. "The firm looks to hire primarily from [the] top 20 law schools, with particular emphasis on schools nearest the firm's offices." During the interview, recruiters want to see how well-rounded you are, looking for "intelligence, communication skills, interpersonal abilities [and] motivation." After the initial screening interview, callbacks generally entail five or six 30-minute partner interviews and "lunch with junior-level associates." But be careful what you say while eating your sandwich: "All attorneys (including junior associates) evaluate the candidates they interview."

OUR SURVEY SAYS

Overall, associates describe their experience at LB&B as "extremely satisfying." The Chicago office is "friendly" and "laid-back," although some say it is "becoming more uptight" due to management changes and streamlining. "The firm is somewhat conservative in its operation, yet is comprised of an eclectic mix of personalities. On the whole, lawyers get along well," says one seasoned associate. "There are no (or few) yellers," which makes for a more pleasant atmosphere, and the firm even hosts after-hour "firm dinners and social outings."

Lord Bissell attorneys spend plenty of time in the office, too. The firm requires a minimum of 2,000 billable-hours annually. While not all attorneys meet that goal, some far exceed it. According to a few new associates, however, too many of those hours are spent in the office and not out "in the field." Nevertheless, "the work is, for the most part, challenging and interesting." "I have been at several firms in the past and have practiced in several areas of the law and I cannot imagine a better working environment and more interesting work," gushes one newcomer. Associates praise their firm's "very real commitment to pro bono work." Not only do all pro bono hours count toward the billable requirements, but the firm "strongly encourages" attorney participation.

As for compensation, salary levels are at or above market for starting associates. "They are paying me a lot of money and I understand that I need to put in a lot of hours in order to earn that pay," says one first-year. But a few experienced attorneys find cause for complaint. According to one litigator, "Compensation is a bit low compared to other Chicago firms this size." Moreover, raises aren't awarded until March, "retroactive to January." Insiders report that the firm recently changed its bonus policy. While bonuses used to be tied to billable requirements, the firm now has a "vague, subjective bonus policy." Bonuses "generally require 2,000 billable-hours to 'qualify' and then the bonus is discretionary according to department leaders and politics," says one attorney. Associates say that they're also required to meet a "nonchargeable guideline" of 150 hours for business development, recruiting and professional activities. If this time is well spent and you bring in new work, expect to be compensated handsomely. "The best part about working for Lord Bissell is the firm's commitment to client development and the firm's client development bonus," raves one attorney.

LB&B has "extensive formal training programs for first- and second-year associates." But for more senior associates, training is generally a "hands-on" process. "From my perspective, the training is essentially on-the-job training. I am assigned tasks and I am supposed to complete them," says one attorney. The firm does "encourage associates to attend seminars," however, and "is extremely generous in paying for outside training if you seek it out." Luckily, most associates feel comfortable asking the attorneys they work with for guidance. In fact, associates give Lord Bissell's informal training and mentoring programs high marks. "This has been the most useful form of training for me. I believe training and mentoring obligations are included in the criteria for partnership consideration," explains one senior associate. According to a newer associate, "All partners and senior associates here are willing to train and mentor, but only about half of them make time or have time to really do an effective job."

Marshall, Gerstein & Borun LLP

233 South Wacker Drive
6300 Sears Tower
Chicago, IL 60606-6357
Phone: (312) 474-6300
www.marshallip.com

LOCATION

Chicago, IL

MAJOR DEPARTMENTS & PRACTICES

Copyrights
Internet/Cyberlaw
Licensing & Business Transactions
Litigation
Opinions & Counseling
Patent Prosecution
Technologies
Trade Secrets
Trademarks

THE STATS

No. of attorneys: 76
No. of offices: 1
Summer associate offers: 5 out of 5 (2004)
Managing Partner: Jeffrey S. Sharp
Hiring Partner: Sandip H. Patel

NOTABLE PERKS

- Profit-sharing plan
- $7,500 summer stipend for bar exam study
- Payment of all bar exam-related expenses
- Regular firm-wide social events

BASE SALARY

Chicago, IL (2005)
1st year: $130,000
Summer associate: $2,500/week

EMPLOYMENT CONTACT

Ms. Michele J. Gudaitis
Recruiting Coordinator
Phone: (312) 474-6300
Fax: (312) 474-0448
E-mail: mgudaitis@marshallip.com

THE SCOOP

As an intellectual property boutique with over a half-century of experience, Marshall, Gerstein & Borun has long been making the world safe for innovation and invention. The 76-lawyer firm has a highly specialized practice, advising clients on all aspects of obtaining and protecting copyrights, trademarks, patents and trade secrets. From its single office in Chicago, Marshall Gerstein reaches clients around the country and has litigated in virtually every state in the union.

In one recent case in the fall of 2004, Marshall Gerstein obtained a $3.5 million judgment on behalf of client Golden Voice Technology & Training, LLC, against Rockwell Electronic Commerce Corporation. The Florida-based Golden Voice won the damages award when a jury in the U.S. District Court for the Middle District of Florida, Orlando Division, concluded that Rockwell had infringed upon Golden Voice's patent for a telephone call-center technology that allows operators to use recorded messages to respond to incoming calls. Chief Judge Patricia Fawsett awarded enhanced damages, prejudgment interest, and attorneys' fees and expenses.

Another of the firm's recent wins came in October 2004, when a Marshall Gerstein team garnered a favorable ruling in another patent dispute for client Amgen, Inc. after almost seven years of litigation. In a nearly 300-page decision, a federal district judge in Massachusetts held that Amgen's patents for four pharmaceutical products were valid and enforceable, and that defendants Aventis Pharmaceuticals, Inc. and Transkaryotic Therapies Inc. had infringed those patents. Outside of the patent area, the firm won an appellate decision against the city of Chicago in which it succeeded in striking down a zoning ordinance that violated the constitutional due process rights of the residents of a nine-block area in Lincoln Park.

A few months earlier, in July 2004, the firm scored yet another major victory. In *Stevens v. Tamai*, a unanimous panel of the U.S. Court of Appeals for the Federal Circuit reversed the decision of the U.S. Patent and Trademark Office, Board of Patent Appeals and Interferences, which had awarded judgment against Marshall Gerstein's client, Sanford, L.P., in an interference proceeding involving a hand-held correction tape dispenser. The circuit court ruled that the board incorrectly awarded priority of invention to the plaintiff, Seed Rubber Company, because the company had "failed to establish a proper claim to the priority benefit of its original Japanese patent application."

Recent successes like these landed the firm in 39th place in *Intellectual Property Today* magazine's March 2005 ranking of the nation's 390 top patent firms.

Unfortunately, not all the firm's rankings are so rosy. In *Chicago Lawyer*'s 2004 Diversity Survey, Marshall Gerstein ranked dead last in the percentage of female partners among the 64 Illinois law firms with 20 or more attorneys that participated in the magazine's poll. While women accounted for 18.6 percent of the partners at these 64 mid-size and large firms, they only comprised 2.6 percent of the total at Marshall Gerstein. (The second-to-last place firm, Segal McCambridge Singer & Mahoney, still had a rate more than three times higher than Marshall Gerstein's, at 8.3 percent.) However, as an IP boutique with a heavily science-centered client base, Marshall Gerstein practices in an area that does not traditionally attract large numbers of women, so the firm's hiring and promotion practices aren't necessarily to blame for its poor diversity ranking.

On the lighter side, at least one of the firm's partners claims – and proves – that the firm allows enough "down time" to pursue such outside interests as, say, having a family or writing a novel. Thomas A. Miller, an engineer-turned-patent-attorney has been compared, with the publication of his novel *Snow White's Lies*, with such other successful lawyer-writers as Chicago's own Scott Turow.

GETTING HIRED

It's not enough to be a lawyer to practice at Marshall Gerstein. You need also to be an engineer or a scientist. Because technology is essential to this IP boutique's practice, all entry-level candidates must take the U.S. Patent and Trademark Office bar exam and hold undergraduate degrees in engineering, chemistry or one of the biological sciences. And if you've got an advanced degree in medicine, molecular biology or chemistry or prior work experience in a technical field, you've got a leg up. Beyond technical criteria, the firm looks for "strong writing ability and an excellent academic background." Moot court participation and clerkship experience are additional assets.

For laterals, the firm is especially interested in attorneys with patent prosecution experience in computer or mechanical engineering and seasoned lawyers with at least three years of patent litigation under their belt.

Mayer, Brown, Rowe & Maw LLP

190 South LaSalle Street
Chicago, IL 60603-3441
Phone: (312) 782-0600
www.mayerbrownrowe.com

LOCATIONS

Charlotte, NC • Chicago, IL • Houston, TX • Los Angeles, CA • New York, NY • Palo Alto, CA • Washington, DC • Brussels • Cologne • Frankfurt • London • Manchester • Paris

MAJOR DEPARTMENTS & PRACTICES

Bankruptcy & Reorganization • Corporate & Securities • Employee Benefits • Environmental • Finance • Global Government & Trade • Intellectual Property • Litigation • Real Estate • Tax Controversy • Tax Transactions • Trust Estates & Foundations

THE STATS

No. of attorneys:
 firm-wide: 1,300
 Chicago: 474
No. of offices: 13
Summer associate offers:
 firm-wide: 90 out of 90 (2004)
 Chicago: 44 out of 44 (2004)
Managing Partner: Debora de Hoyos
Hiring Partner: J. Thomas Mullen

UPPERS
- Firm prestige
- Associate autonomy

DOWNERS
- Opacity surrounding partnership prospects
- High billable-hour requirement

NOTABLE PERKS
- "Top-notch" pastries and bagels for breakfast
- Monthly cocktail parties
- Six weeks paid paternity leave
- Free dinner and cab fare after 8 pm

BASE SALARY

Chicago, IL (2005)
1st year: $125,000
2nd year: $135,000
3rd year: $150,000
4th year: $165,000
5th year: $185,000
6th year: $195,000
7th year: $205,000
Summer associate: $2,400/week

EMPLOYMENT CONTACT

Ms. Laura Kanter
Attorney Recruitment Administrator
Phone: (312) 701-7003
Fax: (312) 701-7711
E-mail: lkanter@mayerbrownrowe.com

THE SCOOP

Over a hundred years ago, Mayer Brown helped Bank of America and Sears Roebuck incorporate. Like those early clients, the firm itself has expanded into something of an empire. The transatlantic merger that resulted in the creation of Mayer, Brown, Rowe & Maw in 2002 also created one of the 10 largest law firms in the world – a 1,300-attorney firm that represents one-third of all the banks in the United States and well over half of the companies on the Fortune 500. With close to 500 lawyers, the Chicago office stands as the biggest law practice in the city and, established in 1881, the oldest branch of the firm.

Given the firm's heft, it's not surprising that Mayer Brown handles top-shelf matters on a daily basis. This September, nine lawyers from the firm closed a $191 million, all-cash deal by which client Capital One Finance Corporation acquired Onyx Acceptance Corporation. As a result of the transaction, Capital One's auto finance division will expand exponentially in its geographical presence and its product offerings. In a complex deal finalized in May 2004, lawyers from Mayer Brown's corporate, tax, benefits, real estate and labor departments collaborated on the creation of a partnership between client ProLogis, Inc. and several companies run by Eaton Vance Management, as well as the partnership's subsequent acquisition of Keystone Property Trust for $1.6 billion. The closing added millions of square feet and several new markets to the distribution facilities and services managed by ProLogis and Eaton Vance.

GETTING HIRED

Mayer Brown associates consider their firm to be among the most selective in Chicago. Pedigree matters a great deal. "The firm is definitely infatuated with the blue-blood Ivy Leaguers," says one insider. According to another, "The firm tends to put much greater stock in where a candidate went to school than how well that person did at school." Nevertheless, says a midlevel associate, "high GPA is extremely important, with personality somewhat important but not nearly at the same level as GPA." Even so, Mayer Brown values well-rounded candidates. "I believe the firm is strict about its grade cut-off," offers a first-year, "but aside from grades, I think we look for individuals with personalities, who can work well with clients and other attorneys, and who offer more than book-smarts." In the words of a litigator, "The firm wants the best of the best, and a certain self-selection tends to weed out those who are looking for something less thoroughbred than Mayer Brown."

OUR SURVEY SAYS

As a group, associates at Mayer Brown enjoy working at this top-shelf firm – if only they could work just a bit less. A senior associate raves, "I am very, very pleased with Mayer Brown. The people are great and the work is absolutely top-notch. But for a very short list of Wall Street firms, I think the work that comes across my desk on a day-to-day basis is as interesting as at any firm in the country." Attorneys like one another, but the focus is on work, not play. One source describes the firm as "friendly and relatively laid-back, but it is understood that you have a responsibility to do quality work and bill your hours."

In fact, most insiders find the hours requirements at Mayer Brown fairly rigorous. One associate notes that the "expectation is that midlevel/senior associates are billing at least 2,200 hours (more is better) with the obvious result that a lot of time needs to be spent at the office. Also, if there is work that needs to be done, working late hours and weekends is expected." To some, the problem is one of predictability: "Hours ebb and flow with the demands and deadlines of the case/deal. Some weeks it's a strictly 9-to-6 affair, other weeks may require all-nighters." Many realize that the grass is probably not any greener elsewhere, though. "I work at a big law firm," acknowledges a Chi-town lawyer. "I'd rather not be here so much, but I can't imagine that it would be significantly different elsewhere."

Mayer Brown provides so much formal training that associates can't possibly take advantage of all of it. According to one inside source, "The firm provides a good amount of training during your first year, not only legal training, but also effective life skills to manage stress and succeed in your career. The firm also pairs new associates with a partner advisor who serves as a mentor and makes sure the associate gets meaningful work and is not falling through the cracks." Some say that the training could be "more geared to specific practice areas." On an informal level, some initiative is required: "It really is up to the individual associate to find senior attorneys that they feel comfortable with and can serve as informal mentors. As almost everyone here is friendly and accessible, the pickings are endless."

When it comes to payday, Mayer Brown operates primarily on a lockstep system, with bonuses tied to hours. Some appreciate the predictability; others would prefer less rigidity. The firm says that a 25-percent discretionary bonus rewards teamwork and subjective contributions, but some associates aren't convinced. "Compensation (including bonuses) is highly tied to billable-hours)," complains a midlevel associate. "I would prefer a system that recognizes the importance of non-billable work (such as pro bono, training, administrative)." Mayer Brown reports that it revised its bonus consideration criteria in 2004 to include up to 60 hours of pro bono work toward hours bonus thresholds.

McDermott Will & Emery

227 West Monroe Street
Suite 4400
Chicago, IL 60606
Phone: (312) 372-2000
www.mwe.com

LOCATIONS

Boston, MA
Chicago, IL
Irvine, CA
Los Angeles, CA
Miami, FL
New York, NY
Palo Alto, CA
San Diego, CA
Washington, DC
Brussels
Dusseldorf
London
Milan
Munich
Rome

MAJOR DEPARTMENTS & PRACTICES

Corporate
Employee Benefits
Health
Intellectual Property
Private Client
Regulation & Government Affairs
Tax
Trial

THE STATS

No. of attorneys:
  firm-wide: 1,000
  Chicago: 251
No. of offices: 15
Summer associate offers:
  firm-wide: 51 out of 56 (2004)
  Chicago: 6 out of 6 (2004)
Chairman: Harvey W. Freishtat
Hiring Partner: Linda M. Doyle

UPPERS
- Big-firm talent with "vast network of experience"
- Ability to work with different partners

DOWNERS
- Excessive focus on bottom line
- High ratio of attorneys to support staff

NOTABLE PERKS
- Bar review reimbursement
- Certain moving expenses
- Judicial clerkship bonus

BASE SALARY
Chicago, IL (2005)
1st year: $125,000
2nd year: $135,000
3rd year: $150,000
4th year: $165,000
5th year: $185,000
6th year: $195,000
Summer associate: $2,400/week

EMPLOYMENT CONTACT
Ms. Karen Mortell
Legal Recruiting Manager
Phone: (312) 984-7784
Fax: (312) 984-7700
E-mail: kmortell@mwe.com

THE SCOOP

Last spring, McDermott Will & Emery lawyers won a landmark case on behalf of the Illinois Clean Energy Community Foundation when the U.S. District Court for the Northern District of Illinois invalidated a state law, finding it unconstitutional. The statute in question was intended to reduce the state budget deficit and would have required the foundation to hand over more than half of its endowment, to the tune of $125 million. The state argued that the foundation's monies were public funds, and thus available for the state's use as a "contribution" to the deficit reduction plan. The court disagreed with this argument, and ruled that the law violated both procedural and substantive due process rights. On the corporate side of the firm, in May 2004, McDermott-Chicago advised Hillcrest HealthCare System on the sale of 10 of its 14 hospitals located in Oklahoma. The buyer in the $281.2 million transaction was Ardent Health Services, a for-profit health care system based in Nashville, Tenn.

Now a 1,000-lawyer international firm, McDermott Will & Emery's first office opened in Chicago. Launched in 1934 by Edward H. McDermott and William M. Emery (Howard A. Will came along in 1941), the firm originally concentrated solely on tax law. As the firm branched out to 14 additional cities, its practice evolved, and today the 250 attorneys in the Windy City office engage in a diverse practice that excels in everything from securities law to antitrust to government relations.

GETTING HIRED

Most insiders agree that it's tough to get hired at McDermott Will & Emery. Like other top firms, McDermott looks for an "excellent academic record and superior writing skills." While some feel that "the firm has gotten too caught up in top-10 schools and is ignoring amazing candidates which come through from schools outside of the top 10," others say that recruiters favor "personality over pedigree." "Personality, work experience and general polish seem to be highly valued," says one associate. "Fit is very important."

If you are selected for an interview, don't expect to receive an offer right away. Sources say that candidates go through one to three callback interviews, followed by a final internal group evaluation. Only if a candidate passes all of these steps do they receive an offer.

OUR SURVEY SAYS

If you're looking for a great party, you've come to the wrong spot. But if you want hands-on experience working with reputable and knowledgeable attorneys, McDermott Will & Emery may be the place for you. Opinions vary as to the firm culture, but no one describes it as a fraternity house. Some say the firm is "friendly," with "a generally good working environment," while others complain that "over the last couple of years, it has gotten extremely formal and uptight." In any event, the general consensus is that attorneys work hard, resulting in "not a lot of water-cooler talk around the office." Still, "everyone is very friendly and respectful." In some departments, you'll even find laid-back, "cool Midwestern people."

One other thing is certain: "The firm is extraordinarily cost-conscious." "There is a perception that they 'nickel and dime' you for everything," says one associate. This doesn't mean that salaries are low. On the contrary, most associates feel that their "compensation is current with what is typical in the marketplace." Bonuses are tied to hourly requirements and can be tough to obtain, particularly because pro bono and training hours count for bonus purposes only after associates meet their yearly requirements. But most associates feel the benefits and perks could be better. According to one lawyer, "The firm eliminates programs that make associate life better in the name of cost-cutting. There seems to be too much focus on the bottom line and not enough focus on making sure that the associates are happy." "We used to have bagel/donut Mondays, but that was eliminated to save costs," laments another insider.

Views about hours are also inconsistent. Some consider the hours "totally manageable" and "current with what is expected in the marketplace." One senior associate even says that "McDermott is among the most livable of the large Chicago shops for associates." Nevertheless, the firm's minimum billable requirement is 2,000 hours per year, which many consider "too high" and unattainable, especially because "there is often a very tight limit placed on hours for individual assignments, resulting in unbilled time." Luckily, however, "there is no formal face time required in the office." More good news: the firm cultivates a "free-market environment," which allows associates some flexibility to work with partners of their choice.

The level of formal training at McDermott varies according to department. One associate says that his department does not provide any sort of training program, while another says that McDermott "has recently improved and increased the amount of formal training within the corporate department," which now has "excellent" training sessions. Unfortunately, even where the firm does offer education programs, some feel they are "difficult to attend due to billing requirements."

The level of informal training tends to vary by department as well. "Upper-level associates and lower-level partners in my department are willing to give their time in informal mentoring," says one attorney. But "it really depends on who you work for and the type of case. If you have a good relationship with a partner and the work allows for it, this can be good. Otherwise it could be absolutely nonexistent."

McGuireWoods LLP

77 West Wacker, Suite 4100
Chicago, IL 60601
Phone: (312) 849-8100
www.mcguirewoods.com

LOCATIONS
Richmond, VA (HQ)
Atlanta, GA
Baltimore, MD
Charlotte, NC
Charlottesville, VA
Chicago, IL
Jacksonville, FL
New York, NY
Norfolk, VA
Pittsburgh, PA
Tysons Corner, VA
Washington, DC
Almaty
Brussels

MAJOR DEPARTMENTS & PRACTICES
Commercial Litigation
Complex Products Liability & Mass Tort Litigation
Corporate Services
Financial Services
Health Care
Labor & Employment
Real Estate & Environmental Services
Taxation & Employee Benefits

THE STATS
No. of attorneys:
  firm-wide: 700+
  Chicago: 155
No. of offices: 14
Summer associate offers:
  firm-wide: 33 out of 35 (2004)
  Chicago: 12 out of 13 (2004)
Chairman: Robert L. Burrus Jr.
Hiring Partner: Jacquelyn E. Stone

UPPERS
- Top-of-the-market compensation
- High-quality work, attorneys and resources

DOWNERS
- Post-merger frustration and anxiety
- Office culture becoming more formal

NOTABLE PERKS
- Skybox access for Bulls games
- Reimbursement of cell phone bill (up to $100)
- Bar expenses and substantial continuing education stipend
- Free breakfast on Fridays

BASE SALARY
Chicago, IL (2005)
1st year: $125,000
Summer associate: $2,400/week

EMPLOYMENT CONTACT
Ms. Kristina Snell
Attorney Recruiting Manager
Fax: (312) 849-3690
E-mail: ksnell@mcguirewoods.com

THE SCOOP

In July 2003, the Chicago office of the Richmond-based firm, McGuireWoods, merged with the 155-lawyer shop of Ross & Hardies. The combined firm now comprises 14 offices, primarily concentrated in the mid-Atlantic region, but reaching as far as Belgium and Kazakhstan. In addition, the merger created one of the country's largest labor and employment practices, while bolstering McGuireWoods's litigation and corporate departments. The Second City branch of McGuireWoods also boasts a renowned health care practice group, the seventh-largest in the nation. This fall, the firm hosted its second annual Hospital and Health Care Systems Conference in Chicago, bringing together legal specialists and clients to discuss ways to improve hospital performance.

Early in 2004, a team of litigators from McGuireWoods-Chicago represented the Ohio Valley Coal Company and Robert E. Murray, one of the company's executives, in a defamation lawsuit against *The Akron Beacon Journal* and several related defendants, including the newspaper's owner, Knight-Ridder, Inc. The suit, which seeks $1 billion in damages, arose out of an article in the paper in which the writer made statements regarding Murray's health and character and allegedly falsified comments made by Murray in an interview. After three years of litigation, the Ohio Court of Appeals ruled in favor of the McGuireWoods team this past February, reversing a lower court's grant of summary judgment for defendants. The court held that the statements in the article were defamatory per se and, accordingly, the action could proceed to trial.

GETTING HIRED

The firm's national reputation has led to ever-rising standards, associates report. McGuireWoods "has become more competitive in hiring and has changed its policy on interviewing," reports a senior associate in Chicago. According to one insider, the firm "will now only interview at top schools." But there are no tricks or surprises in the firm's hiring criteria, associates say. The firm is looking for good grades from good schools. Indeed, it's "very hard to get looked at here if you are not at a top law school," says one midlevel associate.

OUR SURVEY SAYS

The Chicago office of McGuireWoods has been experiencing some post-merger pains. According to one associate, "It is a time of transition in the Chicago office (due to the recent merger with Ross & Hardies), with a lot of factions within the firm trying to vie for associate alliances." The merger has left a lot of former R&H attorneys less than pleased with the results. As the once "laid-back" environment of Ross & Hardies combines with the "more formal" atmosphere of McGuireWoods, "the resulting culture is anybody's guess." But many Chicago associates already see fallout from this culture clash, complaining that their office is "becoming more uptight by the day." "Over the past few years," adds a senior associate, "the culture has become slightly more stressful as the firm has placed a stronger emphasis on billable-hours."

Some associates also complain that the merger and ongoing "power struggle" between firm factions leaves them feeling somewhat insecure. "I like the people I currently work for," says one Chicago lawyer, "but there have been many changes since the merger and the future is uncertain." Another source agrees: "I also think there is a lot of fear among associates and partners as to whether layoffs are on the horizon." McGuireWoods notes that the firm is putting into effect a 2005–2006 strategic growth plan for the Chicago office.

Those who can tolerate the increased formality and stress, however, say that McGuireWoods has much to offer. In addition to an impressive client roster, the firm provides "great diversity in terms of [practice] areas and in terms of tasks," according to one attorney. Most Chicago associates also praise the guidance they receive from more senior attorneys. "I have had great mentoring and informal training from the partners I work for," says a litigation associate. Although one lawyer sees "more distance and formality between partners and associates at McGuireWoods" than there had been at the former Ross & Hardies, another attorney reports that "partners and senior associates are always willing to take time to provide additional guidance on an issue."

In general, insiders' negative comments seem triggered more by the merger itself than by unhappiness with individual attorneys or workloads. According to one Chicago lawyer, "On a firm level, associates receive full disclosure of firm financials and other sensitive information on a regular basis. On an individual level, my experience is that partners treat the associates with great respect." Yet even in this area, some of the lingering ill will bleeds over. "Post-merger, most partners are worried about their piece of the pie, their office size and so on," grumbles one source. "Associates are fungible billing units."

The hours, respondents say, are typical for a big firm, though partners appear to be flexible about the specific hours associates work. The 1,950 billable-hours requirement, which includes approved pro bono, is "on par with all other major firms." Still, says one wistful attorney, "it would be great to see a reduced-hour track." One thing that virtually no one complains about: the compensation. As one contented midlevel associate says, "Let's face it – the money's sick."

"I have had great mentoring and informal training from the partners I work for."

- *McGuireWoods LLP associate*

Michael Best & Friedrich LLP

100 East Wisconsin Avenue
Suite 3300
Milwaukee, WI 53202
Phone: (414) 271-6560
www.michaelbest.com

LOCATIONS
Milwaukee, WI (HQ)
Chicago, IL
Lehigh Valley, PA
Madison, WI
Manitowoc, WI
Waukesha, WI

MAJOR DEPARTMENTS & PRACTICES
Business
Employment Relations
Health Care
Intellectual Property
Land & Resources
Litigation
Tax
Wealth Planning

THE STATS
No. of attorneys:
  firm-wide: 308
  Milwaukee: 141
  Chicago: 59
  Madison: 61
No. of offices: 6
Summer associate offers:
  firm-wide: 10 out of 11 (2004)
  Milwaukee: 4 out of 4 (2004)
  Chicago: 1 out of 1 (2004)
  Madison: 5 out of 6 (2004)
Managing Partner: Thomas E. Obenberger
Management Committee Chair: Tod B. Linstroth
Hiring Attorneys:
  Milwaukee: Katherine W. Schill and Alexander P. Fraser
  Chicago: Sarah E. Swartzmeyer and Jeffrey S. Torosian
  Madison: John C. Scheller and Amy O. Bruchs

UPPERS
- Relaxed atmosphere and "family-friendly" hours
- Lots of responsibility and opportunity for client contact

DOWNERS
- Too much non-billable work
- Pro bono doesn't count toward billable-hours

NOTABLE PERKS
- First-time homebuyer program
- Free tickets to local plays, concerts and sporting events
- Progressive flex-time program
- 12 weeks paid family leave

BASE SALARY

Madison and Milwaukee, WI (2005)
1st year: $105,000
Summer associate: $1,850/week

Chicago, IL (2005)
1st year: $115,000
Summer associate: $2,200/week

EMPLOYMENT CONTACTS

Milwaukee (3L and laterals) and Chicago (1L – 3L and laterals)
Ms. Joyce M. Nordman
Recruitment Director
Phone: (414) 271-6560
Fax: (414) 277-6656
E-mail: jmnordman@michaelbest.com

Milwaukee (1L – 2L)
Ms. Tracy L. Dati
Recruitment Coordinator
Phone: (414) 271-6560
Fax: (414) 277-6656
E-mail: tldati@michaelbest.com

Madison (1L – 3L and laterals)
Ms. Liina A. Keerd
Recruitment Coordinator
Phone: (608) 257-3501
Fax: (608) 283-2275
E-mail: lakeerd@michaelbest.com

THE SCOOP

Michael Best owes its existence to Edward Ryan, a trial lawyer who ultimately became chief justice of the Wisconsin Supreme Court, and Matthew Hale Carpenter, a young attorney who later served as a U.S. senator. The two set up shop in Milwaukee in 1848, and their practice has bloomed into a multi-state, six-office firm made up of more than 300 legal professionals. In October 2004, the firm announced the hiring of 18 new associates in its Wisconsin offices. Michael Best's overarching practice areas subdivide into several industry and specialty groups, which include communications, energy, international law and venture capital, among others. The firm has attracted banner clients such as Sears, Roebuck & Co., which relies upon Michael Best for counsel on intellectual property matters, as reported in *The National Law Journal*'s 2004 list of "Who Represents Corporate America." The firm's IP group, with more than 80 members, is one of the largest in the Midwest.

Unsurprisingly, given its Midwestern location, the firm has built a flourishing agribusiness practice. This highly interdisciplinary area assists clients such as Wholesome Dairy, Smithfield Beef and Seneca Foods Corporation with everything from land use permits to biotechnology licensing. Another of the firm's prominent practices serves the health care industry, advising insurance companies, hospitals, clinics and laboratories on a wide range of corporate and litigation matters. In 2004, Michael Best hosted several seminars on salient issues and developments in the law; the subjects of the colloquia included worker's compensation, asset protection for medical professionals, and federal and state tax laws.

GETTING HIRED

When it comes to getting hired, say firm insiders, "personality is very important." "The applicant needs to be interesting and needs to get along well with people," says a litigator. The firm also "emphasizes a strong academic background," and looks at "community involvement and work ethic." According to a midlevel associate, "While personality is a huge factor in hiring decisions, it is also clear that grades (and pedigree, for laterals) matter quite a bit as well." Moreover, she adds, "The firm takes its hiring practices very seriously. Every person who comes in contact with a recruit has the ability – and in fact is encouraged – to comment on the candidate." Given that practice, "it always helps to have a friend on the inside."

Although one source suggests that "the firm should really work on hiring and retaining more minorities," another notes that "Milwaukee is a tough environment for minority recruitment."

OUR SURVEY SAYS

Michael Best attorneys generally don't mind the hours they work. As a junior transactional associate says, "There are times when I work more than I would like, but I am usually able to ease up a bit after those work-intensive times." The major complaint among associates is that the firm requires 400 "non-billable-hours." The minimum billable level is 1,850 hours, which many associates feel is "fine," but the additional non-billable requirement isn't too popular. (According to the firm, the non-billable requirement includes time spent for CLE/training programs, pro bono activities, client development events, bar functions, practice group meetings and the like.) At least one lawyer is "a bit surprised that a 'Milwaukee firm' is as conscious about the number of hours each associate bills each month as this firm is," noting that "a monthly report is circulated where every person's hours and receivables are listed." Another issue is that "pro bono work does not count toward billable work." Despite being "unwilling to discuss a meaningful way of counting pro bono hours," the firm "expects a high commitment to various pro bono activities."

The firm "sponsors a number of in-house CLE programs," and the formal training offered is "practical and very helpful," but "formal training is often replaced by 'on-the-job' training and guidance from a partner or senior associate." The firm has a formal mentoring program, and insiders say that "partners and senior associates here are overwhelmingly willing to field questions and provide guidance – you just have to ask." One associate suggests that there is room for improvement in the system for feedback, since associates may feel "blindsided by several poor ratings" in their annual review.

When it comes to money, "We are among the highest-paid associates in the surrounding area," boasts one insider, "so there is little to complain about." Others say that their salaries "are slightly lower than other large firms," but feel that "the work-schedule flexibility, the work quality and the wonderful people … make up for the slightly lower salary." But one litigator argues that Michael Best hasn't achieved the right balance since, despite lower salaries, the firm still "requires hours like those big Chicago firms." Even though most attorneys feel that they are "paid a nice base salary," a few voice complaints about the bonus system, which is "entirely quantity-based."

An experienced attorney describes the firm environment as "formal, professional and focused." Associates generally agree that the atmosphere is "relaxed" and "lawyers here certainly socialize together." A "large number of the partners are young," and the firm "sponsors and supports sports leagues and social events that promote associate and partner interaction outside of the office." A few attorneys worry that the culture is changing and one lawyer laments that the firm "does not seem to be as friendly and laid-back as it used to be." While Michael Best can be a "terminally cheery" place to work, at least one attorney feels that "there is so much pressure on billing and hours that people keep to themselves more than [they] used to."

Miller, Canfield, Paddock and Stone, P.L.C.

150 West Jefferson, Suite 2500
Detroit, MI 48226-4415
Phone: (313) 963-6420
www.millercanfield.com

LOCATIONS
Detroit, MI (HQ)
Ann Arbor, MI
Grand Rapids, MI
Howell, MI
Kalamazoo, MI
Lansing, MI
Monroe, MI
New York, NY
Pensacola, FL
Troy, MI
Washington, DC
Gdansk, Poland
Katowice, Poland
Windsor, Ontario (Canada)

MAJOR DEPARTMENTS & PRACTICES
Bankruptcy
Business & Finance
Environmental & Regulatory
Federal Tax & Employee Benefits
Financial Institutions & Transactions
Health Care
Immigration
Intellectual Property & Information Technology
International Business
Labor & Employment
Litigation
Personal Services
Public Law
Real Estate

THE STATS
No. of attorneys:
  firm-wide: 349
  Detroit: 148
  Ann Arbor: 36
  Grand Rapids: 18
  Kalamazoo: 36
  Lansing: 16
  Troy: 50
No. of offices: 14
Summer associate offers:
  firm-wide: 7 out of 8 (2004)
Chief Executive Officer: Thomas W. Linn
Hiring Partner: Deborah W. Thompson

UPPERS
- Great people and environment
- High level of responsibility

DOWNERS
- "Big fish-small pond mentality"
- Lack of training

NOTABLE PERKS
- Free on-site parking
- Bar membership dues
- Subsidized cell phone expenses
- Gym subsidy

BASE SALARY
Detroit, MI (2005)
1st year: $95,000*
Summer associate: $1,800/week

*Includes $5,000 starting bonus

EMPLOYMENT CONTACT
Ms. Mary Wassel
Manager of Professional Recruitment
Phone: (313) 496-7685
Fax: (313) 496-7500
E-mail: wassel@millercanfield.com

THE SCOOP

Miller, Canfield, Paddock and Stone has been a fixture in Detroit since 1852. Now, with over 300 attorneys, the firm has offices in several Michigan cities, along with branches in the Big Apple, Washington, D.C., and Pensacola, Fla. During the 1990s, the firm gained an international foothold by opening three offices in Poland, and in 2002 Miller Canfield added an office in Windsor, Ontario.

For the last 25 years, Miller Canfield has been ranked the No.-1 bond counsel in Michigan by Thomson Financial. With 26 attorneys, the firm's public law group is the largest such group in the Great Lakes State. In 2004, *Chambers USA* ranked Miller Canfield the No.-1 firm in Michigan in the areas of banking and finance, employment and general commercial litigation. Miller Canfield also snagged the second-place slot for its corporate/M&A and real estate practice groups. Such high ratings are not surprising, given that the firm represents eight of the top-10 Fortune 500 companies.

Based in the automotive industry capital, the firm has a long history of representing automobile manufacturers and suppliers. Firm attorneys serve as sole discovery counsel for all Daimler-Chrysler Corp. non-airbag product liability litigation in America. In fact, Miller Canfield has developed a unique practice niche in corporate discovery management. Using a specialized team of lawyers and support staff (and a 10,000-square-foot "war room" in its Kalamazoo office), the firm tackles complex discovery issues on behalf of big-name clients such as the National Collegiate Athletic Association and Comerica Bank. The firm is currently supporting lead counsel Cravath, Swaine & Moore in a complex, discovery-driven patent-infringement lawsuit filed by IBM Corp. against Compuware Corp.

In 2004, a team of Miller Canfield attorneys represented the Coalition of Independent Filmmakers to settle a dispute with the Motion Picture Association of America. The entertainment giants had been engaged in a two-year battle over the so-called "screener ban," which restricted film distributors' ability to determine the dissemination of promotional screeners. The parties settled after Miller Canfield won a court order directing the MPAA to lift the ban.

GETTING HIRED

Getting into the largest law firm in Michigan's largest city is a tall order. Because "turnover is relatively low" and entering classes relatively small, there's not a lot of wiggle room for would-be Miller Canfield lawyers. "Among the crop of Detroit-area applicants, it's extremely competitive," says a first-year associate. According to another insider, the degree of competitiveness "depends on the associate's school. People from top law schools will find it fairly easy to be hired. Not so for less prestigious institutions, unless you're at the top of your class."

In terms of personality, the firm looks for "smart, interesting people who work hard." It helps to be "friendly and outgoing." Conversely, in this congenial environment, it'll hurt your cause to act "snobby or pretentious."

OUR SURVEY SAYS

Aspects of Miller Canfield life that please associates include early responsibility, interesting projects and the opportunity to work with a "diverse group of people" who are both friendly and smart. A junior litigator gushes, "This job surpasses all my expectations for my first year at a law firm. I look forward to going to work every day.... I work with smart, interesting people and get challenging and exciting assignments." Another insider offers a similarly glowing review: "In the public law department, the work is extraordinarily dynamic. Public finance is the central focus, but clients also seek general counsel-type work that involves a broad menu of policy-related work, even for the newest associates." At least one associate, however, would like to see the firm become more "competitive outside the state."

Sources agree that the firm's culture is "very friendly," if not exactly "laid-back." The degree to which attorneys socialize together seems to depend on both the office and the practice group. According to one associate, there are "plenty of spontaneous happy hours and informal practice-group get-togethers, but not so much where it gets annoying." Another insider describes an open-door environment: "If a door is closed, you can bet there's an important phone call going on."

Most sources praise their relationships with partners, some of whom are reportedly "fantastic." "Firm-wide," says one lawyer, "associates are treated with respect." "The crazy partner thing is a rarity here," adds another associate. "If folks are unreasonable, everyone knows it." Partners often work closely with new associates, which can be "very cool." In fact, say insiders, there are "great mentors at this place, especially if you're willing to forge the relationships."

But forge them you must; associates need to take initiative to get the most guidance. Otherwise, "expect to learn by doing," cautions one insider. Asked about the quality of formal training, a litigator responds, "Training is as formal or informal as you want it to be. If you want help and instruction, you ask for it and it is given. If you don't feel you need it, you finish writing the brief or the motion or the memo and you get feedback." This "baptism-by-fire" method doesn't satisfy everyone. One transactional lawyer laments the limited instruction, noting that "training is so important, especially in a highly specialized or complex field."

Although one young associate boasts, "This is a lifestyle firm," others disagree. "The 'promise' of having a balanced life is a bit misleading," claims one lawyer. "I feel I work a lot of hours for a mid-sized firm." Another insider who also reports working long hours shrugs, "But this comes with the territory in terms of working for a firm."

Associates are not of one mind when it comes to money. One overworked attorney grumbles, "I could work at a much larger firm and make more money billing these kinds of hours." Others complain that there is "too much compression between [salary] levels." But several insiders find the pay appropriate for the market. According to one associate, compensation is "competitive with the other five or 10 major Detroit firms," while another says, "The money is good, especially in a state like Michigan where cost of living is so low."

Miller, Johnson, Snell & Cummiskey, P.L.C.

Calder Plaza Building
250 Monroe Avenue, NW
Suite 800
Grand Rapids, MI 49503-2250
Phone: (616) 831-1700
www.millerjohnson.com

LOCATIONS

Grand Rapids, MI (HQ)
Kalamazoo, MI

MAJOR DEPARTMENTS & PRACTICES

Administrative
Banking
Bankruptcy
Business Counsel
Communications
Corporate & Securities
Education
Employment & Labor
Environmental
Finance
Health Care
Intellectual Property
Litigation & Dispute Resolution
Probate & Estate Planning
Real Estate
Tax
Workers' Compensation & Employee Benefits

THE STATS

No. of attorneys:
   firm-wide: 96
   Grand Rapids: 82
No. of offices: 2
Managing Partner: Jon G. March
Hiring Partner: Alan C. Schwartz

NOTABLE PERKS

- Firm pays 100 percent of premiums for medical/dental insurance
- Bar review/exam expenses and reasonable moving expenses
- Federal, state and local bar association dues
- Free parking

BASE SALARY

All offices (2005)
1st year: $85,000*
Summer associate: $1,500/week

*Includes $5,000 graduation bonus

EMPLOYMENT CONTACT

Ms. Michelle D. Smith
Recruitment & Development Manager
Phone: (616) 831-1866
Fax: (616) 988-1866
E-mail: smithm@mjsc.com

THE SCOOP

Despite its relatively small size, Miller, Johnson, Snell & Cummiskey is a veritable jack-of-all-trades. From its home base in Grand Rapids, Mich., where it employs more than 80 lawyers, Miller Johnson provides legal services in a diverse array of practice areas; the firm advises individual clients, major corporations and entities of all sizes in between on matters concerning adoption, securities, employee benefits, products liability and health care, to name just a few. Miller Johnson was founded in 1959, and the firm's second office, in Kalamazoo, opened for business 20 years later.

Many of Miller Johnson's specialty groups span several disciplines, bringing together litigators and transactional attorneys as well as tax and labor lawyers. For example, the construction group can counsel clients, from architects to financiers, on all aspects of a building project. A team in this area might handle the establishment of a joint venture, the procurement of applicable permits and licenses, and the litigation of a contract dispute, all related to one construction project or for a single client in this area. By the same token, attorneys at Miller Johnson gain experience in any number of fields – a litigation associate might work on aviation, family law, manufacturing and energy matters simultaneously.

In recent years, the firm has landed numerous prestigious clients, both in and out of the state's bread-and-butter industry, automobiles. A representative list includes Benteler Automotive, Gordon Food Service and Steelcase, the furniture manufacturer. Indeed, in *Corporate Board Member*'s 2003 edition of "Leaders in 50 Metro Areas," the magazine ranked Miller Johnson as the third-best firm in Grand Rapids, ahead of much larger Michigan firms such as Miller, Canfield, Paddock and Stone (which boasts more than 300 attorneys) and Dickinson Wright (which employs about 200). But while the firm grows, it also stays true to its small-town roots: for example, Miller Johnson remains small enough that it releases announcements not only when it lands a new big-name partner, but even when it hires a new associate.

Even though the firm is located outside Michigan's capital, a number of its lawyers have risen to positions of state-wide prominence. In 2003, for example, partner Dustin P. Ordway was appointed the chair of the Membership Committee of the State Bar's Environmental Law Section. That same year, Ordway was also elected secretary of the Alternative Dispute Resolution Section of the Grand Rapids Bar Association. The Michigan Occupational Safety and Health Administration's book, *Occupational Safety and Health: A Guide For Michigan Employers*, was written by Miller

Johnson partner Brent Rector, whom the agency calls "the" source for Michigan managers regarding health and safety laws. The firm also reaches beyond its home state to have an international presence. As a member of Meritas, the international alliance of nearly 200 business law firms, the firm offers clients the ability to access legal service in more than 50 countries worldwide.

Miller Johnson strives to make its environment "a place to enjoy," not merely a place to work. The firm has a relatively low billable requirement of 1,800 hours per year; and most associates who meet that target earn performance-based bonuses. Miller Johnson prides itself on a high level of community involvement as well as high-quality client service. Its people, according to the firm, "live in the real world, not inside dusty law books." As lawyers, performers, pilots, coaches, Big Brothers and Big Sisters, they maintain active lives outside the office. And this emphasis on community emanates from the top. In 1982, the State Bar of Michigan established the annual John W. Cummiskey Award in honor of one of the firm's founders and in recognition of his lifelong commitment to public service. Each year, the State Bar presents the prestigious award to a Michigan lawyer who has made significant pro bono contributions.

GETTING HIRED

If you've got a sense of humor, an interest in your community and a desire to excel, Miller Johnson might just be the place for you. According to the firm, "We take the practice of law, but not ourselves, seriously." The firm values diverse backgrounds and considers personal and family interests an asset, "not a threat." Miller Johnson's goal is to recruit and train "excellent" lawyers "without stifling their personalities." Accordingly, the firm's hiring criteria are fairly broad and include "superior personal qualities and academic performance," with "extra consideration" for extracurricular activities, like moot court and law review, as well as prior work experience.

Much Shelist Freed Denenberg Ament & Rubenstein, P.C.

191 North Wacker Drive
Suite 1800
Chicago, IL 60606
Phone: (312) 521-2000
www.muchlaw.com

LOCATION

Chicago, IL

MAJOR DEPARTMENTS & PRACTICES

Bankruptcy, Reorganization & Creditors' Rights
Business Litigation
Class-action Litigation
Corporate Finance & Securities
Corporate Law
E-Commerce & Internet Practice
Employee Benefits
Environmental Law
Health Care
Intellectual Property
Labor & Employment
Real Estate
Secured Lending
Taxation & Business Planning
Wealth Transfer & Succession Planning

THE STATS

No. of attorneys: 81
No. of offices: 1
Chair of Management Committee: David T. Brown

NOTABLE PERKS

- Matching 401(k) plan
- Profit-sharing plan
- Reimbursement of bar review/exam fees
- Business casual dress code

EMPLOYMENT CONTACT

Ms. Carol Restivo
Director of Human Resources
Phone: (312) 521-2000
Fax: (312) 521-2100
E-mail: crestivo@muchshelist.com

THE SCOOP

Founded in 1970, Chicago's Much Shelist Freed Denenberg Ament & Rubenstein has a national practice centered on business and litigation. Although the firm has a client roster including major public corporations, Much Shelist focuses on the needs of small and medium-sized businesses and individuals. In fact, the firm has a thriving class-action practice that boasts of having obtained over $4 billion in verdicts, judgments and settlements for plaintiffs in lawsuits against big-name corporations such as American Airlines, SmithKline Beecham (now Glaxo SmithKline), H&R Block and Prudential Life Insurance.

The firm represents plaintiffs in litigation involving antitrust, securities, consumer fraud and environmental remediation. Much Shelist has spearheaded several price-fixing lawsuits in the food and drug industries. In the automotive arena, the firm brought a class-action suit against DaimlerChrysler Corporation for allegedly manufacturing cars with defective seatbelts and is currently involved in litigation against Bridgestone/Firestone and Ford Motor Company regarding the tires used in the popular Ford Explorer.

In July 2004, the firm garnered a settlement with the last remaining defendant in a high-fructose corn syrup price-fixing class-action that had at one time included PepsiCo and Coca-Cola among its defendants. That litigation had been ongoing for nine years and had seen three rounds in the 7th U.S. Circuit Court of Appeals and two appearances before the U.S. Supreme Court. The settlement for the plaintiffs totaled $531 million. In other food-related litigation, Much Shelist principal and class-action lawyer extraordinaire, Michael B. Hyman, represented a plaintiff class of vegetarians in a suit challenging McDonald's use of beef by-products in the preparation of French fries and hash browns. The parties reached a settlement; since then, however, some members of the vegetarian community have appealed a 2003 court ruling on the disbursement of settlement funds. In 2004, Much Shelist once again faced the fast-food giant when it filed a shareholder class-action against McDonald's Corp. in the U.S. District Court for the Northern District of Illinois.

Much Shelist also helped resolve another long-running dispute in 2003 as counsel for the plaintiffs in a right-of-way lawsuit filed in Illinois federal court against Sprint and three other telecommunications carriers. Two years of negotiations concluded in a $142.5 million settlement for some 360,000 landowners who claimed that the carriers had laid down fiber cables without getting the landowners' permission. Most recently, in January 2005, the firm announced a pending shareholder class-action against OfficeMax, which had allegedly released misleading statements to the market, thereby artificially inflating the market price of its securities.

Even as it represents the little guy against the spoils of big business, Much Shelist manages to sustain a thriving corporate practice. In recent months, the firm has handled substantial M&A transactions, including several complex, tax-advantaged acquisitions of manufacturing concerns by client Home Products International, Inc. Much Shelist also counseled LaSalle Bank, N.A., on the organization and financing of its new corporate equipment leasing division. Other areas of firm practice include bankruptcy, employee benefits, health care, real estate, taxation and intellectual property. In September 2002, the IP practice gained additional heft when the firm acquired the intellectual property boutique Hamman & Benn.

Neal, Gerber & Eisenberg LLP

2 North LaSalle Street, Suite 2200
Chicago, IL 60602
Phone: (312) 269-8000
www.ngelaw.com

LOCATION
Chicago, IL

MAJOR DEPARTMENTS & PRACTICES
Association Law
Bankruptcy, Reorganizations & Creditors' Rights
Commercial Leasing
Corporate & Securities
Employee Benefits & Executive Compensation
Environmental
Estate Planning & Administration
Finance
General Litigation
Health Law
Information Technology
Intellectual Property
Labor & Employment
Private Wealth Services
Real Estate
Securities & Commodities Litigation
Taxation

THE STATS
No. of attorneys: 173
No. of offices: 1
Summer associate offers: 5 out of 5 (2004)
Managing Partner: Jerry H. Biederman
Hiring Partner: Robert A. Bedore

UPPERS
- Quality and sophistication of work
- Congenial environment with good balance between work and play

DOWNERS
- Minimal formal training
- Firm too small for privacy

NOTABLE PERKS
- Same-sex partner insurance
- Bar association dues
- Free dinner and cabs when working late
- Jeans on Fridays

BASE SALARY
Chicago, IL (2005)
1st year: $125,000
Summer associate: $2,400/week

EMPLOYMENT CONTACT
Ms. Sonia Menon
Director of Professional Recruitment & Development
Phone: (312) 269-8079
Fax: (312) 269-1747
E-mail: smenon@ngelaw.com

THE SCOOP

Last year, Neal, Gerber & Eisenberg added 40 new attorneys to its employment rolls, doubling the size of its intellectual property and bankruptcy departments and significantly expanding its litigation and labor and employment groups. Continuing its "opportunistic growth plan," Neal Gerber also expanded its health law practice early in 2004, when two partners from Michael Best & Friedrich LLP joined the firm. The firm added an information technology practice with the addition of two attorneys from Gordon & Glickson. Neal Gerber offers a range of interdisciplinary business practices, among them commercial leasing, real estate, finance and association law.

Last August, the firm represented shopping mall giant General Growth Properties in its $12.6 billion acquisition of The Rouse Company – the largest retail transaction nationwide in 2004. One of Neal Gerber's cases captured the attention of MTV News last year, when the firm represented Ticketmaster in a lawsuit brought by disappointed concertgoers who sued the ticket company, the rock band Creed and the band's manager after the lead singer of Creed appeared to be too intoxicated or otherwise impaired to perform during a scheduled Chicago show. A Cook County judge declined to hold the defendants culpable for any damages, stating that to do so would be to impose subjective standards and undefinable "audience expectations" on artists in performance. In other words, as a lawyer for Creed stated, "you can't bring a lawsuit against a band for sucking."

In a less publicized case, in March 2004, the firm successfully defended client Engineered Controls International, Inc., against a product liability suit brought by Pratt & Whitney, which claimed that a device made by Engineered was defective and that the defect caused an ammonia leak at the company's plant. After a six-week trial, the jury returned a verdict for the defense, denying Pratt & Whitney any recovery on its $2.5 million claim.

GETTING HIRED

Because the firm "elects to have a smaller summer associate class" – just six to eight students, according to one source – "it is relatively difficult to secure an interview or callback at the firm." On the other hand, "This is beneficial to those fortunate enough to get an offer for a summer associate position because it virtually assures those students that they will receive a full-time offer of employment." It also ensures "significant interaction between the students and attorneys."

As part of its "rigorous" hiring process, Neal Gerber demands "top grades and participation in legal activities." But the firm also "looks beyond the numbers." According to one insider, "We are looking for a candidate who is a bright, articulate, positive, energetic, independent go-getter to fit in with the young, entrepreneurial spirit of the firm."

OUR SURVEY SAYS

Neal Gerber associates seem to have little to complain about. It's an "amazing place to work," says one associate. "The firm culture here is fabulous," raves a recent hire. Insiders describe the atmosphere as "casual," "eclectic" and "friendly." A senior attorney says that Neal Gerber has "the most friendly, collegial work environment I've ever known." A midlevel notes that attorneys "work hard and care about doing high-quality work and being responsive to clients' needs," but without sacrificing the laid-back atmosphere. The firm appreciates both "good judgment and a good sense of humor," and there's a general welcoming feeling to the office. "People are on a first-name basis, leave their doors open and discuss their ideas with each other," says a litigator.

Insiders also voice satisfaction with salaries that are "competitive with other top firms in the marketplace." "I tend to view salary more holistically than most," reports one source. "Let's face it: Almost all of the attorneys answering this survey for Chicago firms receive 'superior compensation' in terms of dollars. If the quality of work assignments, people and ability to balance work and family are factored into the equation, I would judge NG&E to have the highest compensation in the city." Another associate says, "I could never complain with the amount that I am being paid to learn how to practice law." A few attorneys suggest that the firm could spend a bit more money on the office space. And the firm has listened. "The older offices are being redone to match the new offices in terms of décor and furniture," reports a midlevel associate.

Associates are pretty satisfied with their hours as well. A litigator reports, "I don't feel pressure to bill." Another attorney agrees: "There are no unreasonable expectations placed on associates to bill an extraordinary number of hours." While "there are periods when the work requires exceptional hours," the firm "has recognized the need for additional associates and has thus hired more people in the last two years." Moreover, "the firm encourages its associates to seek a balance between work and play." Pro bono work can count toward the billable-hour target, but it is done "very much on an individual basis" rather than firm-appointed.

Many attorneys feel that Neal Gerber is weak when it comes to training. "We mostly learn by doing," says one associate. But the firm appears to be trying to remedy the situation. It "encourages associates to attend external seminars such as NITA" and "has stepped up formal training for its younger associates." The firm has "developed a formal in-house program for young litigation associates to learn basic pre-trial skills," says one midlevel. Associates can also "practice trial skills by participating in an in-house mock trial program." Each associate "is assigned one associate mentor and one partner mentor." More generally, says an intellectual property attorney, "I receive feedback and mentoring on a daily basis." "Comments, suggestions and constructive criticism are not limited to the review period," says a source. Another attorney finds the "camaraderie and informal guidance to be extraordinarily helpful."

Pattishall, McAuliffe, Newbury, Hilliard & Geraldson LLP

311 South Wacker Drive
Suite 5000
Chicago, IL 60606
Phone: (312) 554-8000
www.pattishall.com

LOCATIONS

Chicago, IL (HQ)
Alexandria, VA

MAJOR DEPARTMENTS & PRACTICES

Advertising & Promotions
Alternative Dispute Resolution
Copyright
Due Diligence & Audits
Internet, E-Commerce & Computer Technology
Rights of Publicity & Privacy
Trade Secret
Trademark

THE STATS

No. of attorneys:
   firm-wide: 33
   Chicago: 31
No. of offices: 2
Senior Partner: David C. Hilliard
Hiring Partner: Bradley L. Cohn

NOTABLE PERKS

- Reimbursement of bar review course and exam fees
- Profit-sharing plan
- Allowance for out-of-town meetings and client development
- Business casual attire

EMPLOYMENT CONTACT

Ms. Deborah A. Trnovec
Human Resources Manager
Phone: (312) 554-8000
Fax: (312) 554-8015
E-mail: hr@pattishall.com

THE SCOOP

For the last 121 years, Pattishall, McAuliffe, Newbury, Hilliard & Geraldson has provided learned counsel in intellectual property law to clients in industries ranging from toys to pharmaceuticals to sporting goods. The firm eschews patent law in favor of a practice focusing on trademark, copyright, advertising, Internet and e-commerce, trade secrets and unfair trade practices. With its 31-lawyer headquarters in Chicago and a toehold in Alexandria, Va., Pattishall has positioned itself to serve a national base of clients. And these clients are no small potatoes – in the snack food industry alone, Pattishall represents Frito-Lay, Brach & Brock Confections, Nabisco and PepsiCo; other household-name clients include St. Ives, Jaguar, Anheuser-Busch, BASF, Encyclopaedia Britannica and AT&T.

The firm has litigated an impressive number of cases that led to published decisions for clients that include J. Crew and Ford Motor Company. Outside the courtroom, Pattishall frequently conducts due diligence reviews and audits to assist clients in preparing for mergers, acquisitions and other corporate transactions. The firm has counseled clients in transactions involving such big names as London Fog, Planters, Del Monte and Everyday Learning Corporation.

Pattishall recently won an appeal for Deutsche Wurlitzer in *Baldwin Piano, Inc. v. Deutsche Wurlitzer GmbH*. In 1985, Deutsche Wurlitzer was spun off from The Wurlitzer Company (parent of Baldwin Piano) and received a license to continue using the Wurlitzer name on its jukeboxes and associated products. In March 2003, Baldwin Piano terminated the license, arguing that it could be terminated at will. Persuaded by Pattishall attorneys, who argued that the license could only be terminated on account of material breach, the U.S. Court of Appeals for the 7th Circuit ruled in favor of Deutsche Wurlitzer in December 2004.

Not only do Pattishall attorneys play lead roles in individual cases; they have also helped shape the development of intellectual property law. One early member of the firm became a primary drafter of the United States Trademark Act of 1946, more commonly known as the Lanham Act. More recently, Pattishall lawyers have assisted in drafting legislation such as the Trademark Revision Act of 1989 and participated as expert panelists for the World Intellectual Property Organization. In April 2004, Robert W. Sacoff, Pattishall partner and chair of the American Bar Association Section of Intellectual Property Law, testified before the House Subcommittee on Courts, the Internet and Intellectual Property on proposed amendments to the

Federal Trademark Dilution Act. The amendments were proposed largely in response to the U.S. Supreme Court's 2003 decision in *Moseley v. Victoria's Secret Catalogue*, in which the high court unanimously ruled that a little Kentucky sex shop called Victor's Little Secret didn't infringe on the trademark held by lingerie titan Victoria's Secret. Sacoff had co-authored the ABA's amicus curiae brief in favor of a "likelihood of dilution" standard rather than the "actual dilution" requirement eventually upheld by the Supreme Court.

Throughout the firm's history, many of its lawyers have been regarded as leaders in IP law. In 2004, eight Pattishall attorneys were selected as "Leading Lawyers" in intellectual property law in a survey of more than 50,000 practicing Illinois attorneys. The survey, conducted by the Law Bulletin Publishing Company, selects fewer than 5 percent of attorneys in their field. Pattishall attorneys have served in leadership positions in the Chicago Bar Association, the Intellectual Property Law Association of Chicago and the U.S. Group of the Association Internationale pour la Protection de la Propriete Industrielle. They have chaired the Intellectual Property Section of the American Bar Association and participated on the Public Advisory Committee for Trademark Affairs. Lawyers from Pattishall McAuliffe have lectured at law schools throughout the Midwest. Most recently, in January 2005, the University of Chicago Law School announced that Pattishall partner Uli Widmaier would teach a new course entitled "The First Amendment and the Media."

GETTING HIRED

Pattishall seeks "motivated individuals with high scholastic achievement and demonstrated advocacy skills." The goal is to produce attorneys who "are authorities in their field" and "excel at federal court litigation." To this end, the firm conducts on-campus interviews at top law schools including Chicago, Michigan, Virginia, Harvard, Northwestern and Yale. Although it's certainly not easy to get a job at this firm, Pattishall's application process has one advantage over many other IP boutiques: because the firm's practice is non-patent, candidates needn't have a technical background. Summer associates receive hands-on exposure to many aspects of litigation and may even travel to other cities to participate in hearings or trials.

Pedersen & Houpt

161 North Clark Street, Suite 3100
Chicago, IL 60601-3224
Phone: (312) 641-6888
www.pedersenhoupt.com

LOCATION
Chicago, IL

MAJOR DEPARTMENTS & PRACTICES
Corporate & Business Counseling
Employment Law
Intellectual Property
Litigation & Dispute Resolution
Real Estate & Financing
Wealth Preservation

THE STATS
No. of attorneys: 37
No. of offices: 1
Chairman: Peer Pedersen
Managing Partner: John H. Muehlstein

EMPLOYMENT CONTACT
Director of Human Resources
Phone: (312) 641-6888
Fax: (312) 641-6895
E-mail: humanresources@pedersenhoupt.com

THE SCOOP

After serving in World War II in the U.S. Navy and practicing with Arrington & Healy in Chicago, Peer Pedersen struck out on his own to found his eponymous firm in 1957. Still active as the 37-lawyer firm's chairman, Pedersen also serves on the boards of directors for many corporations and nonprofit organizations in the Chicago area. Known for his strong business sense, Pedersen was among the first to invest in video rental giant Blockbuster Entertainment and fast food company Boston Chicken.

By the firm's own description, Pedersen & Houpt chiefly focuses its practice on the representation of "closely-held middle market businesses" in the manufacturing, distribution and service industries. However, not to be pigeonholed, the firm also counsels entrepreneurs, financial institutions and real estate developers on matters that are by no means mid-sized. Pedersen & Houpt's M&A team, for example, recently advised a video retail-chain franchisee on the $250 million sale of its business – the largest in the chain – to the franchisor, a publicly traded company.

The firm also has an impressive real estate department. Over the past five years, Pedersen & Houpt attorneys have handled approximately 800 lease transactions for two specialty food chains and a national laundromat chain. In addition to several multi-state acquisitions, dispositions and leasing projects throughout the United States, the real estate department recently represented an investment fund that was created to buy office developments in Florida. The Pedersen lawyers' role was to establish a four-tier plan for the equity, financing and ownership of the $150 million fund. As a result of that project, the fund has purchased more than $200 million in property. But Chicago is where the firm's closest ties are, with firm attorneys having worked with several of Chicago's largest developers on mixed-use city developments costing close to $500 million.

Despite its successes in most corporate and legal arenas, the firm is currently facing a lawsuit by ex-Bulls star Scottie Pippen. Last year, Pippen filed a complaint for $5.7 million against Pedersen & Houpt over the firm's representation in an airplane purchase that left Pippen with a hefty $5 million loan. In another lawsuit against a different Chicago-based firm (Katten Muchin Zavis & Rosenman), Pippen alleged that he lost $20 million because of a fall-out with financial guru Robert Lunn, whom many ex-clients seem to have a beef with. According to the suit, Pippen lost nearly $20 million because of Lunn and, by extension, Katten Muchin. Now, news reports say that Pippen's complaint against Pedersen & Houpt may be amended to include claims resulting from Pedersen's close investment and legal ties to Lunn. Pedersen itself also has a few claims pending against Lunn.

Pedersen & Houpt litigators, for their part, have acted as counsel to plaintiffs in several massive class-action lawsuits. The firm has served as lead counsel for the plaintiffs in class actions against companies in the industrial gas, glass container and brand-name pharmaceutical drug industries. These cases have recovered over $700 million in damages for plaintiffs' class members based upon antitrust claims such as price fixing and unfair competition.

The firm also counsels clients on employment law and offers on-site seminars on sexual harassment and working conditions and federal and state safety laws. In one precedent-setting employment law case before the Illinois Supreme Court, Pedersen & Houpt attorneys successfully defended their client, a medical products manufacturer, against a wrongful discharge suit filed by the company's former in-house attorney. The court determined that the company had a right to fire the attorney despite his allegations that the company illegally fired him after he "blew the whistle" on products he claimed were dangerously defective.

GETTING HIRED

As a relatively small Chicago firm, Pedersen & Houpt keeps its recruiting processes close to the vest. But that doesn't mean that it doesn't have standards. Pedersen recruiters look for candidates with great resumes who fit in well with the firm's culture. And they're always happy to review resumes even if there aren't any open positions – they may just create one for you if you're the right match.

Wondering what it's like to work at a specific employer?

Read what EMPLOYEES have to say about:
- Workplace culture
- Compensation
- Hours
- Diversity
- Hiring process

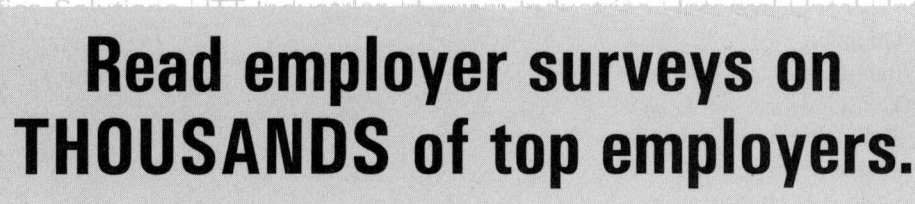

Read employer surveys on THOUSANDS of top employers.

VAULT

> the most trusted name in career information™

Go to www.vault.com

Porter Wright Morris & Arthur LLP

41 South High Street, Suite 2800
Columbus, OH 43215-6194
Phone: (614) 227-2000
www.porterwright.com

LOCATIONS

Columbus, OH (HQ)
Cincinnati, OH
Cleveland, OH
Dayton, OH
Naples, FL
Washington, DC

MAJOR DEPARTMENTS & PRACTICES

Antitrust & Trade Regulation
Business & Securities
Construction
Employee Benefits
Environmental Law
Finance & Commerce
Financial Institutions
Governmental Affairs
Health Care
Immigration
Insurance & Financial Services
Intellectual Property
International Business
Labor & Employment
Litigation
Real Estate
Tax
Technology
Trusts & Estates
Utilities & Energy
White-Collar Crime & Government Enforcement

THE STATS

No. of attorneys:
   firm-wide: 306
   Columbus: 200
   Cincinnati: 11
   Cleveland: 38
   Dayton: 22
No. of offices: 6
Summer associate offers:
   firm-wide: 20 out of 27 (2004)
   Columbus: 12 out of 14 (2004)
   Cleveland: 3 out of 5 (2004)
   Dayton: 1 out of 1 (2004)
Managing Partner: Robert W. Trafford
Hiring Partner: Richard G. Terapak

UPPERS
- Diverse and challenging work
- Emphasis on quality of life

DOWNERS
- Comparatively low starting salaries
- Expensive health insurance plan

NOTABLE PERKS
- Associate retreats
- Window offices for all associates
- Frequent cocktail parties and lots of food

BASE SALARY

Columbus and Cincinnati, OH (2005)
1st year: $100,000
Summer associate: $1,923/week

Cleveland, OH (2005)
1st year: $110,000
Summer associate: $1,923/week

Dayton, OH (2005)
1st year: $90,000
Summer associate: $1,923/week

EMPLOYMENT CONTACT

Mr. David G. Zimmerman
Professional Personnel Coordinator
Phone: (614) 227-1907
Fax: (614) 227-2100
E-mail: dzimmerman@porterwright.com

THE SCOOP

Porter Wright Morris & Arthur LLP has won quite a collection of laurel wreaths in 2004. First, for the fourth year running, the firm landed a spot among the top law firms in Columbus as the result of a survey conducted by *Corporate Board Member* magazine. The publication bases its rankings upon the responses of CEOs and boards of directors of major corporations, who weigh in on the top five law firms in a given geographic region. Then, in October, two Porter Wright attorneys gained recognition as among the "Best of the Bar" in the *Dayton Business Journal*. The following month, the Columbus Bar Association honored the firm for its extensive pro bono work, particularly in the area of domestic violence; Porter Wright frequently provides legal assistance to victims of abuse who need representation in court hearings or help filing for divorce. To top it all off, 51 of the firm's 300 attorneys were selected for inclusion in *The Best Lawyers in America 2005–2006*.

With 158 years of legal experience under its belt, Porter Wright Morris & Arthur has established itself as a premier law firm. Over the years, it has diversified from its single Columbus location, adding satellite locations around Ohio as well as in Naples, Fla., and the nation's capital. Porter Wright's practice is varied as well, offering legal services in 22 general areas which divide into many specialized or industry-based subgroups.

GETTING HIRED

Porter Wright's hiring practices are fairly typical for a corporate firm, according to its associates, including on-campus recruitment followed by in-office callback interviews. The firm's combination of longevity and recent prominence allows it to be rather selective. According to one newcomer, getting hired is "easy if you are from a top-tier East Coast or Chicago law school," but "hard and very competitive otherwise." Another associate elaborates, explaining that the firm seeks candidates among the "top 10 to 15 percent from first- and second-tier law schools" and from the "top 3 percent of local, lower-tier law schools." Although one insider claims that it's "mostly grades" that "get you in past the on-campus interviews," a seasoned associate insists that "the firm looks for well-rounded individuals."

OUR SURVEY SAYS

Among its associates, Porter Wright has a reputation for being fairly casual, with occasional glaring exceptions. "It is seemingly pretty laid-back, but there are pockets of uptightness," reports one third-year. "The problem is, you never really know where (who) they are until you've already made the mistake." Another midlevel lawyer agrees: "We have a very mixed culture, even within my small practice group. We can be formal but also laid-back, and we can be friendly but also uptight. I almost wish we would pick one or the other because sometimes it is hard to know which to be."

Just as the firm culture seems to fluctuate, so does associates' overall satisfaction with their firm. As one young attorney says, "I go back and forth, depending in large part on the people with whom I'm working on any given case." In any event, nearly all responding associates feel that one of the firm's greatest strengths is its partners. The "partners here are very encouraging," reports a first-year.

Among the other areas in which associates give Porter Wright high marks are diversity and pro bono work. The firm employs a diverse work force, attorneys say, and is increasingly sensitive to issues of gender and race. "There are a number of very powerful female partners in the firm," says one young attorney. While acknowledging that the firm, like the legal profession as a whole, can still be "insensitive to issues that uniquely affect women," she believes "that if you are a good attorney and female, you can succeed at this firm." Porter Wright offers both "a part-time partnership track program and flex-time opportunities." With respect to pro bono, attorneys give somewhat mixed responses as to how pro bono time is credited. According to one source, pro bono hours are counted "on a one-to-one basis for billable-hour targets," while another asserts that they count only "up to a certain number of maximum hours."

The firm is not without its drawbacks. A common complaint among associates is the pressure to bill. "We are commanded to make the billable hours," says a first-year associate. Others, however, say that billing is not the firm's top priority. "There is an emphasis on doing quality work first and foremost," states an experienced lawyer. "Our billable goal is secondary (but yet important)." Most sources report billing between, on average, between 151 and 175 hours each month.

Some associates also feel aggrieved about salaries which, they argue, are "not on par with other similar firms in our area." (The firm disputes this view, insisting that its salaries are competitive in each city.) But one lawyer shares a different view: "The salary is wonderful, but the remaining benefits package is not as good as I think it could be if we could figure out a way to be more creative."

Quarles & Brady LLP

411 East Wisconsin Avenue
Milwaukee, WI 53202
Phone: (414) 277-5000
www.quarles.com

LOCATIONS
Milwaukee, WI (HQ)
Boca Raton, FL
Chicago, IL
Madison, WI
Naples, FL
Phoenix, AZ
Tucson, AZ

MAJOR DEPARTMENTS & PRACTICES
Bankruptcy
Corporate & Securities
Environmental
Health Care
Immigration
Intellectual Property
Labor & Employment
Litigation & Product Liability
Public Finance
Real Estate & Land Use
Tax, Employee Benefits & Exempt Organizations
Trusts & Estates

THE STATS
No. of attorneys:
  firm-wide: 411
  Milwaukee: 188
  Chicago: 47
  Madison: 35
No. of offices: 7
Summer associate offers:
  firm-wide: 13 out of 16 (2004)
  Milwaukee: 6 out of 6 (2004)
  Chicago: 2 out of 2 (2004)
  Madison: 1 out of 2 (2004)
Managing Partner: Patrick M. Ryan
Hiring Partners:
  Milwaukee: Rachel A. Schneider
  Chicago: Patrick J. Bitterman
  Madison: Sarah E. Coyne

NOTABLE PERKS
- Flexible work schedule
- Democratic environment
- Health club reimbursement
- First-time home buyers program

BASE SALARY
Milwaukee and Madison, WI (2005)
1st year: $105,000
Summer associate: $2,025/week

Chicago, IL (2005)
1st year: $125,000
Summer associate: $2,400/week

EMPLOYMENT CONTACT
Chicago, Milwaukee and Madison
Ms. Michelle Bigler
Legal Recruiting Coordinator
Phone: (414) 277-5290
Fax: (414) 271-3552
E-mail: mbigler@quarles.com

THE SCOOP

Quarles & Brady traces its roots all the way back to 1892. In 2000, the firm merged with Streich Lang PA, which expanded its Phoenix office and added a Tucson office to the Quarles & Brady roster. (In Arizona, the firm is known as Quarles & Brady Streich Lang LLP.) With over 400 attorneys, Quarles & Brady now stands among the 60 largest firms in the country. A substantial portion of those attorneys work out of the firm's Milwaukee office. Ninety-four Q&B lawyers – nearly a quarter of the firm's attorneys – have been named to the 2005–2006 edition of *The Best Lawyers in America*, including 45 attorneys who have been recognized for 10 years or more. Of the top 100 firms on the *NLJ 250*, Quarles & Brady has the highest percentage (23.7 percent) of listed attorneys.

The firm houses 50 diverse practice areas in its seven offices. A small sampling of the firm's clientele includes household names such as Harley-Davidson Motor Company, Miller Brewing Company and Wells Fargo Bank. Over the last few years, the firm has acted as defense counsel to numerous insurers, manufacturers and distributors on massive class action and product liability suits regarding asbestos, tobacco, tires, vaccines and forklifts, to name just a few. Quarles & Brady's bankruptcy practice has also thrived in recent years. On the debtor side, the firm has handled the insolvency filings of a major airline, several resorts and casinos in Nevada, a $4 billion retail convenience-store chain, a $1.5 billion department-store chain and several dot-com companies. Quarles & Brady lawyers also had a hand in saving the Heisman Trophy. In a Chapter 11 proceeding, the firm represented the "white knight" acquirer of the failing Downtown Athletic Club, the founder of the Heisman Trophy.

Recently, Ave Bie, the former chairwoman of the Public Service Commission of Wisconsin, joined the Madison office as a partner. Bie brings extensive experience to the public utility and government relations practices, although the move was not without controversy. Some consumer groups that support a proposal for a two-year moratorium barring commissioners and senior staff from working for utilities regulated by the agency have argued that the appointment reflects a conflict of interest for a senior staff member who worked to regulate industries now to join a law firm that represents them. (To date, the legislature has not passed the moratorium proposal.) In other recent public-to-private-sector moves, Cory Nettles rejoined the firm as a partner in the Milwaukee office in December 2004, after serving two years as Governor Jim Doyle's secretary of commerce.

Quarles & Brady is well known for and proud of its community involvement. To Habitat for Humanity, Q&B's largest pro bono client, the firm has donated more than $1 million in legal real estate services in Wisconsin and Arizona. Among the firm's many pro bono activities, the Milwaukee, Madison and Chicago offices participate in the volunteer panel of attorneys at the U.S. Court of Appeals for the 7th Circuit; the Milwaukee office is currently involved in three death penalty appeals. Lawyers in the Milwaukee office also work with the state public defender's office to represent parents who face termination of their parental rights and volunteer at the restraining order clinic staffed by the Task Force on Family Violence at the Milwaukee County Courthouse. In recognition of the firm's assistance to victims of domestic abuse through its collaboration with the Task Force on Family Violence, the Milwaukee Office Clinic Support Project received the Volunteer Lawyer's Project 2004 Outstanding Pro Bono Special Project Award.

In other honors accorded the firm last year, partner Rachel Schneider received the Milwaukee Bar Association's Distinguished Service Award for her service as chair of the MBA's Legal Services for the Indigent Committee. In 2004, the firm's Phoenix office was honored with two community service awards from the Volunteer Lawyers Program of Arizona: Large Firm of the Year and Children's Law Center Firm of the Year. And in December 2004, *In Business* magazine named four Q&B partners to the 2004 Honor Roll of Greater Madison's Most Civic-Minded Leaders.

GETTING HIRED

"Superior intellectual ability" is the firm's top criterion, but Quarles & Brady also cites "character, motivation [and] maturity" as important factors. The ideal candidate has the ability to work both independently and as part of a team. The firm hires people who it believes have what it takes to become partners. So, while demonstrated performance matters, candidates should also have the ability to maintain and attract clients. In other words, strong interpersonal skills are just as important as academic criteria.

Reinhart Boerner Van Deuren S.C.

1000 North Water Street
P.O. Box 2965
Milwaukee, WI 53201-2965
Phone: (414) 298-1000
www.reinhartlaw.com

LOCATIONS

Milwaukee, WI (HQ)
Madison, WI
Waukesha, WI

MAJOR DEPARTMENTS & PRACTICES

Appellate
Banking & Finance
Bankruptcy & Creditors' Rights
Business Law
Employee Benefits & Executive Compensation
Entertainment Law
Environmental
Government Relations
Health Care
Intellectual Property
Labor & Employment
Litigation
Product Distribution & Franchise Law
Real Estate
Securities
Tax
Trusts & Estates

THE STATS

No. of attorneys:
  firm-wide: 219
  Milwaukee: 186
  Madison: 22
  Waukesha: 11
No. of offices: 3
Summer associate offers:
  Milwaukee: 6 out of 9 (2003)
President and CEO: Richard W. Graber
Hiring Partners: Larri J. Broomfield and William T. Shroyer

NOTABLE PERKS

- Bar dues, bar exam/review course fees
- Loan guarantee for purchase of home
- 401(k) plan
- Transition stipend for summer associates

BASE SALARY

Milwaukee, WI (2004)
1st year: $95,000
Summer associate: $1,775/week

EMPLOYMENT CONTACT

Ms. Sandra W. Faull
Manager of Attorney Recruiting
Phone: (414) 298-8528
Fax: (414) 298-8097
E-mail: swfaull@reinhartlaw.com

THE SCOOP

Over the course of the firm's history, the Milwaukee-based Reinhart Boerner Van Deuren has provided legal services with a conscience, having accomplished everything from saving the jobs of more than 800 workers at the financially troubled Emmber Foods to rescuing the Sargento Cheese company from tax liabilities that threatened its status as a family-run business. Name partner Richard A. Van Deuren presides over the firm as chairman of the board of directors. A graduate of Harvard Law School, Van Deuren has been practicing with the firm since 1956, when it had just three partners. Although his practice largely focuses on corporate law, particularly mergers and acquisitions and corporate finance, Van Deuren also established the firm's employee benefits practice, which now comprises 10 percent of the firm's attorneys. Reinhart Boerner has served the Milwaukee community for over a century and is now the fourth-largest firm in Wisconsin. Remaining true to its roots, the firm has not yet expanded beyond its home state of Wisconsin, but maintains branch offices in Madison and Waukesha.

Reinhart Boerner offers a broad array of practice groups. Of particular note is the bankruptcy department, which has served clients including Banc One Wisconsin Corporation, Harley-Davidson Motor Company, Northwestern Mutual Life Insurance Company and Swiss Bank Corporation in connection with insolvency proceedings. Other significant practices include health care, real estate, appellate litigation and entertainment law. In 2004, five firm attorneys were cited by *Chambers USA* for their expertise in areas including litigation, real estate and corporate law. Twenty-six Reinhart attorneys appeared in the 2005–2006 edition of *The Best Lawyers in America*; more than half of those listed have appeared regularly in the publication for at least a decade.

Firm attorneys are routinely recognized for their contributions to the community, as well as for their professional achievements. In 2004, the firm represented Impact Seven, Inc. to close a $10.5 equity investment by Park Bank in Impact Seven's Wisconsin Impact Fund. The fund will distribute loans to businesses in need of mortgage financing, with the aim of revitalizing economically-depressed communities. The fund was the first Wisconsin entity last year to receive an allocation from the federal New Markets Tax Credit program, which encourages private investment and job creation in targeted communities. The NMTC allocated $21 million to the new fund.

In February 2005, the firm embarked on an unusual kind of pro bono project in which it will donate partner Robert E. Meldman's time to the Low Income

Tax Payers Clinic (LITC) at the University of Wisconsin-Milwaukee. A member of the American College Tax Counsel and a former member of the Internal Revenue Service Taxpayer Advocacy Panel, Meldman will serve as "executive in residence" and work with graduate tax students to provide free tax counseling to those who otherwise could not afford it. UWM students will receive course credit for their work at the LITC and will handle issues such as earned income credit claims, dependency deductions, filing status, and resident and non-resident alien tax questions. The LITC, which is funded by an IRS grant and matching in-kind contribution from Reinhart Boerner, is one of only two tax controversy clinics in Wisconsin, and the only one with an academic affiliation.

In addition to its legal expertise, Reinhart is proud of its innovative use of technology. The firm boasts that it was among the first to provide desktop computers to all employees and to launch its own web site. Reinhart is also among only a few law firms in the country to have its own high-tech courtroom, complete with three jury deliberation rooms. The Trial Science Institute allows attorneys to prepare for major trials by videotaping and reviewing witness testimony, practicing oral arguments and watching mock juries deliberate over the issues.

GETTING HIRED

If you want to work at Reinhart, be prepared for client contact "immediately." The firm believes in giving associates "primary responsibility for projects within the first few months of their tenure." In other words, if you plan to hide behind your desk or under a stack of papers, this is not the firm for you. Reinhart wants go-getters with good grades; the firm says it prefers students in the top 20 percent of their class. Other assets include experience on law review or other journals and participation in moot court.

The firm recruits at schools throughout the Midwest and the eastern half of the United States. In order to increase minority recruitment, Reinhart also participates in the BLSA Midwest Minority Recruitment Conference and the Cook County Bar Association Minority Student Job Fair.

Sachnoff & Weaver, Ltd.

10 South Wacker Drive, 40th Floor
Chicago, IL 60606
Phone: (312) 207-1000
www.sachnoff.com

LOCATION
Chicago, IL

MAJOR DEPARTMENTS & PRACTICES
Business Services
Complex & Commercial Litigation
Employment & Human Resources
Financial Services
Insurance Coverage
Intellectual Property, Internet & Technology
Private Client/Estate & Wealth Planning
Product Liability

THE STATS
No. of attorneys: 142
No. of offices: 1
Summer associate offers: 9 out of 9 (2004)
Co-Managing Partners: Austin L. Hirsch and Michael A. LoVallo
Recruiting Committee Chair: Robert A. Roth

UPPERS

- Collegial culture that encourages both individuality and teamwork
- Substantive responsibilities "from day one"

DOWNERS

- Not-so-generous expense account
- Concern that firm's growth might affect collegial atmosphere

NOTABLE PERKS

- Free BlackBerries for all associates
- "Food treats all the time"
- Twice-yearly associate dinners and frequent social events
- Business casual dress

BASE SALARY

Chicago, IL (2005)
1st year: $125,000
2nd year: $132,500
3rd year: $142,500
4th year: $150,000
5th year: $160,000
6th year: $165,000
7th year: $170,000
Summer associate: $2,163/week

EMPLOYMENT CONTACT

Ms. Nikki Silvio
Director of Legal Recruiting/Professional Development
Phone: (312) 207-6445
Fax: (312) 207-6400
E-mail: nsilvio@sachnoff.com

THE SCOOP

Sachnoff & Weaver, a Chicago firm with over 140 lawyers, made headlines in October 2004 when it won a jury verdict for client Eastman Kodak Company in a patent infringement suit against Sun Microsystems. Before the parties entered the damages phase, they reached a settlement in which Sun agreed to pay Kodak $92 million. According to the *Chicago Daily Law Bulletin*, after the trial, U.S. District Judge Michael A. Telesca called the litigants and their attorneys into his chambers in order to praise counsel for their extraordinary professionalism throughout the case.

In other recent litigation, Sachnoff won the appellate reversal and subsequent favorable settlement for a group of associate members of the Chicago Board of Trade – a result that significantly increased the clients' ownership in the CBOT prior to its proposed initial public offering. On the transactional side, in 2004 Sachnoff lawyers helped Standard Parking Corporation with its IPO, advised MultiPlan, Inc. in its $250 million acquisition of BCE Emergis Inc. and handled a high-yield debt offering for VICORP Restaurants, Inc., owner and operator of Bakers Square® and Village Inn® restaurants.

Aside from intellectual property and litigation, Sachnoff & Weaver offers services in corporate finance, insurance coverage, employment and estate planning to clients from middle-market companies to high-net-worth individuals.

GETTING HIRED

"For a mid-sized firm, it is rather difficult to get a job here," reports an associate at Sachnoff & Weaver. "This firm is looking for people with strong academic credentials and good judgment and skills, yet also with good interpersonal skills," explains one attorney. "This is not a place for the lawyers who are uber-smart, yet lack a personality or interpersonal skills." The firm values "experiences that demonstrate motivation, leadership and outside interests" and seeks "self-starters who are highly motivated and able to run with a lot of responsibility."

As for the actual interviews, according to one experienced associate, "The interview and callback process is extremely thorough but not delayed. I went through three sets of interviews over the course of a five-day period."

OUR SURVEY SAYS

Responding associates report great satisfaction with their firm. "I am very satisfied and feel that this is a terrific place to practice law," says one Sachnoff source. "The members [partners] treat associates like equals and involve them in decision-making. Individuality is encouraged and the firm is well managed and entrepreneurial." Other attorneys agree that "partners make a concerted effort" to create "a positive environment for associates." "The quality of work is fantastic and the caliber of the attorneys is great," raves one happy lawyer. Another associate says, "I cannot imagine working at any other firm."

The firm's casual and friendly vibe contributes to associates' praise. "Many attorneys wear jeans," and lawyers enjoy "cookies and snacks" as well as "lots of banter" throughout the day. (According to the firm, its daily style is "business casual," not jeans and sneakers.) "Attorneys come to Sachnoff because their individuality is not only allowed, it is expected," declares one litigator. In fact, a transactional attorney believes that "the culture is the best part of S&W. If you are going to work this hard, you might as well be in a place that is fairly laid-back with respectable colleagues."

Another point of agreement among insiders: the "approachability" of the firm's partners. "I feel very comfortable walking into any partner's office with questions or concerns about a case I am working on," reports a junior associate. "The partners treat the associates very well," adds a more seasoned lawyer. "The partners seem to respect not only us, but our personal lives."

The small-firm flavor doesn't appear to have a negative effect on associates' paychecks. "We strive to be right around the market rate and, so far as I know, succeed," says one satisfied source. "There are also bonuses designed to pay those who work significantly more – that means that the firm's compensation is relatively fair, even when you work a lot of hours." As one attorney explains, "Associates can get bonuses for every 50 hours they bill over the 1,950 hour minimum requirement. As the 50-hour increments increase, the bonuses get bigger."

Even the nearly universal source of ire among young attorneys everywhere – billable hours – doesn't seem to faze Sachnoff & Weaver associates. "There is no face time requirement at Sachnoff," reports a midlevel lawyer. "While I have worked very long hours to prepare for trial, the hours, generally, are great." But don't idealize the place, associates warn: it's still a law firm. "Our firm has very reasonable hours with no face time whatsoever, but 1,950 hours plus non-billable time still takes up a significant portion of your life," cautions one insider.

Many sources praise the firm's "excellent" training opportunities, which range from in-house seminars to out-of-office workshops. Sachnoff has a formal mentoring program, in addition to which, associates receive informal guidance from more senior attorneys. The "opportunities in both areas are significant," says one source. Another reports that the firm has hired outside consultants to address "a distinct need for improvement in this area." One area in which associates see little need for improvement is pro bono. "This is one of the strong points of the firm," boasts one lawyer. Another attorney agrees: "Pro bono work counts towards billable hours targets, and the firm couldn't be more supportive of pro bono work."

Schiff Hardin LLP

6600 Sears Tower
Chicago, IL 60606
Phone: (312) 258-5500
www.schiffhardin.com

LOCATIONS

Chicago, IL (HQ)
Atlanta, GA • Lake Forest, IL • New York, NY • Washington, DC • Dublin

MAJOR DEPARTMENTS & PRACTICES

Antitrust & Trade Regulation • Bankruptcy, Workouts & Creditors' Rights • Class Action • Construction • Corporate & Securities • Employee Benefits & Executive Compensation • Energy, Telecommunications & Public Utilities • Environmental • Estate Planning & Administration • Finance • Financial Institutions • Government Contracts • Health Care • Insurance • Intellectual Property • International • Labor & Employment • General Litigation • Private Equity & Venture Capital • Product Liability • Public Law • Real Estate • Reinsurance Litigation • Securities & Futures Market Regulations • Sports & Entertainment • Taxation • White-Collar Defense

THE STATS

No. of attorneys:
  firm-wide: 329
  Chicago: 276
No. of offices: 6
Summer associate offers:
  firm-wide: 23 out of 23 (2004)
  Chicago: 23 out of 23 (2004)
Managing Partner: Ronald S. Safer
Hiring Partner: Robert D. Campbell

UPPERS

- Collegial, respectful working environment
- Lean staffing means hands-on experience and early client contact

DOWNERS

- Disparity in salaries
- Firm politics

NOTABLE PERKS

- Wine and cheese get-togethers
- Taxis and dinner reimbursements when working late
- Relocation reimbursement
- Liberal reimbursement policy for client entertainment

BASE SALARY

Chicago, IL (2005)
1st year: $125,000
Summer associate: $2,400/week

EMPLOYMENT CONTACT

Ms. Lilly Tuller
Law Student Recruitment Coordinator
Phone: (312) 258-4832
Fax: (312) 258-5600
E-mail: ltuller@schiffhardin.com

THE SCOOP

Over the course of its 140-year history, Schiff Hardin LLP has been counsel to major players in the transportation industry, including longstanding clients such as the Chicago Transit Authority. The firm played a role in the early days of the El; and, more recently, Schiff Hardin counseled the city of Chicago on the expansion of O'Hare Airport. For over half a century, the firm has also been involved in the field of sports law. Over the course of four decades, the firm counseled Bill Veeck on matters relating to his ownership of the Chicago White Sox, St. Louis Browns and Cleveland Indians. Schiff Hardin also represents Michael Jordan on trademark and litigation matters, and counsels the Chicago Bears on transactional projects, including the financing and governmental relations work needed for the renovation of Soldier Field.

Another of Schiff Hardin's blue-chip clients is PepsiCo. A few years ago, the firm represented the soft-drink titan in a widely publicized litigation against one of its former employees, who left Pepsi to work for a major competitor. The case hinged upon the theory of "inevitable disclosure," a novel theory developed by the Schiff Hardin team. Ultimately, the court applied the new theory and granted PepsiCo's injunction. Today, that case is an important precedent, often cited by litigants and courts in similar cases.

Of the firm's more than 300 lawyers, 276 work in its Windy City office. Firm-wide, the litigation and corporate/securities departments are the largest practice groups, at least in sheer numbers; but Schiff Hardin offers quite a few strong practice areas, such as intellectual property, bankruptcy, labor and employment, and products liability.

GETTING HIRED

Associates seem split over whether hiring attorneys care more about "fit" or pedigree. An experienced lawyer observes, "I've noticed over the last several summers a tendency to recruit only at the top 10 to 15 schools, where it is easy to fill an interview schedule but hard to convince a student to take a job here." But according to others, Schiff Hardin "looks for a good fit, not just a qualified candidate." "A 'good fit,'" explains one associate, "means genuine, down-to-earth and bright." According to another, the firm seeks "bright, personable, outgoing" people who pay "meticulous attention to detail." Yet another insider weighs in on the desired qualities: "Candidates must be intelligent, but not just book-smart. Common sense, interpersonal communication skills and the ability to work as a self-starter are important."

OUR SURVEY SAYS

There's much to praise about Schiff Hardin, say associates. For example, there's "excellent work in a growing firm," "thoughtful, pedagogical partners" and an "innovative coaching program." To top it off, "everyone is, on balance, just very nice."

Among the biggest reasons for associate satisfaction is the laid-back culture in which "everyone is on a first-name basis." If Schiff Hardin were any more relaxed, associates say, it would be sleeping. "The firm is laid-back, friendly and informal. Attorneys socialize together some and generally wish they could do so more, but most have lives, family and friends outside of work," reports a first-year working in the Windy City. Another associate agrees: "Lawyers socialize from time to time, especially younger lawyers, but for the most part people go home, especially if they have families. The place is dead by 6:00 p.m."

How they manage to empty the office by 6:00 and still meet their billable hours is something of a puzzle. "Despite the 2,000-hour requirement, this is not a late-night and all-weekend sort of place," says a corporate associate. Even that relatively high billable requirement does not seem to faze attorneys, who find positive ways to spin it. "One important thing about Schiff is that unlike other firms that say 2,000 [hours] and mean 2,400, 2,000 means 2,000," says a third-year attorney. "An associate who does 2,000 hours of fantastic work will be viewed just as positively as an associate who does fantastic work but billed 2,200 hours the past year, although," the source adds, "the associate who billed more hours will certainly receive a larger bonus, which is only fair."

While, in principle, such financial rewards are fair, many associates voice concern over the opacity of the compensation system. "Associates would perceive the firm as more fair if the firm had objective, consistent criteria for salary increases and was upfront about which practice groups or associate attributes are rewarded more or less," remarks one attorney. (Schiff Hardin reports that, in response to such concerns, the firm now provides associates with more information about the compensation process.) Still, others regard the pay as "satisfactory." "All lawyers are overpaid if you ask me," says a second-year, "but the compensation package fits the market with the possible exception of lower bonuses than comparably-sized firms."

The firm's training program – elsewhere, a frequent source of associate ire – scores high marks at Schiff Hardin. Formal training for litigation and corporate departments is extensive. "[The] introduction-to-litigation program for first-year associates teaches the basics of discovery, filing practices in local state and federal courts, and document review. Second- and third-year associates alternate between a comprehensive pre-trial [program] and a trial program that culminates in a mock trial before a judge, witnesses and a real jury. The partners put a great deal of effort into the program, and it shows." Some associates say, however, that there can be too much of a good thing. There's "too much required, formal training," complains a seasoned attorney. "It's like a security blanket for the firm and the bureaucracy has taken on a life of its own."

Schwartz, Cooper, Greenberger & Krauss

180 North LaSalle Street
Suite 2700
Chicago, IL 60601
Phone: (312) 346-1300
www.scgk.com

LOCATION
Chicago, IL

MAJOR DEPARTMENTS & PRACTICES
Banking & Finance
Corporate & Business
Franchise & Distribution
Insolvency & Bankruptcy
Litigation
Private Wealth Services
Real Estate
Technology & Intellectual Property
Trusts & Estates

THE STATS
No. of attorneys: 74
No. of offices: 1
Summer associate offers: 3 out of 3 (2004)
Managing Partner: Ronald B. Grais
Hiring Partner: Patrick T. Stanton

NOTABLE PERKS
- Bar association dues and attorney registration fees
- Bar exam review fees
- Profit-sharing plan
- $10,000 entry-level signing bonus

BASE SALARY
Chicago, IL (2005)
1st year: $100,000
Summer associate: $1,923/week

EMPLOYMENT CONTACT
Patrick T. Stanton, Esq.
Hiring Committee Chairman
Phone: (312) 346-1300
Fax: (312) 782-8416

THE SCOOP

Schwartz Cooper is the product of the 1993 merger of two Chicago firms that dated back to the Depression era. The firm employs approximately 75 attorneys in its single Chi-town office. The firm's clients represent more than 200 industries, including automotive, business-to-business, professional services, hotel, health care, child care, retail, upscale restaurants and real estate brokerage.

A representative list of Schwartz Cooper clients spans a number of fields. In financial services, the firm represents such powerhouses as LaSalle Bank, BankOne, SunTrust Mortgage Corp. and Washington Mutual Bank. Manufacturing clients include Eltek Energy and the Wickes Lumber Company. In real estate, the firm counsels Freestone Realty Advisors and Pacific Security, among others. The firm's client roster boasts a number of other household names in retailing, the service industries, technology and communications. Clients range from individuals to emerging businesses to successful Fortune 500 companies.

The firm's sophisticated real estate department represents all types of clients, including developers, institutional lenders, real estate investors and landlords throughout the country. Among other recent matters, Schwartz Cooper has represented a lender in a $90 million condo development in Arizona, counseled a Canadian investment company in the purchase of a $65 million office-building portfolio in Indiana and advised a lender in a $180 million condo conversion loan in Florida. In transactions closer to home, the firm recently represented a lender in a $100 million apartment building acquisition loan in Chicago, a developer in a $60 million condo project in the city and a developer in two build-to-suit leases of new office buildings in downtown Chicago.

Among its many practice areas, Schwartz Cooper features a franchise and distribution department, which subdivides into specialty areas such as litigation, finance, and mergers and acquisitions. The franchise litigation team has represented Mickey D's in numerous disputes, including the termination of a franchisee in Paris who controlled a McDonald's site worth more than $350 million. Schwartz Cooper has also represented familiar food chains such as Godfather's Pizza and Sizzler Restaurants International in franchise-related disputes.

The firm also boasts a nationally known bankruptcy practice. The firm is counsel to LaSalle Bank National Association, the largest creditor in the liquidation and bankruptcy proceedings for the Chicago-based law firm of

Altheimer & Gray. The debtor firm owes its creditors more than $40 million. A liquidation plan was filed in U.S. Bankruptcy Court in Chicago in October 2004.

GETTING HIRED

Schwartz Cooper's hiring program doesn't deviate much from the law-firm norm: an initial, on-campus interview followed by an all-day, in-office callback at which candidates typically meet several partners and associates and get to struggle with the interview-over-lunch ritual. The firm accepts applications from second-year law students at schools outside the firm's on-campus recruiting program as well as those participating in on-campus interviews; it typically does not hire first-year law students.

Beyond a search for academic credentials, professional achievements and "interpersonal skills," the firm's goal is to hire "students who will be a 'good fit' at Schwartz Cooper." The firm therefore urges students to let their real personalities shine through their "interviewee demeanor."

Seyfarth Shaw LLP

55 East Monroe Street, Suite 4200
Chicago, IL 60603-5803
Phone: (312) 346-8000
www.seyfarth.com

LOCATIONS

Chicago, IL (HQ)
Atlanta, GA
Boston, MA
Houston, TX
Los Angeles, CA
New York, NY
Sacramento, CA
San Francisco, CA
Washington, DC
Brussels

MAJOR DEPARTMENTS & PRACTICES

Bankruptcy, Workouts & Business Reorganization
Business Immigration
Construction
Corporate
Employee Benefits & ERISA
Environmental & Toxic Torts
Government, Commercial & International Contracts
Intellectual Property
International
Labor & Employment
Litigation
Real Estate
Tax
Trusts & Estates

THE STATS

No. of attorneys:
    firm-wide: 605
    Chicago: 261
No. of offices: 10
Summer associate offers:
    Chicago: 8 out of 8 (2003)
National Managing Partner: J. Stephen Poor
Hiring Partner: James L. Curtis

NOTABLE PERKS

- Domestic partner health insurance
- Bar review course and exam fees
- Leave of absence and alternative work arrangement policies
- Summer stipend while studying for the bar

BASE SALARY

Chicago, IL (2004)
1st year: $120,000
Summer associate: $2,300/week

EMPLOYMENT CONTACT

Ms. Dawn M. Patchett
Legal Hiring Coordinator
Phone: (312) 739-6458
Fax: (312) 269-8869
E-mail: dpatchett@seyfarth.com

THE SCOOP

Seyfarth Shaw started out in 1945 as a three-man labor and employment boutique in Chicago. Today, the firm still maintains a substantial labor practice and has kept its headquarters in the Windy City; but Seyfarth has also expanded to over 600 lawyers in 10 offices, including one in Europe, and has branched out into 14 major practice areas. Even so, labor and employment work remains the firm's bread and butter. Over one-third of Seyfarth's attorneys work on labor and employment matters. In 2004 the firm was deemed the No.-1 employment practice in Illinois by *Chambers USA*, and the firm regularly appears on The NLJ Client List, *The National Law Journal*'s survey of "Who Represents Corporate America." Seyfarth is, along with Littler Mendelson and Morgan Lewis, one of the most frequently used outside counsel for labor and employment matters. Among the many Fortune 250 companies on Seyfarth's client roster are Costco, Dell, The Dow Chemical Company, Motorola, New York Life Insurance, Caterpillar Inc., Merck & Co., Comcast and Abbott Laboratories.

As part of its work in the employment arena, the firm has developed a unique program called Seyfarth Shaw at Work™, which provides training sessions for clients on labor law issues through interactive presentations without all the legal jargon. In March 2004, the firm scored a big coup when Kenneth R. Dolin left nearby Jenner & Block LLP to join the Chicago office as a partner. Dolin, who brings more than two decades of experience to Seyfarth, had chaired Jenner's labor practice for nearly seven years.

Seyfarth Shaw does not exist on employment law alone, however; other areas of the firm's expertise include corporate, litigation, intellectual property and environmental law. In 2003, Seyfarth participated in one of the largest law firm mergers of the year when it combined with D'Ancona & Pflaum, a century-old shop with 60 lawyers. The addition of D'Ancona's personnel and clients helped to diversify Seyfarth's practice in areas such as securities, mutual funds, venture capital and estate planning. Seyfarth management cited the merger as part of the firm's strategic growth plan, through which the firm has also established stronger footholds in other U.S. cities like Atlanta and Boston. In June 2004, the firm added two new partners to its litigation, media/entertainment and international practices in New York.

In late 2003, the firm was instrumental in negotiating the $1.3 billion Meadowlands Xanadu Development in New Jersey. New York partners John Napoli and Stephen Epstein led the legal team representing Mack-Cali Realty Corporation in structuring its joint venture with development partner Mills

Corporation. The Meadowlands Xanadu project, which has been approved by the New Jersey Sports and Exhibition Authority, features a variety of sports facilities, including a minor league sports stadium and a sports entertainment complex complete with a surfing pool, a mini-Formula One Racing Oval and the country's first indoor skiing slope.

Seyfarth Shaw is a member of ius laboris, an international law alliance for firms specializing in employee benefits, pensions, labor and employment law. Established in 2001, ius laboris now includes 24 member firms and over 1,000 attorneys in 74 cities throughout Europe, North and South America.

"Although the law is our vocation, it is not our life," announces the firm's recruiting page. In keeping with that philosophy, the firm has a business casual dress policy and relatively low (for big-firm life, that is) billable requirement of just 1,950 hours per year. Moreover, all time spent on approved pro bono projects counts toward that target. In another effort to address the perennial issue of life-work balance, 15 years ago Seyfarth instituted a formal policy permitting alternative work arrangements. Such arrangements are determined on a case-by-case basis, and associates who work alternative schedules still remain on track for partnership.

A second aspect of Seyfarth Shaw's philosophy is its "'free-market' approach to the practice of law." The firm neither assigns associates to a particular practice group nor doles out individual work assignments. Under the free-market system, associates actively seek out the matters that interest them or the partners with whom they'd like to work.

GETTING HIRED

Seyfarth's summer associate program is at the core of the firm's hiring program. When Seyfarth looks for summer associates, it does so "with the expectation that they will later return to the firm as associates." The firm sets high standards, requiring that candidates be in the top 25 percent of their law school class. They must also demonstrate "character, intelligence and training." "Excellent writing, analytical and interpersonal skills" are obvious assets and the firm prefers candidates who have journal experience. However, in looking for well-rounded attorneys-to-be, the firm also gives weight to judicial clerkships, prior work experience and extracurricular activities. Like summer clerks, lateral associates should have "excellent" academic credentials, analytical and communication skills.

Shefsky & Froelich Ltd.

444 North Michigan Avenue
Suite 2500
Chicago, IL 60611
Phone: (312) 527-4000
www.shefskylaw.com

LOCATION

Chicago, IL

MAJOR DEPARTMENTS & PRACTICES

Banking & Financial Institutions
Construction
Corporate Finance
Estate Planning & Probate
Food Industry
Gaming
Government Regulation
Health Care
Insolvency & Creditors' Rights
Insurance
Litigation
Real Estate
Securities
Tax
Technology
Venture Capital

THE STATS

No. of attorneys: 70
No. of offices: 1
President/Chairman: Cezar Froelich
Managing Partners: Anthony R. Licata and Michael J. Schaller
Hiring Partner: John F. Kennedy

NOTABLE PERKS

- Profit-sharing plan
- Free fitness center
- Professional dues and seminars

BASE SALARY

Chicago, IL (2005)
1st year: $110,000
Summer associate: $2,115/week

EMPLOYMENT CONTACT

Ms. Susan M. Cristiano
Human Resources Manager
Phone: (312) 836-4141
Fax: (312) 527-9285
E-mail: SCristiano@shefskylaw.com

THE SCOOP

Shefsky & Froelich opened its doors in 1970 when 29-year-old Lloyd Shefsky recognized a need for attorneys who could assist developing companies with ever-increasing business and finance changes. Today, Shefsky still specializes in advising entrepreneurs and their companies at every stage of development – "from the billion-dollar corporation looking for overseas or new business expansion to the young person with rich dreams and limited resources." But the firm that started out with a focus on complex commercial transactions now also offers advice in nine major practice areas, including estate planning, health care and litigation, which accommodates the majority of the firm's attorneys.

The mid-size, Midwestern law firm has developed several specialty areas in which it has gained a national reputation. One of these industry-specific, interdisciplinary groups focuses on construction law, combining the talents and resources of lawyers in every one of Shefsky's substantive practice areas. The construction group has worked on all kinds of matters, from licensing and government relations to performance bonds, for clients such as architects, engineers and contractors.

Meanwhile, Shefsky & Froelich's insolvency practice provides a similar level of expertise. The firm has represented creditors including AIG Risk Management, LaSalle Bank and the Illinois Department of Commerce and Community Affairs in recent bankruptcy-related matters. Not to be outdone, the firm's real estate department just nabbed Chicago's top land-use expert, Edward J. Kus, who was the executive director of the city's Zoning Reform Commission. This is good news for clients, who will benefit from Kus's in-depth understanding of the Windy City's new zoning ordinance that was adopted last year.

The partner-heavy firm (there are almost two partners for every associate) has also built a distinctive food industry practice. What started with a few clients in the firm's corporate finance department turned into a unique and lucrative practice that is now served by the firm at large. The firm caters to industry giants including the Hess Food Group, Blind Faith Restaurants and Arena Food Distribution Company.

Apart from its service to the corporate world, Shefsky & Froelich provides valuable legal representation to public service clients in the Chicago community. The firm has counseled nonprofit organizations such as the Make-A-Wish Foundation, the Chicago Music & Dance Theatre and the Chicago Youth Hostel on a pro bono basis. Although the firm demands a minimum of 2,000 billable hours before associates can be eligible for a bonus, all pro bono hours count toward this requirement.

GETTING HIRED

According to Shefsky's web site, *"This* is the place to get really good experience, so why start somewhere else?" And it's true. If you want to get in, you'd better be ready to get your hands dirty. Shefsky & Froelich wants "bright, creative and hard-working professionals who are looking for hands-on experience and training from the outset." The firm conducts on-campus interviews locally. But that doesn't mean that you have to be from Chicago to get hired. Some of Shefsky & Froelich's attorneys also hail from Villanova, Harvard, Duke and Yale.

Sidley Austin Brown & Wood LLP

10 South Dearborn Street
Chicago, IL 60603
Phone: (312) 853-7000
www.sidley.com

LOCATIONS

Chicago, IL
Dallas, TX
Los Angeles, CA
New York, NY
San Francisco, CA
Washington, DC
Beijing
Brussels
Geneva
Hong Kong
London
Shanghai
Singapore
Tokyo

MAJOR DEPARTMENTS & PRACTICES

Business & Financial Transactions
Corporate Reorganization & Bankruptcy
Corporate/Securities
Derivatives
Employee Benefits
Employment & Labor
Environmental
Health Care
Intellectual Property & Technology
Litigation
Real Estate
Tax
Trusts & Estates

THE STATS

No. of attorneys:
    firm-wide: 1,532
    Chicago: 510
No. of offices: 14
Summer associate offers:
    firm-wide: 177 out of 184 (2004)
    Chicago: 77 out of 81 (2004)
Executive Committee Chair: Thomas A. Cole
Management Committee Chair: Charles W. Douglas
Hiring Partners:
    Firm-wide chair: John G. Levi
    Chicago co-chairs: Holly A. Harrison and Jon A. Ballis

UPPERS
- Demanding and interesting work
- Top-of-the-market salary

DOWNERS
- "Too many hours, not enough direction"
- Big-firm bureaucracy

NOTABLE PERKS
- Bar and moving expenses
- Transportation subsidies
- BlackBerries and monthly service fees
- Free lunch every other week

BASE SALARY

Chicago, IL (2005)
1st year: $125,000
2nd year: $135,000
3rd year: $150,000
4th year: $165,000
5th year: $185,000
6th year: $195,000
7th year: $200,000
Summer associate: $2,400/week

EMPLOYMENT CONTACT

Ms. Jennifer L. Connelly
Legal Recruiting Manager
Phone: (312) 853-7495
Fax: (312) 853-7036
E-mail: jlconnelly@sidley.com

THE SCOOP

Sidley Austin Brown & Wood was launched in May 2001 when two major law firms merged. Sidley & Austin, which was founded in Chicago in 1866, housed more than 900 lawyers in offices from the Windy City to the Pacific Rim, while the New York-based Brown & Wood had been dominating the capital markets and financial institutions field since 1914. Together, the firm now employs more than 1,500 legal professionals and boasts a truly global, fully diversified practice with specialties in everything from college and university law to postal services.

When *The American Lawyer* released its "Corporate Scorecard" in April 2004 for the previous year, Sidley Austin Brown & Wood won its share of bragging rights. The firm appeared in 14 categories within the top 10, and in more than half of the rankings Sidley placed in the top five. The firm earned the No.-1 slot for its roles as issuer's counsel in equities offered by U.S. corporations, issuer's and underwriter's counsel for investment grade debt, and underwriter's counsel for REIT debt. Not to be outdone, Sidley's litigation department garnered the spotlight as the winner of *AmLaw*'s top defense verdict of the year. The firm achieved this recognition for its successful representation of Tyson Foods against a claim that the company had been smuggling illegal aliens into the country to work at its poultry processing plants. Among the 10 firms most often relied on by Fortune 250 companies, according to *The National Law Journal*'s "Who Represents Corporate America," Sidley boasts a client roster that includes AIG, Fannie Mae, Morgan Stanley, Microsoft, CVS and Honeywell International. In recognition of its initiatives to retain and promote female lawyers, Sidley received the 2005 Catalyst Award. Catalyst is an independent, nonprofit member organization dedicated to expanding opportunities for women in business.

Unfortunately, over the last year the firm has also made headlines for less celebratory reasons. Sidley has faced criticism and several lawsuits by clients over allegedly bad tax-shelter advice given by a former Brown & Wood partner several years ago. The IRS has assessed millions of dollars in back taxes against the clients. Other firms embroiled in related litigation include Dallas-based law firm Jenkens & Gilchrist, Deutsche Bank, Ernst & Young and KPMG.

GETTING HIRED

You stand the best chance of getting hired at Sidley if you come from a top-10 school. Even then, "Harvard ain't enough – better to be on law review, too." Insiders say that the firm is "very selective" and takes only the best. Although recruiters look for "well-rounded individuals with interests outside of the law" and "genuinely nice people who are nice to be around," these attributes won't make a difference if you aren't at the top of your class. "Best advice: show that you're smart, friendly and can write well, but don't be pretentious or arrogant. That," declares one associate, "is the kiss of death at Sidley."

OUR SURVEY SAYS

According to one associate, "the single most important part of Sidley's culture (and it is very important) is that everyone here at Sidley is extremely nice and considerate. Everyone is treated with respect at the office, whether you are a lawyer, secretary or the janitor." Insiders describe the firm as soft on the inside, but hard and crunchy on the outside. While attorneys are "overall friendly" and "somewhat laid-back" in the office, the firm can be "intense when it has to be." Nevertheless, Sidley "deals with pressure in a very professional manner," says one new associate. "I believe the personalities come together to lighten the environment despite the high-impact work that is being done," he adds. Although most sources agree that there "is not a lot of socializing after hours," some practice groups are more sociable than others.

As one Sidley associate aptly puts it: "There is no getting around the fact that working at a big firm means a lot of hours." And Sidley is no exception. But most associates don't mind. For this type of firm, "work hours are completely reasonable," says one second-year. "Although some associates are busier than others, there is room both for people who happen to be going through slow periods and [for] people who just don't want to work atrocious hours." And the firm doesn't care about "face time." "If I am caught up at work so that I can leave at 4:00, I take advantage of that and no one has ever told me that I could not do so," says one midlevel associate. While the firm's pro bono program gets high marks (pro bono hours are counted toward billable requirements), the part-time program gets mixed reviews. Insiders say that, in some cases, "the boundaries of part-time arrangements" have not been respected, with part-timers working just as hard as full-timers.

The goods news is that if you work hard, you'll get paid well. "Sidley really appreciates associates that have, for whatever reason, worked hard (or under difficult circumstances – i.e., out of the office)," says one associate. "For hard-working associates, there is no other law firm in the country where you will make more money. Period." But even though some Chicago associates feel their "bonuses are very generous," others claim that the bonus system is "way behind market." "Bonuses are tied to hours as opposed to substantive work product, which I find somewhat demeaning," complains a senior associate.

The only area where there is a significant difference of opinion among associates is the firm's training program. One junior associate says that the firm "offers a Litigation Trial Skills Training program for new litigation associates, which is both personally helpful and provides the necessary credits to qualify" for the trial bar. But another attorney in a different department complains that limited formal training is the "weakest point of being a young to midlevel associate at Sidley." Most insiders say that training is "hands-on." Many associates boast that they get to "work on interesting and challenging matters" very early in their careers, although a few grumble that they're stuck with "a lot of document review." According to one litigator, "Job satisfaction depends greatly on the partners for whom you are working. Some are excellent lawyers and managers who seek to keep associates involved and attempt to get them experiences that will allow them to develop. Others are just the opposite."

"Best advice: show that you're smart, friendly and can write well, but don't be pretentious or arrogant. That is the kiss of death at Sidley."

- Sidley Austin Brown & Wood associate

Skadden, Arps, Slate, Meagher & Flom LLP and Affiliates

333 West Wacker Drive
Chicago, IL 60606
Phone: (312) 407-0700
www.skadden.com

LOCATIONS

New York, NY (HQ)
Boston, MA
Chicago, IL
Houston, TX
Los Angeles, CA
Palo Alto, CA
San Francisco, CA
Washington, DC
Wilmington, DE
Beijing
Brussels
Frankfurt
Hong Kong
London
Moscow
Munich
Paris
Singapore
Sydney
Tokyo
Toronto
Vienna

MAJOR DEPARTMENTS & PRACTICES

Banking & Institutional Investing
Communications
Corporate
Corporate Restructuring
Litigation
Mass Torts & Insurance Litigation
Real Estate
Tax

THE STATS

No. of attorneys:
  firm-wide: approx. 1,700
  Chicago: 165
No. of offices: 22
Summer associate offers:
  firm-wide: 148 out of 152 (2004)
  Chicago: 18 out of 18 (2004)
Executive Partner: Robert C. Sheehan
Hiring Partners: Marian P. Wexler, Thomas A. Hale, Charles F. Smith, Maxwell M. Miller, Rodd M. Schreiber (Chicago)

UPPERS
- "The best-quality legal work"
- The salary

DOWNERS
- Long hours and unpredictable schedule
- "Firm should be your life" attitude

NOTABLE PERKS
- In-house gym with personal trainer
- Catered lunch on weekends
- $3,000 technology allowance
- Regular attorney lunches

BASE SALARY

Chicago, IL (2005)
1st year: $140,000
Summer associate: $2,400/week

EMPLOYMENT CONTACT

Ms. Lena R. Gonzales
Legal Hiring Coordinator
Phone: (312) 407-0909
Fax: (312) 407-0411
E-mail: legonzal@skadden.com

THE SCOOP

Perhaps the most ubiquitous outside counsel among the Fortune 250, Skadden Arps consistently ranks high on *The National Law Journal*'s list of "Who Represents Corporate America." In litigation, corporate transactions and corporate governance, top-drawer clients such as Pfizer, Lockheed Martin, Alcoa, Gap Inc., Office Depot and Abbott Laboratories regularly rely on Skadden's expertise.

Worldwide, the firm employs nearly 1,700 lawyers. Although it only comprises about 10 percent of the total size of the firm, the Chicago office of Skadden Arps is as high-powered as they come. Skadden-Chicago's handling of landmark insolvency cases recently won one partner the title of "Dealmaker of the Year." John Butler Jr., a partner in Skadden's Second City office, earned this title in April 2004 from *The American Lawyer*, which profiled his leadership efforts in the Chapter 11 matters of Kmart and US Airways and the firm's unique transactional approach to the restructuring process. Butler has also counseled clients including Rite Aid and Xerox in their corporate reorganizations.

In the firm's litigation practice, lawyers in the Chicagoland office have handled mass tort cases including lawsuits centered on silicone breast implants, cell phone radio frequency emissions and genetically modified corn. The corporate transactions group at Skadden has long been a member of the billion-dollar club, having closed mergers and acquisitions for Sears, Roebuck & Co. and Ameritech, Inc., among others. Similarly, the Skadden-Chicago tax group frequently weighs in on multibillion-dollar deals. This office also boasts a communications practice that has represented SK Telecom, the largest cellular carrier in Korea, on expansion efforts across Southeast Asia and in the United States and Brazil. Other areas of Chicago attorneys' expertise include negotiated acquisitions and leveraged buyouts, contested takeovers, communications, and real estate finance, development and restructuring.

GETTING HIRED

It's never easy to land a job at this firm, and some Chicago associates think it's getting even harder. According to one insider, "I've noticed that Skadden-Chicago is even more selective when it comes to hiring than it was when I was hired in 2001. Most, if not all, of the summer associates speak two languages and have had experience between college and law school."

If the firm is looking for something beyond "book smarts," it still cares about pedigree. "Top grades are a must," says one lawyer. According to another, the firm recruits from a wider range of schools than "places like Cravath or Wachtell. But even at less-recognized schools they only take the top of the class." A Chicagoland associate reports that the firm has "minimum grade requirements that vary depending on which law school you attend." These requirements may not be "set in stone, but they are definitely given strong consideration in evaluating which candidates should be called back to interview at the firm."

OUR SURVEY SAYS

In many respects, the stereotypes associated with BigLaw practice seem to hold true for Skadden-Chicago. The work is "high-profile and complex," the hours are long and hard, and the salary is staggering. According to one insider, Skadden offers "the best New York-style litigation in Chicago" as well as "cutting-edge securities, corporate control, corporate governance work." Others agree that the work is "fabulous." But, warns a litigator, "in exchange for excellent work, great experience and really top-notch partners to learn from, you'll work really, really hard and you won't make partner." For many, that's a fair trade. "I work really hard and they pay me a ton in salary," says one associate, who shrugs, "I knew the deal when I signed on."

But it is good to know what you're getting into. Long hours may be an inherent "part of big-firm life," but that doesn't mean they're not exhausting. In fact, what many associates complain about more than the long hours is the inconsistency and unpredictability of their schedules. "It's not the hours per se," explains a Chicago source, "but the fact that you never know any given day when you will be working until... Could be 6:30 or 3 a.m. and you won't know until 6:30." On the other hand, "when the workload is light, people do leave early." And if the "feast or famine" nature of the work can be difficult, respondents aren't exactly surprised: "I took a job at Skadden Arps; what kind of hours do you think I expected?"

For those up to the challenge, the payoffs can be substantial. With starting salaries at $140,000 and third-year associates pulling in $170,000, most insiders are understandably "pleased" with base compensation. Nevertheless, some associates "continue to be disappointed by the class-based bonus system" in which all associates in the same class receive the same bonus based on "firm profitability" rather than hours billed. Others think the lockstep system "is a huge advantage," especially when work in their area is slow.

As far as training, "most of it is on the job, which is fine" with many associates. One source explains, "My general impression is that if you ask for a certain type of training it will be provided but that informal, hands-on training is much more beneficial to one's development as an attorney." Insiders give the firm's formal mentoring program mixed reviews. But if you crave more personal guidance, ask and ye shall receive. "I have found people here open to sharing their experience, strength and hope in a very candid way," says one associate. "I pretty strongly sought it out, though."

The culture in the Chicago office is described as "fairly collegial" and "friendly," though "professional." Some departments may be more sociable than others. While an attorney in the real estate group says that "people at all levels (partners, associates and support staff) are laid-back and friendly, both in a work and [a] social environment," a litigator sees a "definite divide between the partnership and associates." Partners are respectful, according to this attorney, "but they're not going to become your friends." Still, if some associates have been "barked at ... in stressful situations," others are "grateful for the mentoring and friendships" they've developed with individual partners.

"I took a job at Skadden Arps; what kind of hours do you think I expected?"

– *Skadden Arps associate*

Sonnenschein Nath & Rosenthal LLP

8000 Sears Tower
Chicago, IL 60606
Phone: (312) 876-8112
www.sonnenschein.com

LOCATIONS

Chicago, IL (HQ)
Kansas City, MO
Los Angeles, CA
New York, NY
San Francisco, CA
Short Hills, NJ
St. Louis, MO
Washington, DC
West Palm Beach, FL

MAJOR DEPARTMENTS & PRACTICES

Bankruptcy • Corporate & Securities • Corporate Diversity Counseling • Employee Benefits & Executive Compensation • Energy & Environmental • Government Contracts • Health Care • Information Security & Internet Enforcement • Insurance • Intellectual Property & Technology International • Labor & Employment Life Sciences • Litigation • Media & Entertainment • Public Finance • Public Law & Policy Strategies • Real Estate • Taxation • Telecommunications • Trusts & Estates • Venture Capital • White-Collar Investigations & Trial

THE STATS

No. of attorneys:
 firm-wide: 699
 Chicago: 229
 Kansas City: 57
 St. Louis: 45
No. of offices: 9
Summer associate offers:
 firm-wide: 48 out of 50 (2004)
 Chicago: 16 out of 17 (2004)
 Kansas City: 9 out of 9 (2004)
 St. Louis: 5 out of 5 (2004)
Chairman: Duane C. Quaini
Hiring Partners:
 Chicago: Jordan Sigale
 Kansas City: Steven L. Rist
 St. Louis: Stephen J. O'Brien and Stacey L. Murphy

UPPERS
- Sophisticated work and big-firm prestige
- Exposure to a variety of practice areas

DOWNERS
- Holdbacks in associate salaries
- Limited training

NOTABLE PERKS
- Free donuts and pizza on certain days
- Window offices for all associates
- Free dinners and cab rides for late nights
- Free legal assistance in connection with home sale/purchase

BASE SALARY

Chicago, IL (2005)
1st year: $125,000
2nd year: $135,000
3rd year: $150,000
4th year: $165,000
5th year: $185,000
6th year: $195,000
7th year: $200,000
Summer associate: $2,400/week

Kansas City, MO (2005)
1st year: $85,000
Summer associate: $1,500/week

St. Louis, MO (2005)
1st year: $90,000
Summer associate: $1,550/week

EMPLOYMENT CONTACTS

Chicago
Ms. Nicole L. Foster
Recruitment Coordinator
Phone: (312) 876-8112
Fax: (312) 876-7934
E-mail: nfoster@sonnenschein.com

Kansas City
Ms. Danielle M. Gibbons
Marketing and Recruiting Coordinator
Phone: (816) 460-2434
Fax: (816) 531-7545
E-mail: dgibbons@sonnenschein.com

St. Louis
Ms. Kimberly P. Morgan
Recruitment Coordinator
Phone: (314) 259-5869
Fax: (314) 259-5959
E-mail: kmorgan@sonnenschein.com

THE SCOOP

In late April 2004, a team of Sonnenschein litigators persuaded a jury to return a complete defense verdict in a 30-state, class-action lawsuit. The action, which sought over $400 million in damages from the firm's client Allstate Insurance Company, was initiated by a plaintiff class made up of more than 387,000 policyholders. The plaintiffs alleged that Allstate had refused to reimburse them for the lost value of their automobiles. After a three-week trial in St. Clair County Circuit Court, the jury sided with Allstate, finding that the company had lived up to the terms of the auto insurance policies in question. In another high-profile case, lawyers from several of Sonnenschein's offices, including its Chicago headquarters, represented Sun Microsystems in an antitrust suit against Microsoft. Thanks in large part to Sonnenschein's efforts, the parties settled the dispute in April 2004; Microsoft paid Sun $2 billion in cash up front and will provide future payments worth up to $450 million. This deal has been touted as the largest settlement in history in a private antitrust litigation.

Sonnenschein Nath & Rosenthal LLP dates back to 1906 and now comprises approximately 700 attorneys in nine offices across the country. The firm is particularly well known for its practices in antitrust, corporate and securities, bankruptcy, entertainment and litigation. Its client roster includes Abbot Laboratories, Aon Corporation, The Boeing Company, McDonald's Corporation, Sears and The Tribune Company, to name just a few.

As part of the firm's upcoming centennial celebration, a team of Sonnenschein staff and lawyers founded the Legacy Charter School in Chicago; the firm is also sponsoring the school, which will open in an inner-city neighborhood in August 2005. And, in what may be a law-firm first, in 2004 Sonnenschein formed an alliance with one the nation's largest minority-owned and -managed law firms, Pugh, Jones, Johnson & Quandt, PC, to provide clients with more diverse legal talent.

GETTING HIRED

"Only the best get hired at Sonnenschein," according to insiders. The firm looks for "very intelligent people" (say, top 5 percent of their class) who are "friendly" and "self-starters." Of course, "law clerks are popular," and the firm also appreciates "top-tier law schools and applicants with good grades or interesting backgrounds." For graduates of regional schools, "ranking and background must be very strong." On the plus side, the firm "seeks diversity in attorneys, including gays and lesbians." According to insiders, the firm has several openly gay partners and associates.

OUR SURVEY SAYS

Insiders voice varying degrees of satisfaction with life at Sonnenschein. A Missouri associate declares, "Of all the employers I've worked for, in many different industries, Sonnenschein is the best employer I've ever had. The work is fun and challenging, and my mentors are brilliant practitioners who are an endless source of advice and knowledge." A junior attorney in Chicago agrees that "Sonnenschein is a wonderful place to work." On the other hand, several Windy City sources grumble that there is a perception "among new and lower-level associates that the firm is not invested in us."

In fact, most insiders think the firm's training program could stand improvement, although "this is an area that the firm has recently identified as lacking and it has hired someone to focus on formal training." (The firm hired a chief learning officer in May 2004 to oversee training in all offices.) While some attorneys complain that training is "nonexistent," an intellectual property lawyer asserts, "My practice area has regular training sessions and I have been approved to attend third-party training seminars whenever I've requested to do so." Most associates learn through "hands-on experience," and the firm assigns a partner to mentor more junior associates. Although a few insiders insist that the "attorney mentor quality is incredibly high," others claim that "only a small handful of partners and senior associates take the time to train and mentor."

Opinions also vary as to the firm culture. In the Chicago office, some associates say that, "generally, doors are closed during the day," and if you're not part of the "in" crowd, you probably won't find much in the way of socialization. But others in the same office consider it "friendly" and say that "most partners tend to have an open-door policy." The smaller Missouri offices seem to be more laid-back. The St. Louis office may rate as the friendliest, with one associate gushing that it's a "fantastic work environment," combining "a smaller-office feel" with the "resources of large firm."

Regardless of the location, one thing is certain: "There is enormous pressure on billing hours." Some say that this "has resulted in an unpleasant competitiveness in particular practice areas." According to one attorney, "New associates are afraid to turn down work or take significant vacation time," and there is a pervasive fear of not "making the hours." The firm requires a minimum of 1,950 hours annually (1,900 hours for St. Louis and Kansas City), "but don't think you'll get anywhere in the firm on those hours," warns one associate. Another disagrees, however, boasting, "I bill 1,950 and have plenty of time to spare for community work and business development. Easy!" The good news is that the firm is committed to pro bono work and counts these hours toward billable requirements. It even "has a full-time partner dedicated to developing pro bono opportunities."

Fueling the resentment of many associates is the "Sword of Damocles" that sources say the firm "dangles" over associates' heads by "holding back a portion of their annual salary which is then paid in one lump sum in the next year as a 'productivity bonus'" for meeting required hours (the firm refuses to call it a "holdback"). But "all big firms require big hours, which usually corresponds to higher pay, so there is a balance," reasons one associate. In general, associates say that the firm pays at or near the top of the market, with lock-step salary increases that take the uncertainty out of yearly raises.

"I bill 1,950 hours and have plenty of time to spare for community work and business development. Easy!"

– *Sonnenschein Nath & Rosenthal LLP associate*

Squire, Sanders & Dempsey L.L.P.

4900 Key Tower
127 Public Square
Cleveland, OH 44114-1304
Phone: (216) 479-8500
www.ssd.com

LOCATIONS

Cleveland, OH (HQ)
Cincinnati, OH • Columbus, OH • Houston, TX • Los Angeles, CA • Miami, FL • New York, NY • Palo Alto, CA • Phoenix, AZ • San Francisco, CA • Tampa, FL • Tysons Corner, VA • Washington, DC • Beijing • Bratislava • Brussels • Bucharest* • Budapest • Dublin* • Hong Kong • Kyiv* • London • Madrid • Milan • Moscow • Prague • Riyadh* • Rio de Janeiro • Shanghai • Tokyo

* Independent offices affiliated with Squire, Sanders & Dempsey

MAJOR DEPARTMENTS & PRACTICES

Bankruptcy & Restructuring • Communications • Corporate • Corporate Finance • Economic Regulation • Energy • Environmental, Health & Safety • Financial Services • Health Care/Life Sciences • Intellectual Property • International Dispute Resolution • Labor & Employment • Litigation • Project Finance • Public Revenue Finance • Public Securities • Real Estate • Taxation • Transportation

THE STATS

No. of attorneys:
  firm-wide: 679
  Cleveland: 149
  Cincinnati: 21
  Columbus: 82
No. of offices: 26
Summer associate offers:
  firm-wide: 24 out of 32 (2004)
  Cleveland: 11 out of 14 (2004)
  Columbus: 4 out of 5 (2004)
Chairman: R. Thomas Stanton
Hiring Partners:
  Cleveland: Steven A. Friedman
  Cincinnati: James J. Barresi
  Columbus: William A. Nolan

UPPERS
- High level of responsibility for complex matters
- Collegial environment

DOWNERS
- Long partnership track
- Emphasis on billable hours

NOTABLE PERKS
- Down-payment assistance for first-time homebuyers
- Cab service after hours
- Generous bar preparation stipend
- Occasional happy hours

BASE SALARY
Ohio offices (2005)
1st year: $110,000
Summer associate: $4,125/semi-monthly

EMPLOYMENT CONTACTS
Cleveland
Ms. Julie M. Gladys
Recruiting Manager
Phone: (216) 479-8017
Fax: (216) 479-8780
E-mail: jgladys@ssd.com

Cincinnati and Columbus
Ms. Brandi L. Hann
Recruiting Manager
Phone: (614) 365-2753
Fax: (614) 365-2499
E-mail: bhann@ssd.com

Vault Guide to the Top Chicago & Midwest Law Firms
Squire, Sanders & Dempsey L.L.P.

THE SCOOP

Squire, Sanders & Dempsey has been quietly achieving worldwide domination over the past 114 years. From its unassuming home base in Cleveland, Squire Sanders has grown from the three-man practice that established its masthead to the 679-lawyer, 26-office empire it is today. The firm has spread around the United States, across Europe and throughout Asia, most recently opening an office in Shanghai in 2004.

Recently, the communications practice group at Squire Sanders handled a particularly notable matter that will make cellular phones available to the Iraqi people for the first time since the beginning of Saddam Hussein's regime. The firm assisted a group of companies in Iraq and Kuwait in obtaining one of the three wireless telephone licenses that were made available by the country's interim minister for communications. In another truly international matter, lawyers from SSD's headquarters are currently part of a team that is representing the government of the Czech Republic and the National Property Fund in arbitration against Japanese investment bank Nomura. The plaintiffs allege that Nomura owes them anywhere between $3.3 billion and $8.5 billion as a result of the collapse of the third-largest bank in the Czech Republic following an attempt to privatize the institution. The case has been allowed to move forward after an UNCITRAL tribunal in Switzerland determined that the Czech Republic could bring suit against Nomura even though the government had not been a party to the underlying arbitration agreement.

GETTING HIRED

Associates describe Squire Sanders as anywhere from "pretty selective" to "very selective" in its hiring standards. A junior lawyer reports, "Especially in economic bad times, the market for associates here is pretty demanding. Lots of qualified people do not get hired. The most important things for first-years are good school plus good grades. For laterals, it's reputation around town plus whatever those intangibles are that make you appear to be a competent person." According to one source, "Candidates that get in and stay in seem to have a combination of intelligence and common sense, along with a good work ethic." Another insider claims that "the firm periodically gets delusions of grandeur about the level of associates it can attract," but notes that "overall we get good people who do good work. Those that can't cut it leave."

OUR SURVEY SAYS

Squire Sanders associates enjoy the best of both worlds: a firm that combines a large international practice with a laid-back Midwestern feel. One enthusiastic insider gushes, "It is a privilege to practice here. I am given a large amount of responsibility and autonomy, but not ignored or left to fend for myself. The work is challenging and difficult, but extremely rewarding and satisfying." Another happy camper remarks, "We work hard, and both the partners and our clients expect and demand high-quality work, but our environment is friendly and supportive. I have never faced a (figuratively) closed door when I have needed help. And because partnership here is hard-won but not beyond reach, associates are not set up to compete against one another for a precious few partnership slots." Although the environment is "friendly and collegial," most attorneys spend down time with their families rather than socializing outside the office.

With respect to associate training, a senior lawyer reports, "We currently have a firm-wide initiative under way to evaluate and recommend improvements in our training and mentoring programs and practices. We have just instituted an electronic firm-wide training calendar, which makes any training session in any office available to all attorneys firm-wide, through teleconference and audio recording." Partners and senior associates are also readily available to act as mentors, "to review individual documents and performances for the purpose of attorney development," as well as "to offer advice on substantive legal issues and marketing and professional issues."

Associates are expected to bill 2,000 hours a year. Most find that this translates into a reasonable work schedule. "I am at the office Monday through Friday from about 9:00 a.m. until 6:00 p.m.," says one litigator. "I work a lot from home, but no one seems to mind that I'm not actually at the office all the time, as long as the work gets done." A junior associate comments, "I have been well above my billable-hour goal and don't feel that I've killed myself or sacrificed my life outside of work." Even when the days get long, say insiders, "the quality of work is good and the partners generally are accommodating and do not abuse the associates' time."

Compensation receives mixed reviews. Although the base pay is generally satisfactory, particularly given the low cost of living in Ohio, one source laments, "The annual increase and bonus system cause me profound aggravation. My department has said two years in a row that the department has had a good year. My salary increase has been low and I received no bonus, despite exceeding the billable goal two years in a row by a modest amount." Another lawyer finds the pay "appropriate for the hourly requirements and demands," although, she adds, "there are not many add-ons – associates pay a large chunk for insurance premiums, there is no 401(k) match and, although we do get a month of vacation time, it's hard to take it all and still make your billables."

Taft, Stettinius & Hollister LLP

425 Walnut Street, Suite 1800
Cincinnati, OH 45202-3957
Phone: (513) 381-2838
www.taftlaw.com

LOCATIONS

Cincinnati, OH (HQ)
Cleveland, OH
Columbus, OH
Covington, KY
Dayton, OH

MAJOR DEPARTMENTS & PRACTICES

Antitrust
Bankruptcy
Business & Finance
Environmental
Health Care
Intellectual Property
Labor & Employment
Litigation
Real Estate
Tax

THE STATS

No. of attorneys:
  firm-wide: 193
  Cincinnati: 129
  Cleveland: 44
No. of offices: 5
Summer associate offers:
  firm-wide: 11 out of 12 (2004)
  Cincinnati: 8 out of 8 (2004)
  Cleveland: 2 out of 3 (2004)
Managing Partner: Thomas D. Heekin
Hiring Partner: Mark J. Stepaniak

NOTABLE PERKS

- Client development account
- Bar review and association dues
- Moving expenses
- Pre-tax parking

BASE SALARY

Cincinnati, OH (2005)
1st year: $95,000
Summer associate: $1,730/week

EMPLOYMENT CONTACT

Ms. Amy C. Bulger
Director of Legal Recruiting
Phone: (513) 381-2838
Fax: (513) 381-0205
E-mail: bulger@taftlaw.com

THE SCOOP

Few law firms can count a Hall of Fame athlete among their attorney ranks, but the Cincinnati-based Taft, Stettinius & Hollister LLP is one of those few. Ross E. Wales, a partner in Taft's business and finance group and chair of the international practice, was recently inducted into the Swimming Hall of Fame in Fort Lauderdale, Fla. Wales medaled in the 100-meter butterfly at the 1968 Olympics and served as the first president of United States Swimming. Outside the pool, his practice at Taft Stettinius focuses on international corporations doing business in the United States and domestic companies seeking to expand into the international sphere.

The rest of the firm's attorneys have received their share of awards and honors, albeit in the legal field. Taft Stettinius was recently named one of the top five law firms in Cincinnati. It's no wonder, since 35 of the firm's attorneys were chosen by their peers for the most recent edition of *The Best Lawyers in America*, and six attorneys are listed in *Chambers USA: America's Leading Lawyers for Business*.

The firm was established in Cincinnati in 1924 upon the merger of two Ohio firms, one of which had been around since 1885. With nearly 200 attorneys, Taft, Stettinius & Hollister has grown to become one of Ohio's largest law firms, with three additional offices in Ohio (Cleveland, Columbus and Dayton) and another office in Northern Kentucky. The general practice law firm is organized into four departments: business and finance; litigation; labor and employment; and tax, probate and estate planning. Within these departments are several industry-specific practice areas, including a new "Brownfield group," which the firm formed to assist clients in the remediation and management of environmentally-impaired "Brownfield" real estate. Another interesting group is Taft's Japanese practice, which advises Japanese companies establishing operations in the United States and U.S. companies looking to branch out or do business in Japan.

The international reach of Taft Stettinius, which employs nearly 250 lawyers in five offices, is substantial; in addition to the firm's unique Japanese practice, Taft Stettinius has a longstanding presence in Italy. Taft Stettinius also provides substantial support in immigration, labor and employment, and tax matters to foreign corporations in America. In addition, the firm offers several industry-specific groups such as its education law, biotech and health care practices. As an example of the interdisciplinary nature of these departments, the health care group combines the talents of attorneys in antitrust, tax, bankruptcy and malpractice litigation, to name just a few.

Through this group, the firm has represented many prestigious clients, including Yale Medical Center, Cedars Sinai Hospital and The Ohio State University Medical Center.

There are two other things that Taft Stettinius has that most other firms do not: a Professional Women's Resource Group and its own university. In an effort to strengthen relationships with female clients and business leaders, the women's group hosts a number of professional activities, including a popular "Women in Leadership" breakfast. Women from all professions join with firm attorneys and summer associates for breakfast four times a year to network and discuss emerging business issues and trends. The firm is also one of the few in the country to have established a "university" for training attorneys. The Taft, Stettinius & Hollister University provides ongoing training and mentoring for all firm attorneys, including senior partners. Seminar topics include effective deposition skills, time management, meeting dynamics and accounting. There's even a course on the traditions and goals of the firm.

GETTING HIRED

Taft, Stettinius & Hollister isn't so concerned about where you come from – it's more interested in where you're headed. The firm interviews at schools all over the country, including Chicago, Harvard and New York University, and looks for candidates with demonstrated commitment and partnership potential. Most entry-level attorneys are hired through the firm's summer associate program. Of course, firm recruiters want the usual: "strong academic achievement, interpersonal skills, initiative, leadership in outside activities and demonstrated maturity." But with an international practice and unique programs like the Taft, Stettinius & Hollister University and Professional Women's Group, the firm clearly wants innovative individuals who can add to each practice's value in the long run.

Thompson Coburn LLP

One US Bank Plaza
St. Louis, MO 63101
Phone: (314) 552-6000
www.thompsoncoburn.com

LOCATIONS

St. Louis, MO (HQ)
Belleville, IL
Washington, DC

MAJOR DEPARTMENTS & PRACTICES

Admiralty
Appellate
Banking & Commercial Finance
Bankruptcy
Business Litigation
Class Action
Construction & Real Estate Litigation
Corporate & Securities
Corporate Compliance, Investigation & Defense
Employee Benefits
Environmental
Government Contracts
Health Care
Intellectual Property & Information Technology
Labor & Employment
Maritime
Product Liability Litigation
Private Client & Tax
Public Finance & Public Law
Railroad Litigation & Toxic Tort
Tobacco Litigation
Transportation & International Commerce/Utilities

THE STATS

No. of attorneys:
   firm-wide: 285
   St. Louis: 260
No. of offices: 3
Summer associate offers:
   firm-wide: 10 out of 31 (2004)
   St. Louis: 10 out of 31 (2004)
Chairman: Thomas J. Minogue
Hiring Partner: Lawrence C. Friedman

UPPERS

- Excellent training from partners
- Formal but friendly culture

DOWNERS

- Workload can be uneven

NOTABLE PERKS

- Friday lunches
- Reimbursement for local club dues
- All associates have window offices

BASE SALARY

St. Louis, MO (2005)
1st year: $90,000
Summer associate: $1,500/week

EMPLOYMENT CONTACT

Ms. Nichole D. Clasquin
Legal Recruiting Manager
Phone: (314) 552-6234
Fax: (314) 552-7000
E-mail:
nclasquin@thompsoncoburn.com

THE SCOOP

Thompson Coburn has had plenty to brag about in the last year. In 2004, the 285-lawyer firm celebrated its 75th anniversary. Thompson Coburn was also named the No.-1 trademark law firm in St. Louis by *NameProtect Trademark Insider* for having made the most trademark filings of any firm in the city, and it was a finalist for a "Stevie" award for "Best Corporate Web Site." The "Stevies" are also known as the American Business Awards and are given out for "great performances in the workplace." Judges in the competition have included Donald Trump and Anthony Robbins. Other finalists in the web site category were Kraft, General Electric and Hewlett Packard.

Among its wide-ranging practice areas, Thompson Coburn has established particular renown for its work in toxic tort litigation. Attorneys in this group collaborate with medical and other specialists on staff at the firm in defending companies such as Shell Oil, Union Pacific Railroad and Goodyear Tire & Rubber against liability actions. Thompson Coburn's experience in mass tort litigation dates back to the dioxin cases against Monsanto. The firm succeeded in defeating every one of those lawsuits, including one that lasted nearly four years and made the *Guinness Book of World Records* as the longest jury trial in history. Thompson Coburn also has the distinction of representing Lorillard, one of four tobacco companies currently involved in the largest civil case (in terms of total dollars) in U.S. history. As for class actions in general, Thompson Coburn has defended more than 250 such actions in the past four years alone and has been singled out by PriceWaterhouseCoopers for its exemplary use of litigation support technology in this area. As a result of its 2001 merger with IP boutique Howell & Haferkamp, Thompson Coburn now houses one of the St. Louis region's largest IP practices, which counsels clients such as Converse, Enterprise Rent-a-Car, Boeing and Washington University.

GETTING HIRED

Thompson Coburn "hires on an 'as-needed' basis," so the selection process is very competitive. The firm looks for candidates who "demonstrate ability, motivation, academic and good interpersonal skills." "We look for well-rounded people who have done well in law school," explains one attorney. Since hiring is need-specific, "a candidate needs to bring a required skill/experience level to the table," says a midlevel associate. Ultimately, as another source reports, the prospect of an offer depends "upon how well the candidate has done and how good the school is."

OUR SURVEY SAYS

Our sources seem to be a happy bunch. The opportunity to learn from high-caliber attorneys is touted as one of the best things about working at Thompson Coburn. "The partners are passionate and knowledgeable about the law and provide younger associates with great opportunities for expanding their careers," reports one inside source. "I have had a great experience at Thompson Coburn," says another associate: "great people, great work and great clients. What more can you ask?"

While the firm does offer formal training opportunities, many associates feel that the best training comes from doing. "Most training comes from one-on-one interaction with partners," reports an intellectual property lawyer. Another source says, "I have received some of the best training anyone could have in the Midwest because I have worked with talented TC lawyers." The firm's formal training sessions cover "a number of legal and technical aspects of practicing law." Early responsibility is common at the firm, and one insider reports that senior associates "have allowed [him] to get involved with cases at all levels."

"As with all major firms," acknowledges one associate, "the bottom line on hours does matter." That said, "it is not the most important thing here by any measure." Most responding associates feel that Thompson Coburn has a humane outlook when it comes to billing and time spent in the office. "Our bonus system is not linked to hours beyond certain milestone requirements," explains one source, "because the partnership wants to [reward] associates for reasons other than just how many hours have been billed." And when work "can be done from home," says an IP attorney, "if you have to work evenings/weekends, you can at least do it from home." While "there is a great deal of litigation work" to keep associates busy, the firm is also committed to non-billable and pro bono work, which "counts for up to 50 hours of our billable targets." Attorneys can choose pro bono projects that appeal to them, and the firm will determine whether they count toward the hours requirement.

Most attorneys give the compensation structure at Thompson Coburn high marks. Associates are similarly pleased with their firm's working environment. A junior associate reports that the firm culture is "organized in a formal manner but comes off friendly overall." In particular, both the intellectual property and litigation departments are described as "collegial," "friendly" and "casual." One insider is impressed with "the commitment lawyers have to their families and the emphasis the firm places on being well-rounded." Thompson Coburn makes sure that associates have plenty of opportunities to socialize, including firm dinners and parties. According to one associate, "the partnership has many events throughout the year to show appreciation for associates." In addition, "the management committee also meets with associates twice a year to keep the channel of communications open."

The firm is committed to diversity in its attorneys, and the associates have noticed. "Our associate classes generally are comprised of 50 percent women," says a midlevel lawyer, "and there are a growing number of partners who are women." An experienced attorney also reports that "diversity is a primarily goal here at TC, and there have always been a number of minority associates in every new associate class since I've been here."

Thompson Hine LLP

3900 Key Center
127 Public Square
Cleveland, OH 44114-1216
Phone: (216) 566-5558
www.thompsonhine.com

LOCATIONS
Cleveland, OH (HQ)
Atlanta, GA
Cincinnati, OH
Columbus, OH
Dayton, OH
New York, NY
Washington, DC
Brussels

MAJOR DEPARTMENTS & PRACTICES
Admiralty & Maritime • Bankruptcy Business Litigation • Business Regulation & Government Affairs • Commercial & Public Finance • Competition, Antitrust & White-Collar Crime • Corporate & Securities • E-Business & Emerging Technologies • Employee Benefits & Executive Compensation • Environmental • Health Care • Intellectual Property • International Labor & Employment • Life Sciences • Personal & Succession Planning • Product Liability Litigation • Real Estate • Taxation

THE STATS
No. of attorneys:
    firm-wide: 355
    Cleveland: 143
    Cincinnati: 62
    Columbus: 45
    Dayton: 48
No. of offices: 8
Summer associate offers:
    firm-wide: 18 out of 25 (2004)
    Cleveland: 10 out of 12 (2004)
    Cincinnati: 4 out of 4 (2004)
    Columbus: 1 out of 3 (2004)
    Dayton: 1 out of 3 (2004)
Managing Partner: David J. Hooker
Hiring Partners:
    Cleveland: Robert F. Ware
    Cincinnati: Deborah S. Brenneman
    Columbus: Peter D. Welin
    Dayton: J. Wray Blattner

UPPERS
- All pro bono hours count as billable
- Low pressure to bill

DOWNERS
- Low pay increases and limited bonuses
- "No perks to speak of"

NOTABLE PERKS
- "Skit Night:" associates make fun of partners, and partners pick up the tab
- Boxes and tickets available for various sporting and cultural events
- Discounts on cars and technology
- Doughnuts every other Friday (in some offices)

BASE SALARY

Cleveland, OH (2005)
1st year: $105,000
Summer associate: $1,750/week

Cincinnati, Columbus, Dayton, OH (2005)
1st year: $95,000
Summer associate: $1,650/week

EMPLOYMENT CONTACTS

Firm-wide, Columbus, New York and Washington, DC
Ms. Jennifer J. Irwin
Manager, Attorney Recruiting and Development
Phone: (216) 566-5558
Fax: (216) 566-5800
E-mail: jennifer.irwin@thompsonhine.com

Cleveland
Ms. Ryan Burns
Recruiting and Development Specialist
Phone: (216) 566-7736
Fax: (216) 566-5800
E-mail: ryan.burns@thompsonhine.com

Cincinnati
Ms. Lynda L. Anderson
Recruiting and Development Specialist
Phone: (513) 352-6792
Fax: (513) 241-4771
E-mail: Lynda.Anderson@ThompsonHine.com

Dayton
Ms. Susan Certo
Recruiting and Development Specialist
Phone: (937) 443-6846
Fax: (937) 443-6635
E-mail: susan.certo@thompsonhine.com

THE SCOOP

Thompson Hine LLP is at the top of its game. In April 2004, *Chambers USA* named the Cleveland shop the No.-1 law firm in Ohio in the areas of construction, environmental law and real estate. Thompson Hine also placed among the top three firms in banking and finance, bankruptcy, corporate/M&A, intellectual property and litigation. That same month, a partner in the Cleveland office, Donald L. Korb, became the chief counsel of the Internal Revenue Service and an assistant general counsel to the Treasury Department. Korb had been tapped by President Bush for the position in late 2003, and in April the U.S. Senate confirmed his appointment. As if all that weren't enough, 59 of Thompson Hine's 353 lawyers were named Ohio "Super Lawyers" for 2004. Super Lawyers® comprise the top 5 percent of legal practitioners around the country, and members are selected through a process of peer review and voting.

Lawyers at Thompson Hine have the opportunity to work on matters with a truly global reach. The firm has provided all types of legal services to domestic and foreign clients in a wide range of industries; for example, multinational representations have included the formation of joint ventures among three U.S. companies and foreign parties in Europe and Asia. Specifically, Thompson Hine attorneys formed ventures through which domestic companies will distribute frozen pizzas in Italy; design, manufacture and distribute hydraulic hammers in Japan; and fabricate metal food cans in Thailand.

GETTING HIRED

When hiring, Thompson Hine looks for "excellent academic performance," with sources suggesting varying criteria for candidates at top-tier schools – ranging from the top 10 percent to the top 25 percent to the upper half of their class. For recruits from local schools, the "requirements are more strict." According to one associate, "Thompson Hine has largely recruited from Ohio law schools, but is definitely interested in recruiting from more prestigious out-of-state schools." Not everyone appreciates the firm's openness to local schools; one attorney complains that the firm spends "too many resources wining and dining fungible law students from non-descript law schools."

In any case, the firm is interested in more than just academics. Thompson Hine "values life experience as much as grades," says one associate. It's very important to be a "team player" and "mix well with clients." The potential for client contact means that associates must be "intelligent, well-spoken [and] mature." And the possibility of working late with colleagues means that candidates should also be "personable and friendly."

OUR SURVEY SAYS

Most associates feel that the 1,800 billable-hour requirement is "not that demanding and easy to meet given the workflow available." According to a first-year, "The firm doesn't care about 'face time.'" Another attorney reports no "pressure to bill above the minimum." However, other lawyers feel some pressure to bill. A midlevel associate claims that "you need to hit 1,950-2,000 [hours] to be seen as successful." Nevertheless, according to a junior litigator, the pressure for hours "is tempered by the realization that pro bono work and community activities are the precursors to successful business development." And Thompson Hine is serious about pro bono. "All our pro bono hours count as billable hours and pro bono work is strongly encouraged," says a junior associate. "The firm is really top-notch in this department," raves another attorney.

Thompson Hine culture hits the "right mix of formality and informality." Most people find the firm "very friendly and close-knit across offices." A second-year associate says that "lawyers tend to socialize together ... and look for opportunities to hang out." Most attorneys "dress casually," and a transactional associate notes that people are "frequently stopping to chat in the halls and the offices." According to a new hire, however, "It's difficult to get to know people outside one's practice group." As a whole, however, most associates feel that partners "are extremely approachable" and "doors are always open."

When it comes to compensation, attorneys voice mixed opinions. The "base salary is competitive," says a senior associate, "but bonuses are not very large, when given." Moreover, "There are not a lot of other compensation perks such as 401(k) or parking." (The firm notes that it offers pre-tax parking benefits.) And, although starting salaries may be "high compared to other firms in the area," as lawyers "progress to a more senior associate status, the increases in pay are minimal." Indeed, according to a midlevel associate, "The salary compression at our firm is always an issue." (The firm reports that after conducting associate focus groups and reviewing market data over the last two years it has adjusted salary ranges to eliminate compression.) On the other hand, several insiders share views like this young lawyer: "Our salary is terrific considering the good quality of life Thompson Hine associates have."

The firm offers limited structured, in-house training. "The actual training on becoming a lawyer is done in the trenches," observes one young associate. "Most of the truly helpful training is on the job," agrees another inside source. But the firm "provides support for external training." And Thompson Hine offers "top-notch" business development training, "networking skills" and "formal training for non-partners"–all evidence that "the firm intends for you to stick with them long enough to make partner." According to the firm, additional internal training programs, including a "university" offering will be available in 2005. A corporate attorney believes that the "low associate-partner ratio means associates aren't as fungible" as they might be in other firms. While mentoring might be "self-initiated," most sources report positive experiences with senior colleagues and partners. A litigator says, "The individuals I work with always try to teach me during every assignment I complete."

Ungaretti & Harris LLP

3500 Three First National Plaza
Chicago, IL 60602
Phone: (312) 977-4400
www.uhlaw.com

LOCATIONS

Chicago, IL (HQ)
Springfield, IL
Washington, DC

MAJOR DEPARTMENTS & PRACTICES

Appellate
Bankruptcy & Creditors' Rights
Corporate, Securities & Finance
Employee Benefits & Executive Compensation
Financial Services
Health Care
Intellectual Property
Labor & Employment
Legislative, Regulatory & Public Policy
Litigation
Products Liability
Public Finance
Real Estate
Tax
Trusts & Estates
White Collar Criminal

THE STATS

No. of attorneys:
  firm-wide: 97
  Chicago: 97
No. of offices: 3
Summer associate offers:
  firm-wide: 4 out of 4 (2004)
  Chicago: 4 out of 4 (2004)
Managing Partner: Thomas M. Fahey
Hiring Partner: Stacey Feeley Cavanagh

NOTABLE PERKS

- Business casual dress
- $9,000 summer stipend for bar study
- Bar admission and review course fees
- College savings program

BASE SALARY

Chicago, IL (2005)
1st year: $125,000
Summer associate: $2,400/week

EMPLOYMENT CONTACT

Stacey Feeley Cavanagh, Esq.
Hiring Partner for the Summer Program
Phone: (312) 977-4400
Fax: (312) 977-4405
E-mail: sfcavanagh@uhlaw.com

THE SCOOP

Ungaretti & Harris made a name for itself when it became the first law firm in the country to provide a written guarantee of satisfaction to its clients. The firm pledges to clients that, although it cannot promise a win or a specific outcome, the lawyers will provide a representation that is open and candid and effectively addresses all of the client's concerns. Ungaretti & Harris backs this bold promise with nearly 100 attorneys, who work in four major practice areas: litigation, business, government and health care. Within each of these core areas are several boutique practices with national scope. In February 2005, veteran federal prosecutor Dean J. Polales joined Ungaretti to launch the firm's white-collar criminal defense practice. Polales had served in the U.S. attorney's office for the Northern District of Illinois for 21 years.

The litigation group at Ungaretti has an outstanding record in trial, appellate and alternative dispute resolution matters. For one client alone, a national brokerage house, the firm has handled the arbitration of over 800 cases involving breach of contract, investment and securities fraud, and breach of fiduciary duty claims. In addition, Ungaretti recently represented a major pharmaceutical company in a dispute with the U.S. Justice Department, which ultimately settled for $110 million. The firm served as national coordinating counsel for recurring products liability litigation for Baxter Healthcare Corp., resolving hundreds of cases involving claims of allergic reaction to the company's latex gloves. The successful verdict in the first latex allergy case to go to trial was cited by *The National Law Journal* as one of the Top Twenty Defense Verdicts for 2002. In another representative matter, the firm served as national coordinating counsel in defending a class action arising out of a spate of more than 25,000 salmonella infections.

On the transactional side, Ungaretti lawyers represent clients in a variety of industries, including manufacturing, financial services, consumer products, gaming, telecommunications and information technology. Clients range in size from established Fortune 100 corporations to mid-sized companies to small startups. The firm has recently handled major deals for private equity firms Wind Point Partners and RoundTable Healthcare Partners. In 2004, Ungaretti represented the Southfield, Mich.-based Wind Point in its $275 million acquisition of United Subcontractors, Inc., a leader in the insulation installation industry. In late 2003, the firm helped form a joint venture between the Illinois-based RoundTable and Marmon Medical Companies, LLC, through which RoundTable became a majority shareholder of American Medical Instruments Holdings, Inc. A few months later, Ungaretti represented RoundTable in its acquisition of the majority interest in New Jersey-based Excelsior Medical Corp.

The firm has a thriving practice serving the health care industry. Led by the managing partner, Thomas M. Fahey, the firm's health care group represents hospitals, individual and group practices, health care associations, clinical laboratories, imaging centers, community-based residential facilities, home health agencies, HMOs and managed care networks, medical device manufacturers and insurance carriers. The firm also counsels clients in related industries, such as health care venture capital funds, financial services companies that lend to health care organizations and technology companies.

In September 2004, Ungaretti made the legal dailies by boosting associate salaries. The starting salary for first-years in the firm's Chicago office jumped to $125,000, placing Ungaretti & Harris among the highest-paying of the city's mid-size firms – comparable, even, with many of the Windy City's most prominent large firms, like Sidley Austin Brown & Wood and Kirkland & Ellis. (Representatives of the firm said that the raise reflected its economic well-being; some industry analysts said Ungaretti was simply keeping pace with the competition.) The base salary is supplemented by both discretionary and hours-based bonuses.

The bigger paychecks have apparently encouraged the firms' employees to open their checkbooks. In early 2005, partner Michael J. Philippi issued a challenge to his colleagues: he would match the first $1,000 the firm raised for the victims of the recent tsunami that devastated a dozen Asian countries, and he encouraged his partners to do the same. Within two days the firm had raised $12,000. The firm also actively encourages its associates to give back to the community through pro bono work. Ungaretti allows its attorneys to count up to 50 hours of their donated time towards their annual billing requirements.

Another aspect of the firm's community involvement lies in its strong ties to the Democratic National Committee. Joseph A. Cari Jr., a member of the firm's executive committee, is a former national finance chair for the DNC, and in the last election cycle Ungaretti & Harris was among the Democratic Party's biggest donors from the Chicago legal community. Joseph Cari alone donated more than $40,000.

GETTING HIRED

Ungaretti's summer program is small and select. The firm looks for candidates who have "strong academic records" and are ready to hit the ground running. "The sophisticated nature of our practice demands attorneys who can take responsibility from the minute they join the firm and who are highly motivated, mature, team-oriented and self-starting," the firm reports. In addition to "academic excellence," applicants should have "a degree of maturity and a sociable personality," since the firm's goal is to maintain its atmosphere of camaraderie and congeniality.

Wondering what it's like to work at a specific employer?

Read what EMPLOYEES have to say about:
- Workplace culture
- Compensation
- Hours
- Diversity
- Hiring process

Read employer surveys on THOUSANDS of top employers.

VAULT
the most trusted name in career information™

Go to www.vault.com

Vedder, Price, Kaufman & Kammholz, P.C.

222 North LaSalle Street
Suite 2600
Chicago, IL 60601-1003
Phone: (312) 609-7500
www.vedderprice.com

LOCATIONS

Chicago, IL (HQ)
New York, NY
Roseland, NJ

MAJOR DEPARTMENTS & PRACTICES

Accounting Law
Antitrust
Bankruptcy & Creditors' Rights
Business Immigration
Capital Markets
Commercial Litigation
Construction Law
Employee Benefits
Employment Class Action
Equipment & Structured Finance
Executive Compensation
Finance & Transactions
Financial Institutions
Health Law
Insurance Coverage
Insurance Law
Intellectual Property
Investment Services
Labor & Employment
Manufacturers' Liability
Professional/Directors & Officers Liability
Real Estate & Land Use
Tax & Estate Planning
Trade & Professional Associations

THE STATS

No. of attorneys:
   firm-wide: 209
   Chicago: 186
No. of offices: 3
Summer associate offers:
   firm-wide: 10 out of 10 (2004)
   Chicago: 8 out of 8 (2004)
Executive Committee: Charles Wolf and Douglas Hambleton
Hiring Partner: James M. Kane

UPPERS

- Challenging, interesting work
- Open management and accessible partners

DOWNERS

- Conservative culture
- No technology stipend for associates

NOTABLE PERKS

- Discretionary commission on business generated
- Free dinners
- Cab rides when working late
- Biannual picnic

BASE SALARY

Chicago, IL (2005)
1st year: $125,000
Summer associate: $2,000/week

EMPLOYMENT CONTACT

Ms. Eileen M. Neis
Legal Recruitment Administrator
Phone: (312) 609-7500
Fax: (312) 609-5005
E-mail: eneis@vedderprice.com

THE SCOOP

Vedder Price has more than a half-century of experience behind it and more than 200 attorneys currently within its fold. In addition to its highly regarded labor and litigation practices, Vedder Price houses diverse practice specialties, ranging from accounting law to structured finance to real estate and land use. Within the corporate area, the firm has notable strengths in the areas of asset-based finance, banking, executive compensation, mutual funds, and aircraft and equipment finance.

In August 2004, a team of litigators from the Chicago-based firm of Vedder, Price, Kaufman & Kammholz, P.C., achieved a significant victory for their client, Amsted Industries, Inc., when they defeated a class action brought by employees of the company. The lawsuit contended that Amsted, which is wholly-owned through its employee stock option plan, and the trustee of the company's stock option plan violated ERISA standards and breached their fiduciary duty when Amsted purchased another company, Varlen Corporation, valuated its own stock price and experienced a liquidity crisis when employees left Amsted in droves. The plaintiffs sought damages over $160 million. Vedder Price filed for summary judgment and won a full dismissal of the action. A federal judge in Illinois ruled that Amsted had not breached its duties or run afoul of ERISA and that the company was not to blame for the cash flow problems it experienced.

Earlier in the year, the 200-lawyer firm won another labor and employment litigation, successfully defending client Sentry Insurance Company against a sex and age discrimination case. There, the plaintiff sued for more than $1 million, alleging that she had been sexually harassed for years and that she was ultimately terminated in retaliation for her refusal of her superior's advances. She also claimed that she had been discriminated against due to her age. After a six-day trial in federal court for the Northern District of Illinois, the jury returned a full defense verdict.

GETTING HIRED

Vedder Price reportedly has a "slow but steady growth plan," and, as a result, say insiders, hiring can be limited. A corporate associate notes that "the summer program is small and therefore quite competitive" to get into. However, hopeful lawyers shouldn't despair, as "there appears to have been a good deal of lateral hiring of late." According to a senior associate, the firm tends to hire "people who are on [a] law journal or who participate in moot court." The firm also looks for "excellent academic credentials, relevant experience and a professional attitude." Another experienced associate describes the ideal candidate as "hardworking, intelligent, outgoing and [with] a good personality." A word of caution to the smug: "Attitude is not tolerated."

OUR SURVEY SAYS

Associates at Vedder Price enjoy working on "complex and challenging matters." An attorney in the labor and employment group boasts that this group is "one of the best in the country. It's a sophisticated practice with great lawyers to learn from." Lawyers in other departments agree that overall, "the people are great." And, say several sources, "the shareholders are fantastic about giving out interesting work to younger associates." According to one insider, "Because there are more partners than associates, almost all associates work directly with partners from the moment they begin here." Moreover, "Senior partners show respect for even the lowliest associates and the talents they bring to the firm."

Insiders describe the firm culture as "professional and cordial, but not overly social." "People certainly work hard and are dedicated to their jobs," says one attorney, but for the most part they are "friendly." Introverts may be relieved that "there are rarely organized functions where socialization is forced," although at least one young associate laments that "attorneys do not associate with each other as much as one would like." "After a long day at the office," explains another lawyer, "most associates want to be with their families, not their co-workers." According to inside sources, "the dress code is business dress four days a week and business casual on Fridays" – a policy not all associates are crazy about. As one lawyer complains, "The firm acts as if I will be less professional if I am dressed in business casual attire."

Many associates feel that the formal training "needs to be revamped," and the firm is starting to make some changes. For example, Vedder Price now has "an excellent mock-trial training program for litigation," and "regular corporate training sessions." (The firm reports that it has instituted a comprehensive labor and employment training program.) There's some disagreement regarding the firm's position on non-firm-sponsored training; one attorney feels that "the firm is generous for paying for attendance at outside seminars," while another complains, "I went to one and had to pay for it myself." Informal training is reportedly "excellent," though it can depend on "with whom the associate is working." A junior attorney comments, "I have both a partner and a senior associate mentor in addition to the informal mentoring relationships that I have developed."

Compensation is "competitive," though associates disagree as to whether it's at or "a little below market." Although one experienced attorney reports that the differences increase "the more senior an associate gets," another senior associate insists that the salary is "commensurate with the number of hours billed and business generated." Similarly, while one source claims that "bonuses are not great compared to other firms," another thinks they are "fairly generous." However, in the words of one insider, "Only those with demonstrated aptitude and higher billable hours can expect to receive the highest raises and bonuses."

"Like all big firms," says an associate, "Vedder requires a substantial time commitment. That being said, partners recognize the need for an outside life and are willing to accommodate the need for time off." According to another attorney, "The billable requirements (target is 2,050 [hours]) are very reasonable compared to similarly-sized firms." But at least one lawyer disagrees. The "days are long," she sighs. "If you are lucky enough, you might be able to take work home with you rather than staying in the office late at night."

Vorys, Sater, Seymour and Pease LLP

52 East Gay Street
P.O. Box 1008
Columbus, OH 43216-1008
Phone: (614) 464-6400
www.vssp.com

LOCATIONS

Columbus, OH (HQ)
Akron, OH
Alexandria, VA
Cincinnati, OH
Cleveland, OH
Washington, DC

MAJOR DEPARTMENTS & PRACTICES

Commercial & Real Estate
Corporate & Finance
Energy & Utilities
Environmental
Government Relations & Lobbying
Health Care
Intellectual Property
International Law
Labor & Employment
Litigation
Probate & Estate Planning
Real Estate
Taxation
Technology
Toxic Torts

THE STATS

No. of attorneys:
 firm-wide: 372
 Akron: 12
 Columbus: 248
 Cincinnati: 50
 Cleveland: 33
No. of offices: 6
Summer associate offers:
 firm-wide: 20 out of 22 (2004)
 Columbus: 15 out of 17 (2004)
 Cincinnati: 4 out of 4 (2004)
 Cleveland: 1 out of 1 (2004)
Managing Partner: Robert W. Werth
Hiring Partner: D. Scott Powell

NOTABLE PERKS

- Bar exam stipend
- Judicial clerk bonus
- European travel plan

BASE SALARY

Columbus, OH (2005)
1st year: $100,000
Summer associate: $1,923/week

EMPLOYMENT CONTACT

Ms. Bobbi J. Shoemaker
Legal Recruiting Coordinator
Phone: (614) 464-6285
Fax: (614) 719-4960
E-mail: bjshoemaker@vssp.com

THE SCOOP

Vorys, Sater, Seymour and Pease LLP started out in 1909 as a four-man law office in Columbus, Ohio. Now the firm employs nearly 400 lawyers in six locations. According to firm lore, the founders of Vorys Sater established the firm on a handshake deal, and to this day, there is no written partnership agreement binding the members of the firm. Among the clients who call upon this foundation of mutual trust for their legal services are Honda of America Manufacturing, Inc., Bob Evans Farms, Inc., The Limited, Inc. and Citibank. Vorys Sater also serves as general counsel to many other Ohio-based businesses including The Scotts Co., Wendy's International, Inc. and the Children's Hospital of Columbus.

The firm's founders included such notables as a United States District Court Judge, an assistant to the U.S. attorney general, a superintendent of insurance for Ohio and a manager of William H. Taft's successful campaign for presidency. But the impressive titles don't stop there. Current notables include partner Gregg Murphy, a regular commentator on CNN, Fox and Court TV, and several attorneys listed in *The Best Lawyers in America*. The firm was also ranked first among Columbus, Ohio's leaders by *Corporate Board Member* magazine.

In November 2004, Vorys, Sater, Seymour and Pease made headlines in connection with the firm's defense of Abercrombie & Fitch against three employment discrimination lawsuits. The claims, which sought up to $50 million in damages, accused the popular retail chain of discriminating on the basis of race and sex in an effort to maintain the corporation's carefully-honed image; specifically, the plaintiffs alleged that the company treated white males preferentially in its hiring and advertising practices. Abercrombie agreed to settle the lawsuits, although Thomas Ridgley, the Vorys Sater lawyer heading the defense team, declined to disclose the terms of the settlement.

On the transactional front, Vorys Sater provides business and real estate advice to corporate clients in wide-ranging matters such as corporate finance, franchise and distribution, corporate takeovers and public finance. Meanwhile, in the firm's insolvency practice, Vorys Sater attorneys have represented IBM as a creditor in the bankruptcy of Phar-Mor, Inc., as well as several unsecured creditors in the Columbia Gas Transmission Company bankruptcy.

One of Ohio's oldest and largest law firms, Vorys Sater has experienced considerable growth over the past few decades. The firm opened an office in

Washington, D.C., in 1975 and now has a significant lobbying practice. In 1982, Vorys Sater opened its Cleveland office to serve a growing client base in Northern Ohio. Two years later, the Cincinnati office opened its doors. The two most recent additions to the Ohio-based firm were the Northern Virginia office, opened in 1998, and the Akron office, opened in 2003 after the firm gobbled up six partners from another Akron firm.

Despite its Ohio roots, the firm has been ranked as one of the world's top law firms in mergers and acquisitions transactions. In the first quarter of 2004 alone, Vorys Sater's attorneys worked on over $1.5 billion in deals. The firm's international interests score a hit with associates, who benefit from Vorys Sater's "European Plan" (also dubbed the "Seymour Plan" on behalf of late partner James Seymour). Established in the late 1970s, the plan pays for six associates and their spouses to take a vacation anywhere in Europe. Another vacation benefit: Vorys also offers a three-month sabbatical to attorneys with more than 10 years of service.

GETTING HIRED

The best way to get into Vorys Sater is to go through the firm's summer associate program. Approximately 75 percent of the attorneys now with the firm participated in the program, which hires over 30 associates each year. The firm actively recruits at 28 law schools across the country and prefers candidates in the top 25 percent of their class with law review experience. But good grades and writing skills aren't enough – you must also fit the firm's personality profile and show leadership and partnership potential. The good news is that if you make it through the door, you're almost certain to become partner eventually. The firm is partner-heavy and associates are considered for partnership after nine and one-half years.

Warner Norcross & Judd LLP

900 Fifth Third Center
111 Lyon Street, N.W.
Grand Rapids, MI 49503-2487
Phone: (800) 752-2401 x 2295
www.wnj.com

LOCATIONS
Grand Rapids, MI (HQ)
Holland, MI
Muskegon, MI
Southfield, MI

MAJOR DEPARTMENTS & PRACTICES
Antitrust & Unfair Competition
Appellate Practice
Banking & Finance
Bankruptcy & Creditors' Rights
Computers & Technology
Corporate
E-Commerce & Internet Law
Employee Benefits
Employment & Labor
Environmental Law
Financial Services
Health Law
Human Resources Law
Intellectual Property
International
Litigation
Real Estate
Securities
Tax Planning & Litigation
Trusts & Estates

THE STATS
No. of attorneys:
  firm-wide: 173
  Grand Rapids: 135
No. of offices: 4
Summer associate offers:
  firm-wide: 7 out of 9 (2004)
  Grand Rapids: 7 out of 9 (2004)
Managing Partner: Alex J. DeYonker
Hiring Partner: Mark J. Wassink

UPPERS
- Reasonable billable-hour target
- Excellent partner-associate relations and overall friendly culture

DOWNERS
- Lower-than-market compensation
- Lousy coffee

NOTABLE PERKS
- Firm pays 75 percent of athletic club membership
- Free parking
- Happy hours on Fridays
- Free laptops and cell phones

BASE SALARY
All offices (2005)
1st year: $85,000
Summer associate (1L): $1,400/week
Summer associate (2L): $1,450/week
Summer associate (3L): $1,500/week

EMPLOYMENT CONTACT
Ms. Cathleen M. Meriwether
Director of Lawyer Recruitment and Development
Phone: (800) 752-2401 x 2295
Fax: (616) 222-2295
E-mail: cmeriwether@wnj.com

THE SCOOP

For two years running, the Grand Rapids firm of Warner Norcross & Judd has been ranked by the Michigan Business & Professional Association as one of the "101 Best & Brightest Companies to Work For" in Western Michigan. Only three law firms made the list, which was compiled based upon factors such as diversity, work-life balance, compensation, recruitment, employee retention, community involvement and strategic planning. In addition, Warner Norcross & Judd has been named in Kimm Walton's 1998 book, *America's Greatest Places to Work with a Law Degree*, alongside such sexy employers as the CIA and the U.S. attorney's office. The firm, which was singled out in part for being highly "tech savvy," was one of only two law firms in Michigan and one of just 115 nationwide to be profiled in the publication.

In early 2004, Douglas A. Dozeman, the head of the litigation practice at Warner Norcross, won a title as one of 10 "Lawyers of the Year" chosen by *Michigan Lawyers Weekly*. He was singled out for his work on a major suit against Taco Bell, which resulted in the largest verdict in Michigan in 2003. Dozeman represented the two creators of the Chihuahua that had been used in Taco Bell's national advertising campaign. The two men, both residents of Grand Rapids, claimed that Taco Bell had breached their contract by using the now-iconic dog without paying the creators a dime. After five years of litigation, the case made it into federal court, where the Warner Norcross & Judd team prevailed, winning more than $42 million for the plaintiffs.

GETTING HIRED

"As a mid-sized firm, there are only so many spots to fill," notes an inside source at Warner Norcross. As a result, this firm can be very selective. "I have a lot of colleagues who did not get called back after their initial interview," adds another attorney. The firm looks for "top-caliber people who not only have great grades but also seem like they will be able to maintain client relationships." Both associates and partners get to weigh in on candidates; one source reports that a job offer requires "two-thirds of the vote of all the attorneys."

While most associates reportedly graduated "in the top quarter of their class at a top-tier law school," the firm also values personality and "good interview presentation." Associates are hired with the expectation that they will make partner, so it is important to find someone who can "do good work as well as be a leader in the community, be able to interact well with clients [and] someday bring in business."

OUR SURVEY SAYS

"Warner is an exceptional place to work," declares one associate, voicing an opinion widely shared by our sources. Despite the smaller Midwestern locale, insiders enjoy a "sophisticated" practice and proclaim that "the lawyers here are as good as any in Chicago [or] Detroit." "While the law can be tedious, challenging and stressful at times," says a Warner associate, "this firm is full of intelligent, supportive people whom you can always turn to."

Attorneys are open to "developing close friendships and spending a lot of time outside the office together." A seasoned lawyer reports, "There is a collegiality here that I have not seen in any other legal environments." The general attitude is "laid-back and friendly." One insider, however, worries that the firm's growth will make this friendly environment "a little more difficult to maintain." But, at least for now, the firm is, as one source puts it, "a unique oasis of very bright attorneys who have fled the insanity of large law-firm law for a place where they can find some semblance of balance."

Part of that balance is achieved by the relatively low billable requirement of 1,750 hours per year. "This is a real number," adds a midlevel associate, "and if you reach it, no one will ask why you did not bill more hours." The firm's belief in efficiency means "less work on the weekends and late at night," according to a litigator. Because billable requirements are so low, the firm doesn't count pro bono hours toward billable targets, under the assumption that associates will make their own time for pro bono. However, one attorney observes that it "doesn't lead many of us [into] doing pro bono." Nonetheless, some insiders consider the firm "a leading donator of services and fees in the area."

When it comes to compensation, Warner attorneys are philosophical. "It's definitely not the most money," says one associate, "but it's fair for the hours." Another lawyer agrees, observing that "the cost of living here is low, and the quality of life is high." Associates are "compensated on a lock-step system," which means that "all associates in the same class receive the same pay, regardless of their hours or accomplishments." The firm "rarely pays bonuses." Although the system is designed "to discourage internal competition," not everyone is happy. "I feel I have pushed myself to work as hard as I would have been working in a bigger city with a salary that has not really grown," complains a senior associate. The absence of an "eat-what-you-kill" system has its benefits, but one source notes that "student loans are the same no matter where you are."

Warner has "an extensive in-house training program" as well as a "practice group-specific training." The firm "also encourages [associates] to attend many local, state and national programs." And while "the programs occur most frequently in the first year," according to a transactional attorney, "there are several programs for more senior associates as well." Comfortable relations between partners and associates means that mentoring occurs often. "I have been fortunate enough to have several partners spend pure non-billable time to mentor," says a trust-and-estates attorney. Both "firm-assigned and informal" mentors are easy to be found; according to one source, "It's part of the culture."

Welsh & Katz, Ltd.

120 South Riverside Plaza
22nd Floor
Chicago, IL 60606
Phone: (312) 655-1500
www.welshkatz.com

LOCATIONS

Chicago, IL (HQ)
Washington, DC

MAJOR DEPARTMENTS & PRACTICES

Intellectual Property
    Counseling & Opinions
    Licensing, Agreements &
      Transactions
    Litigation
    Patent Application Preparation
      & Prosecution
    Trademarks & Copyrights

THE STATS

No. of attorneys:
  firm-wide: 47
  Chicago: 47
No. of offices: 2

NOTABLE PERKS

- Profit-sharing plan
- 401(k) plan
- Flexible benefits plan

EMPLOYMENT CONTACT

Recruiting Coordinator
Phone: (312) 655-1500
Fax: (312) 655-1501
E-mail: careers@welshkatz.com

THE SCOOP

Founded in 1983 by Donald L. Welsh and A. Sidney Katz, Chicago's Welsh & Katz, Ltd. comprises almost 50 attorneys, all of whom are devoted to the practice of intellectual property law. Many of the firm's lawyers hold degrees in scientific disciplines, from engineering to physics to biochemistry. Welsh & Katz deals with all aspects of IP matters, including patent applications and prosecution, trademarks, licensing, copyrights, trade secrets and litigation. In recent years, the firm has handled high-profile licensing matters for clients including Precious Moments and Ty, Inc., the maker of Beanie Babies. Other blue-chip names on the firm's impressive client roster are Mattel, Time, Inc., Atari Games Corp., Intel Corp., the Hard Rock Hotel & Casino and the Walt Disney Company.

With many experienced trial lawyers on staff, including several former assistant U.S. attorneys, Welsh & Katz litigators can be bulldogs in the courtroom. In a recent trade secrets case, a team of lawyers from the firm managed to turn a civil trial into a criminal investigation. In a lawsuit for the misappropriation of trade secrets against a Chicagoland printing company, the plaintiff's lawyer from Welsh & Katz cross-examined the CEO of the defendant corporation. During the course of the questioning, the lawyer uncovered fabrications in the executive's testimony, which prompted the presiding judge to refer the case to the criminal division to prosecute the witness for perjury.

The firm also recently represented Ty, Inc. in a major copyright battle with Peaceable Planets, both of whom sell a plush toy camel that goes by the name of Niles. Peaceable sued Ty in 2001 for infringement and unfair competition practices, alleging that it had a trademark application pending for the name "Niles." U.S. District Judge John W. Darrah granted Ty summary judgment in 2003, holding that a reasonable jury could conclude that consumers would perceive "Niles" to be a personal name and therefore not subject to protection. Since then, however, the decision has been reversed. In 2004, Peaceable Planet's counsel, fellow Chicago IP boutique Banner & Witcoff, Ltd., persuaded the 7th U.S. Circuit Court of Appeals that in this case the name "Niles" is a protectable trademark.

With notable cases such as these, the firm is slowly making its way up the IP rankings. Though it still qualifies as mid-size firm (and on the small side of mid-size at that), Welsh & Katz now ranks at No. 130 among the top 373 intellectual property firms in the country, according to *Intellectual Property Today*, up two spots from 2003. The firm also ranked as the 44th-most prolific trademark firm in 2003, logging 323 trademarks – a rise of 32.9 percent from 2002.

GETTING HIRED

Like other top IP firms, Welsh & Katz professes a desire to hire savvy litigators with technical backgrounds. On the one hand, they look for applicants with experience in licensing, protection and enforcement of intellectual property rights; on the other hand, they also seek out engineers and scientists. The firm's attorneys have degrees in a range of scientific disciplines, including electrical engineering, physics, chemistry, chemical engineering, mechanical engineering, computer science and biochemistry. A number of Welsh & Katz attorneys cut their professional teeth as examiners at the U.S. Patent and Trademark Office. "Ideal candidates" should have both a technical or scientific background and "outstanding law school qualifications, which may be evidenced by participation in law review or a correspondingly high class rank."

And while the job market may be shrinking for IP lawyers in Silicon Valley, in the Midwest business is booming. According to a 2003 interview in *Chicago Lawyer* with one of the firm's name partners, A. Sidney Katz, the burst of the dot-com bubble had no effect on his office. Intellectual property lawyers, particularly patent attorneys, remain in high demand in Chi-town.

Whyte Hirschboeck Dudek S.C.

555 East Wells Street, Suite 1900
Milwaukee, WI 53202
Phone: (414) 273-2100
www.whdlaw.com

LOCATIONS

Milwaukee, WI (HQ)
Madison, WI
Manitowoc, WI

MAJOR DEPARTMENTS & PRACTICES

Bankruptcy
Business & Commercial Finance
Corporate
Employee Benefits & Workers' Compensation
Environmental, Health & Safety
Governmental Affairs
Health Care
Information Technology
Intellectual Property
Labor & Employment
Litigation
Product Liability
Real Estate
Taxation
Telecommunications
Trusts & Estates

THE STATS

No. of attorneys:
　firm-wide: 115
　Milwaukee: 93
No. of offices: 3
Summer associate offers:
　firm-wide: 4 out of 4 (2004)
　Milwaukee: 4 out of 4 (2004)
Chief Executive Officer: Mark A. Miller
Hiring Attorney: Nicole Renouard

NOTABLE PERKS

- Profit-sharing plan
- Associate origination bonus program
- Moving expenses
- Bar review and exam expenses

BASE SALARY

Milwaukee, WI (2004)
1st year: $92,500*
Summer associate: $1,800/week

*2005 salary to be determined

EMPLOYMENT CONTACT

Ms. Tracy L. Jochims
Human Resources Coordinator
Phone: (414) 978-5604
Fax: (414) 223-5000
E-mail: tjochims@whdlaw.com

THE SCOOP

Whyte Hirschboeck Dudek S.C. hung out its shingle in 1943, when the law office consisted of just two partners and one associate. More than a half-century later, the Milwaukee headquarters has expanded exponentially, employing almost 100 lawyers, while the firm has added satellite offices in two other Wisconsin cities, including the state capital. Whyte Hirschboeck has even achieved global reach through its affiliation with a Chinese law firm, Lehman, Lee & Xu. This outpost in Beijing is particularly effective in serving clients that are concerned with trademarks, patent and licensing violations, given the ubiquity of bootlegging and other intellectual property violations in China.

With its increasingly national and international presence, Whyte Hirschboeck counsels top-shelf clients, including Dow Chemical Company, Micron Technology, Inc., Bank One and the Independent Physician's Network, on a wide range of transactional and adversarial matters. Meanwhile, the information technology group has litigated against tech-titans such as Microsoft, Yahoo! and AOL. The firm, however, doesn't neglect its local roots. In December 2004, the firm filed a lawsuit on behalf of the Main Street Coalition in Madison. The Coalition is seeking to stop an increase in the city's minimum wage. The petition argues that such raises should be instigated through uniform statewide action rather than via individual ordinances passed by municipalities.

Each year, Whyte Hirschboeck sponsors and organizes the Midwestern Telecommunications Conference, which brings together executives from companies including Nextel, Cisco and Owens Corning, as well as congressional representatives and legal commentators, to discuss issues currently faced by the industry. For 2004, the topic of the conference was "Telecommunications Security: Key Issues Affecting the Private & Public Sectors" and featured a presentation by the commissioner of the FCC. The firm also boasts a subsidiary, Whyte Hirschboeck Dudek Government Affairs, LLC, which is dedicated to lobbying and advocacy on the local, state and federal levels and provides a liaison between private clients and the public sector.

Over the past year, office- and expansion-related news consistently landed the firm's name in the papers. The opening of the firm's new Milwaukee office in Cathedral Place – a $48 million, 19-story downtown office and condominium – was reported everywhere from the *Business Journal* to the *Milwaukee Journal Sentinel*. The firm occupies part of the 16th floor and all of the 17th, 18th and 19th floors, making it the anchor tenant in the highly acclaimed, new landmark building. The building has 10 soundproof conference rooms, floor-to-ceiling glass panels and a balcony that borders the conference rooms. The firm also broke ground in December 2004 on what will be a 5,000-square-foot office in Manitowoc.

More and more, Whyte Hirschboeck appears to be a big fish in the relatively small Wisconsin sea. In 2004, nine of the firm's attorneys were selected by their peers for inclusion in the annual compendium of *The Best Lawyers in America*. In December 2003, Coachmen Industries, one of the nation's leading manufacturers of recreational vehicles and modular construction, named the firm its Preferred Counsel for the year. Among the firm's noteworthy achievements for Coachmen was an audit of the company's web site in which the firm identified legal exposure relating to intellectual property, privacy, online transactions, regulatory compliance, site terms and conditions, and jurisdictional issues.

GETTING HIRED

Whyte Hirschboeck seeks candidates who want more than just a paycheck. "If you're just looking for a *job* at a law firm, then we're probably not the place for you," according to the firm's practice statement. "We're interested in men and women who are looking for a *career* at our law firm." Summer associates and attorneys alike are expected to be respectful and efficient professionals, as well as "well-rounded individuals." Community service is a plus. The firm demands "a healthy productivity level," but with a realistic billable requirement of 1,800 hours, the firm also leaves time for, and encourages attorneys to pursue, interests outside the office.

Wildman Harrold

225 West Wacker Drive, Suite 3000
Chicago, IL 60606
Phone: (312) 201-2000
www.wildmanharrold.com

LOCATIONS
Chicago, IL (HQ)
Lisle, IL

MAJOR DEPARTMENTS & PRACTICES
Business Continuity & Security
Corporate
Employment & Labor
Environmental
Estate Planning & Family Law
Governmental Affairs
Health Care
Intellectual Property
Litigation
Real Estate
Restructuring & Insolvency

THE STATS
No. of attorneys:
  firm-wide: 212
  Chicago: 198
No. of offices: 2
Summer associate offers:
  firm-wide: 18 out of 22 (2004)
  Chicago: 18 out of 22 (2004)
Managing Partner: Robert L. Shuftan
Hiring Partner: John E. Frey

UPPERS
- Even new associates enjoy "meaningful" work
- Respect for work-life balance

DOWNERS
- Little formal training
- Hours requirements don't reflect kicked-back culture

NOTABLE PERKS
- Firm contributes $50 to any outing of six or more associates
- Subsidized back-up child care
- Social events that include staff as well as attorneys
- Window offices and access to a rooftop patio

BASE SALARY
Chicago, IL (2005)
1st year: $125,000
Summer associate: $2,400/week

EMPLOYMENT CONTACT
Ms. Susan A. Cicero
Recruiting Coordinator
Phone: (312) 201-2574
Fax: (312) 201-2555
E-mail: cicero@wildmanharrold.com

THE SCOOP

Last spring, a team of attorneys from the Windy City firm Wildman Harrold secured an important victory in a class-action suit brought in a Louisiana federal court. The case had commenced in 2001, when a nationwide group of plaintiffs asserted that chromated copper arsenate, a chemical commonly found in the treated wood often used in outdoor decks, had caused contamination of their property. In March 2003, after two years of forum-shopping litigation by the plaintiffs and following a hearing on the issue of class certification, the judge agreed with Wildman Harrold's arguments and denied certification of the plaintiffs' class, holding that the members could not satisfy the requirements of commonality and typicality. The court based its opinion largely on the testimony of defendants' experts and on a precedential case that Wildman Harrold had won for a previous set of defendants in another class action.

In another recent toxic tort case, Wildman Harrold litigators obtained the dismissal of a lawsuit brought by the city of Chicago against a group of paint manufacturers, including the firm's client DuPont. The city had brought the suit seeking payment from the paint companies for cleanup costs incurred in the removal of lead-based paint from municipal buildings and in private homes. A Cook County judge dismissed the suit, finding that its central claim of public nuisance was unfounded.

In 1967 six Chicago attorneys left their big-firm practice to open Wildman, Harrold, Allen & Dixon LLP. Today, Wildman Harrold houses more than 200 attorneys in Chicago and a nearby office in Lisle, Ill. Its broad-based practice goes beyond litigation to encompass corporate and real estate matters as well as intellectual property, tax, labor and governmental affairs work.

GETTING HIRED

Study hard but leave the arrogance at home, if you want to work at Wildman Harrold, advise insiders. In addition to a good sense of humor, the firm values good schools, good grades and other traditional indicia of academic achievement. Associates report that "the hiring process has become more prestige-oriented each year," and Wildman has "recently narrowed the pool of schools from which the firm will interview students, including eliminating on-campus interviewing at some quality local law schools." A third-year calls the firm "snobby," stating, "In contrast to years past, it seems to only want associates from the top-tier law schools with great grades."

"All attorneys from first-years to partners are involved in the recruitment process," says one newcomer. And in his view, personality still matters. "We look for applicants whose qualities complement the firm and its culture," he explains: "lawyers who enjoy their work and have a life outside of the office, but know how to work hard."

OUR SURVEY SAYS

Wildman Harrold provides attorneys with "broad" experience, "fair and competitive" compensation and "a healthy respect for life balance issues." Insiders say that the people are "great" and the firm environment is "extremely laid-back." "Dress is casual, conversation is friendly and not forced," says one source. Another associate adds, "The attorneys are grounded and interested in other things besides their profession. With only a few exceptions, partners care about associates as human beings. The staff is top-notch, very professional, capable and fun."

Partners, in particular, earn high praise. "There are a few exceptions, but for the most part partners treat the associates like their friends and enjoy mentoring and spending time with them," says a midlevel associate. The openness of senior attorneys translates into excellent informal training. As one first-year puts it, "The firm has a mentoring program for new associates, but it's not needed because anyone I ask will take the time to help me with anything." Such guidance is especially important given the limited formal training. The firm does offer "boot camp" sessions for new associates, but most training beyond the first year seems to be on the job. Starting associates needn't worry about being "relegated to mind-numbing document reviews." Instead, they will enjoy "meaningful" work early on. Moreover, the firm's "fluid assignment system" offers "autonomy" to associates who can "gravitate toward partners [they] like to work with."

Even though Wildman promotes a balanced life, you've still got to work. "Like any large law firm in a major market like Chicago," says one seasoned lawyer, "associates often work very hard. However, the intensity depends on your workload at any given time. It is by no means an oppressive work environment." The firm requires 1,950 client-billable hours. One otherwise very happy newcomer who enjoys the work, the atmosphere and the opportunity to weigh in on "complicated issues" worries, "I just started, and I already find the hours daunting." However, as another junior associate says, "You need to reach hours – but at least it's in a good atmosphere."

Part-time and alternative work arrangements are available "on a case-by-case basis." In general, although Wildman suffers from some of the same issues as other large law firms – e.g., "very few women in management positions"–insiders think their firm is "better than most" and are optimistic about the firm's efforts to improve in this area, efforts that include hiring a diversity consultant, creating a diversity committee and launching a "Women in the Practice of Law" group. Another area in which associates look forward to improvement is pro bono. "A lot more time would be spent on pro bono work if Wildman counted the hours toward the billable requirement," observes one attorney. But, say insiders, the firm has "just formed a pro bono committee," the policy "is being evaluated and the issue is being addressed by firm administration." Under the new policy, according to the firm, up to 100 hours of pro bono time will be counted toward the billable-hour requirement of 1,950 hours.

Like the hours, compensation at Wildman is comparable to that at similar-sized firms. Some associates think it a little lower than average, some a little higher. A common theme among responding attorneys' few complaints is that compensation starts off competitively but then gradually falls below market rate. "Starting salary is great," says one source, "but some of the raises are very minimal." Another attorney adds, "My impression is that bonuses are slim at Wildman compared with bonuses at other large firms."

"The firm has a mentoring program for new associates, but it's not needed because anyone I ask will take the time to help me with anything."

– Wildman Harrold associate

Winston & Strawn LLP

35 West Wacker Drive
Chicago, IL 60601
Phone: (312) 558-5600
www.winston.com

LOCATIONS

Chicago, IL (HQ)
Los Angeles, CA
New York, NY
San Francisco, CA
Washington, DC
Geneva
London
Paris

MAJOR DEPARTMENTS & PRACTICES

Corporate & Financial
Employee Benefits & Executive Compensation
Energy
Environmental
Government Relations & Regulatory Affairs
Health Care
Intellectual Property
International
Labor & Employment
Litigation
Maritime & Admiralty
Real Estate
Tax
Trusts & Estates

THE STATS

No. of attorneys:
  firm-wide: 875
  Chicago: 425
No. of offices: 8
Summer associate offers firm-wide: 97 percent (2004)
Chairman: James R. Thompson
Managing Partner: James M. Neis
Hiring Partner: Julie A. Bauer

UPPERS

- Sophisticated work among talented, collegial attorneys
- High-quality resources, technology and support staff

DOWNERS

- Dealing with big-firm bureaucracy
- Firm doesn't match 401(k) contribution or pay bar association dues

NOTABLE PERKS

- Attorney-only dining room with great food and "fantastic" views
- Luxury boxes at United Center and Cellular One Park
- Donuts and bagels on paydays and "really good" cookies at meetings
- "Beautiful offices"

BASE SALARY

Chicago, IL (2005)
1st year: $125,000
2nd year: $135,000
3rd year: $150,000
Summer associate: $2,400/week

EMPLOYMENT CONTACT

Ms. Debby Cusumano
Senior Manager, Attorney Recruitment
Phone: (312) 558-5222
Fax: (312) 558-5700
E-mail: dcusumano@winston.com

THE SCOOP

In 2003, Chicago's Winston & Strawn celebrated its sesquicentennial anniversary with several commemorative events, including the release of a book about the firm and its history and the implementation of new initiatives to promote diversity and public service. Since 1853, the firm has been building a global practice, which is now nearly 900 attorneys strong and includes offices in three major European cities. Over the past five years in particular, Winston & Strawn has executed an ambitious strategic growth plan, opening several new offices and engaging in significant mergers with regional firms. In 1999, the firm opened its Los Angeles office and took on a group of 15 new corporate and tax attorneys in the New York office. The following year, Winston merged with New York's Whitman Breed Abbot & Morgan, adding 80 lawyers to its office there. A 2003 merger added a San Francisco office to the firm's roster and substantially expanded and diversified the Southern California practice. Finally, most recently, Winston & Strawn opened a branch office in London, where the firm specializes in corporate finance and international transactions.

As one of the nation's oldest and largest law practices, Winston & Strawn has established long-running relationships with the likes of American Airlines, Philip Morris USA, JPMorgan Chase, Smurfit-Stone Container and Lear Corporation. The Chicago office is home to one of the nation's leading white-collar defense lawyers, Dan Webb. Webb has represented Wyeth in Fen-Phen diet-drug litigation, Microsoft in the Justice Department's antitrust suit and the New York Stock Exchange in its case against former NYSE Chairman Richard Grasso. Webb is currently lead trial counsel for Philip Morris in the Justice Department's $300 million fraud and racketeering case against the tobacco industry. He also represents former Illinois Gov. George Ryan in a federal racketeering case expected to go to trial in fall 2005.

GETTING HIRED

"It's definitely not easy to get a job here," says a Winston & Strawn associate. While "there's no limitation to Ivy Leaguers," the firm's "selection process is extensive, and decisions are made carefully." Winston looks for a combination of good grades and good "fit," according to inside sources. "The firm is looking to hire people who have done well in law school, although not necessarily top of the class," reports one experienced lawyer. "The firm seems to consider accomplishments other than grades more than other firms of its size and reputation in Chicago. It seems the firm is looking for more than 'brains in jars.'" In fact, according to many insiders, "personality is critical."

Geographically, the firm appears to favor the big-named schools in the east, but not necessarily at the expense of hometown kids. "The firm recruits from the best law schools in the country, but refuses to forget its Midwest roots," says one newcomer. "Midwest alumni dominate, but the Ivies are more than adequately represented."

OUR SURVEY SAYS

Most associates find Winston & Strawn a combination of "friendly and professional." As one senior associate puts it, the firm is "very laid-back. We work hard, but develop good friendships as well." A corporate associate adds, "Although Winston has an external reputation of being a bit stuffy, the internal culture tends to be informal and even a bit laid-back. Interaction among lawyers is almost always cordial and respectful."

Indeed, associates express a high level of satisfaction overall. "The work is high-quality and challenging, and the firm does try to give younger associates courtroom experience with pro bono matters," reports a Chicago litigator. Another associate declares, "My experience at Winston is as good as life can be at a big firm. Any complaints I might have would probably be much worse at any other firm." A litigator echoes that sentiment: "For a big firm, Winston is the best."

Undoubtedly, the accessibility and encouragement of senior attorneys contribute to associates' happiness. "On the whole," agree insiders, "Winston partners treat associates amazingly well." They are approachable and professional and sometimes even eat lunch or play hoops with associates. According to one lucky third-year, "The partners I have worked for have truly been mentors that I feel like I can come back to even if at some point I follow a different career path." "No one is shy about asking for help or giving it freely," says another associate.

Even if some insiders believe that "the most valuable training comes from your interaction with partners and older associates," associates also give high marks to the firm's formal training program. "The firm has in-house litigation training workshops and pays for NITA training," says a fifth-year. "Of course, nothing beats the real thing, and whether you experience the real thing depends on your case load and the people for whom you work." Not everyone, though, thinks the system is perfect; a number of associates complain that "formal training after [the] first year is minimal."

One issue that almost no associate complains about is compensation. "Winston is extremely generous with compensation," says a midlevel associate. Moreover, "the bonus targets are attainable and they don't encourage ridiculous hours through the bonuses." The only concern attorneys express is that the compensation system occasionally seems opaque. As one attorney says, "The firm does spend significant effort trying to explain compensation decisions. Some of the firm's explanations of compensation decisions, however, are cryptic."

Even the billable-hours requirement inspires few gripes. "The hours are manageable, and when the time spent at work is higher than I would prefer, the firm has been generous in compensating me for that time," says one seasoned attorney. Moreover, in the view of one young associate, "Ultimately it's much better to spend 14 hours a day doing work that you truly enjoy than to work six hours on a project you can't stand." Insiders also appreciate that "there is absolutely no face time." However, adds an associate, "As much as I would love to say that work ends when I leave, it does not. BlackBerries, cell phones, good connectivity to servers, all of which are very handy, make it nearly impossible to completely leave work when you walk out the door."

APPENDIX

Alphabetical List of Law Firms

Arnstein & Lehr LLP 10
Baker & Daniels 14
Baker & Hostetler LLP 20
Baker & McKenzie LLP 25
Banner & Witcoff, Ltd. 29
Barack Ferrazzano Kirschbaum Perlman & Nagelberg LLP 32
Barnes & Thornburg LLP 36
Bell, Boyd & Lloyd LLC 42
Bollinger, Ruberry & Garvey 47
Brinks Hofer Gilson & Lione 50
Bryan Cave LLP 54
Butzel Long 59
Calfee, Halter & Griswold LLP 62
Chapman and Cutler LLP 66
Clark Hill PLC 71
Clausen Miller, P.C. 74
Dickinson Wright PLLC 78
DLA Piper Rudnick Gray Cary US LLP 82
Dykema Gossett PLLC 88
Foley & Lardner LLP 92
Freeborn & Peters LLP 97
Frost Brown Todd LLC 102
Gardner Carton & Douglas LLP 107
Godfrey & Kahn, S.C. 111
Goldberg Kohn Bell Black Rosenbloom & Moritz, Ltd. 114
Greenberg Traurig, LLP 118
Hinshaw & Culbertson LLP 123
Holland & Knight LLP 126
Honigman Miller Schwartz and Cohn LLP 131
Husch & Eppenberger, LLC 134
Ice Miller® 138
Jenkens & Gilchrist, a Professional Corporation 142
Jenner & Block LLP 148
Jones Day 154
Katten Muchin Zavis Rosenman 158

Appendix

Kirkland & Ellis LLP 164
Latham & Watkins Illinois LLP 170
Leydig, Voit & Mayer, Ltd. 175
Lord, Bissell & Brook LLP 178
Marshall, Gerstein & Borun LLP 182
Mayer, Brown, Rowe & Maw LLP 185
McDermott Will & Emery 188
McGuireWoods LLP 193
Michael Best & Friedrich LLP 198
Miller, Canfield, Paddock and Stone, P.L.C. 203
Miller, Johnson, Snell & Cummiskey, P.L.C. 207
Much Shelist Freed Denenberg Ament & Rubenstein, P.C. 210
Neal, Gerber & Eisenberg LLP 213
Pattishall, McAuliffe, Newbury, Hilliard & Geraldson LLP 217
Pedersen & Houpt 220
Porter Wright Morris & Arthur LLP 224
Quarles & Brady LLP 228
Reinhart Boerner Van Deuren S.C. 231
Sachnoff & Weaver, Ltd. 234
Schiff Hardin LLP 239
Schwartz, Cooper, Greenberger & Krauss 243
Seyfarth Shaw LLP 246
Shefsky & Froelich Ltd. 249
Sidley Austin Brown & Wood LLP 252
Skadden, Arps, Slate, Meagher & Flom LLP and Affiliates 258
Sonnenschein Nath & Rosenthal LLP 264
Squire, Sanders & Dempsey L.L.P. 270
Taft, Stettinius & Hollister LLP 275
Thompson Coburn LLP 278
Thompson Hine LLP 282
Ungaretti & Harris LLP 287
Vedder, Price, Kaufman & Kammholz, P.C. 292
Vorys, Sater, Seymour and Pease LLP 296
Warner Norcross & Judd LLP 299
Welsh & Katz, Ltd. 303
Whyte Hirschboeck Dudek S.C. 306
Wildman Harrold 309
Winston & Strawn LLP 314

About the Author

Vera Djordjevich

Vera Djordjevich is a law editor at Vault. A former litigator and freelance writer, she holds degrees from Stanford University and New York University School of Law.